Just Memos

Just Memos

Laurel Currie Oates
Director, Legal Writing Program
Seattle University School of Law

Anne Enquist
Writing Advisor
Seattle University School of Law

PUBLISHERS

111 Eighth Avenue, New York, NY 10011
www.aspenpublishers.com

Permissions
Aspen Publishers
111 Eighth Avenue
New York, NY 10036

Printed in the United States of America

2 3 4 5 6 7 8 9 0

ISBN 0-7355-3707-0

Library of Congress Cataloging-in-Publication Data

Oates, Laurel Currie
    Just memos / Laurel Currie Oates, Anne Enquist.
      p. cm.
    Includes index.
    ISBN 0-7355-3707-0 (alk. paper)
    1. Legal composition. I. Enquist, Anne II. Title.

KF250 .O18 2003
808'.06634—dc21   2002038330

About Aspen Publishers

Aspen Publishers, headquartered in New York City, is a leading information provider for attorneys, business professionals, and law students. Written by preeminent authorities, our products consist of analytical and practical information covering both U.S. and international topics. We publish in the full range of formats, including updated manuals, books, periodicals, CDs, and online products.

Our proprietary content is complemented by 2,500 legal databases, containing over 11 million documents, available through our Loislaw division. Aspen Publishers also offers a wide range of topical legal and business databases linked to Loislaw's primary material. Our mission is to provide accurate, timely, and authoritative content in easily accessible formats, supported by umatched customer care.

To order any Aspen Publishers title, go to *www.aspenpublishers.com* or call 1-800-638-8437.

To reinstate your manual update service, call 1-800-638-8437.

For more information on Loislaw products, go to *www.loislaw.com* or call 1-800-364-2512.

For Customer Care issues, e-mail *CustomerCare@aspenpublishers.com;* call 1-800-234-1660; or fax 1-800-901-9075.

Aspen Publishers
a Wolters Kluwer business

To my parents, Bill and Lucille Currie,
my husband, Terry, and my children, Julia and Michael.
Thank you.

To my family, Steve, Matt, and Jeff Enquist,
for their love, support, and patience.

Summary of Contents

Contents

Part I

A Foundation for Legal Writing   **1**

Chapter 1

An Overview of the United States Legal System   **3**

Chapter 6

The Second Memorandum   *151*

Chapter 7

The Opinion Letter   **217**

Preface

After the success of our first derivative work, *Just Writing*, we decided to publish two additional derivative works: *Just Memos* and *Just Briefs*. This book, *Just Memos*, sets out the materials first published in Parts I and II of the third edition of *The Legal Writing Handbook*. In particular, it contains the chapters on the American legal system, on legal reading, and on researching, analyzing, and writing objective memoranda and client letters.

As you work through the materials in this book, keep in mind that writing a memo is a complex task. To do a good job, you must understand our legal system; you must know how to locate, select, and read the applicable statutes and cases; and you must be able to construct and evaluate each side's arguments. In addition, you must be a good writer. You must be able to use conventional organizational schemes to present the law, the arguments, and your predictions clearly, precisely, and concisely. Finally, writing a good memo requires the exercise of judgment. You must exercise judgment in deciding when to stop researching, in deciding which information the attorney needs, and in evaluating each side's arguments.

Instead of presenting each of these skills in isolation, *Just Memos* presents them in context. In Chapter 5, we walk you, step by step, through the process of researching, analyzing, and writing a relatively simple memo. In Chapter 6, we walk you through the process of researching and analyzing a more complex memo. In Chapter 7, we walk you through the process of writing a client letter.

As you read through these chapters, keep your goal in mind. Instead of working to get an "A" on a particular assignment, use your assignments to learn how attorneys think and write about legal issues. By learning how to think and write as a lawyer, you will not only be a good student. You will also develop the skills that you need to be a good attorney.

Acknowledgments

One of the pleasures of writing a derivative work is that it allows the authors to think about all of the people who have helped them along the way. In our case, the preparation of this work has reminded us of all of the people who helped us as we wrote the first, second, and third editions of *The Legal Writing Handbook* and the first edition of *Just Writing*.

We would like to begin by thanking our students and colleagues who, in the eighties, provided the inspiration and insights that lead to the writing of *The Legal Writing Handbook*. We would, however, also like to thank our more recent students and colleagues whose suggestions and corrections made each edition better than the earlier one. In particular, we would to thank the following individuals: Susan McClellan, Connie Krontz, Lori Bannai, Mimi Samuel, Ramona Writt, Janet Dickson, Mary Bowman, Jessica Eaves Matthews, Bill Galloway, Judi Maier, Tom Falkner, Pat Brown, Andrew Carter, Janet Chung, Nancy Wanderer, and Jessie Grearson.

Finally, we would like to thank the editors at Aspen for their support and advice and our administrative assistant, Lori Lamb, for her assistance in preparing the manuscript.

Laurel Oates
Anne Enquist

November 2002

Just Memos

A Foundation for Legal Writing

All knowledge builds on prior knowledge. The ability to understand concept B depends on prior knowledge of concept A; the ability to understand concept C depends on prior knowledge of both A and B.

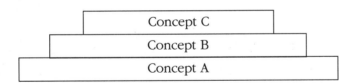

This is particularly true in legal writing. Before you can do legal research, you must know what resources are available and the weight given to each; before you can write, you must possess not only basic writing skills but also an understanding of your audience, your purpose, and the conventional formats.[1]

---

1. Throughout this book, the authors have deliberately used a somewhat more informal writer's style than that which is recommended for legal writing itself. Writing a textbook, like writing anything else, is governed by who the reader is, what the writer's purpose is, what the conventions are for that type of writing, and what relationship the writer wants to have with the reader. Thus, a slightly more informal style seemed appropriate for this textbook. Notice, for example, that the authors use both first and second person, some contractions, some colloquial phraseology, and more dashes than they recommend for legal writing.

Underlying this knowledge, though, must be an understanding of the system in which you are operating. You must understand the United States system of government and, within that larger system, the United States system of law. In addition, you must begin developing the ability to read like a lawyer. The three chapters in Part I lay the foundation for legal writing.

Chapter 3
Reading and Analyzing
Statutes and Cases

Chapter 2
An Introduction to Common
and Enacted Law

Chapter 1
An Overview of the United States
Legal System

An Overview of the United States Legal System

The United States system of government. For some, it is the secret to democracy, the power to elect one's leaders and the right to speak freely. For others, it is a horrendous bureaucracy, a maze through which one must struggle to obtain a benefit, to change a law, or to get a day in court. For still others, it is more abstract, a chart in a ninth-grade civics book describing the three branches of government and explaining the system of checks and balances.

For lawyers, the United States system of government is all of these things and more. It is the foundation for their knowledge of the law, the stage on which they play out their professional roles, the arena for the very serious game of law.

No matter which metaphor you prefer—foundation, stage, arena— the point is the same. To be successful as a law student and a lawyer, you must understand the system. You must know the framework before you can work well within it.

Like most complex systems, the United States system of government can be analyzed in a number of different ways. You can focus on its three branches—the executive branch, the legislative branch, and the judicial branch—or you can focus on its two parts, the federal government and the state governments.

In this chapter, we do both. We look first at the three branches, examining both their individual functions and their interrelationships. We then examine the relationship between state and federal government, again with an eye toward their individual functions and powers.

§1.1   THE THREE BRANCHES OF GOVERNMENT

Just as the medical student must understand both the various organs that make up the human body and their relationship to each other, the law student must understand both the three branches of government and the relationships among them.

§1.1.1   The Executive Branch

The first of the three branches is the executive branch. In the federal system, the executive power is vested in the President; in the states, it is vested in the governor. (See Article II, Section 1, of the United States Constitution and the constitutions of the various states.) In general, the executive branch has the power to implement and enforce laws. It oversees public projects, administers public benefit programs, and controls law enforcement agencies.

The executive branch also has powers that directly affect our system of law. For example, the President (or a governor) can control the lawmaking function of the legislative branch by exercising his or her power to convene and adjourn the Congress (or state legislature) or by vetoing legislation. Similarly, the President or a governor can shape the decisions of the courts through his or her judicial nominations or by directing the attorney general to enforce or not to enforce certain laws.

§1.1.2   The Legislative Branch

The second branch is the legislative branch. Congress's powers are enumerated in Article I, section 8, of the United States Constitution, which gives Congress, among other things, the power to lay and collect taxes, borrow money, regulate commerce with foreign nations and among the states, establish uniform naturalization and bankruptcy laws, promote the progress of science and the useful arts by creating copyright laws, and punish counterfeiting. Powers not granted Congress are given to the states or left to the people. (See the Tenth Amendment to the United States Constitution.) The state constitutions enumerate the powers given to the state legislatures.

Like the executive branch, the legislative branch exercises power over the other two branches. It can check the actions of the executive by enacting or refusing to enact legislation requested by the executive, by controlling the budget and, at least at the federal level, by consenting or refusing to consent to nominations made by the executive.

The legislative branch's power over the judicial branch is less obvious. At one level, it can control the judiciary through its power to establish courts (Article I, section 8, grants Congress the power to establish inferior federal courts) and its power to consent to or reject the

power over Exec

power over courts (judicial)

executive branch's judicial nominations. However, the most obvious control it has over the judiciary is its power to enact legislation that supersedes a common law or court-made doctrine or rule.

The legislative branch also shares its lawmaking power with the executive branch. In enacting legislation, it sometimes gives the executive branch the power to promulgate the regulations needed to implement or enforce the legislation. For example, although Congress (the legislative branch) enacted the Internal Revenue Code, the Internal Revenue Service (part of the executive branch) promulgates the regulations needed to implement that Code.

[handwritten margin note: shared Lawmaking power w/ Exec]

§1.1.3   The Judicial Branch

The third branch is the judicial branch. Article III, section 1, of the United States Constitution vests the judicial power of the United States in one supreme court and in such inferior courts as Congress may establish. The state constitutions establish and grant power to the state courts.

a.   The Hierarchical Nature of the Court System

Both the federal and the state court systems are hierarchical. At the lowest level are the trial courts, whose primary function is fact-finding. The judge or jury hears the evidence and enters a judgment.

[handwritten margin note: Trial court]

At the next level are the intermediate courts of appeals. These courts hear the majority of appeals, deciding (1) whether the trial court applied the right law and (2) whether there is sufficient evidence to support the jury's verdict or the trial judge's findings of fact and conclusions of law. Unlike the trial courts, these courts do not conduct trials. There are no witnesses, and the only exhibits are the exhibits that were admitted during trial. The decisions of the appellate courts are based solely on the written record and the attorneys' arguments.

[handwritten margin note: Appellate Courts]

At the top level are the states' highest courts and the Supreme Court of the United States. The primary function of these courts is to make law. They hear only those cases that involve issues of great public import or cases in which different divisions or circuits have adopted or applied conflicting rules of law. Like the intermediate courts of appeals, these courts do not hear evidence; they only review the trial court record. See Exhibit 1.1.

[handwritten margin note: Supreme Courts]

An example illustrates the role each court plays. In *State v. Strong* the defendant was charged with possession of a controlled substance. At the trial court level, both the state and the defendant presented witnesses and physical evidence. On the basis of this evidence, the trial court decided the case on its merits, the trial judge deciding the ques-

---

| EXHIBIT 1.1 | The Roles of the Trial, Intermediate, and Supreme Courts |

Trial Court

- The trial court hears witnesses and views evidence.
- The trial court judge decides issues of law; the jury decides questions of fact. (When there is no jury, the trial court judge decides both the questions of law and the questions of fact.)

Intermediate Court of Appeals

- The intermediate court of appeals reviews the written record and exhibits from the trial court.
- When an issue raises a question of law, the intermediate court of appeals may substitute its judgment for the judgment of the trial court judge; when an issue raises a question of fact, the appellate court must defer to the decision of the finder of fact (the jury or, if there was no jury, the trial judge).

Supreme, or Highest, Court

- Like the intermediate court of appeals, it reviews the written record and exhibits from the trial court.
- Like the intermediate court of appeals, it has broad powers to review questions of law: It determines whether the trial court and intermediate court of appeals applied the right law correctly. Its power to review factual issues is, however, very limited. Like the intermediate court of appeals, it can determine only whether there is sufficient evidence to support the decision of the jury or, if there was no jury, the decision of the trial court judge.

---

tions of law (whether the evidence should be suppressed), and the jury deciding the questions of fact (whether the State had proved all of the elements of the crime beyond a reasonable doubt).

Both issues were decided against the defendant: The trial court judge ruled that the evidence was admissible, and the jury found that the state had met its burden of proof. Disagreeing with both determinations, the defendant filed an appeal with the intermediate court of appeals.

In deciding this appeal, the appellate court could consider only two issues: whether the trial court judge erred when he denied the defendant's motion to suppress and whether there was sufficient evidence to support the jury's verdict.

Because the first issue raised a question of law, the appellate court could review the issue *de novo*. It did not need to defer to the judgment of the trial court judge; instead, it could exercise its own independent judgment to decide the issue on its merits.

de novo

The appellate court had much less latitude with respect to the second issue. Because the second issue raised a question of fact and not law, the appellate court could not substitute its judgment for that of the jury. It could only review the jury's findings to make sure that they were supported by the evidence. When the question is one of fact, the appellate court can decide only (1) whether there is sufficient evidence to support the jury's verdict or (2) whether the jury's verdict is clearly erroneous—not whether it would have reached the same conclusion.

Regardless of the type of issue (law or fact), the appellate court must base its decision on the written trial court record and exhibits and the attorneys' arguments. Consequently, in *Strong,* the intermediate court of appeals did not see or hear any of the witnesses. The only people present when the appeal was heard were the judges and the attorneys. Not even the defendant, Strong, was present.

based on original trial

If Strong lost his first appeal, he could petition the state supreme court (through a petition for discretionary review), asking it to hear his case. If the state supreme court granted the petition, its review, like that of the intermediate court of appeals, would be limited. Although the supreme court would review the issue of law *de novo,* it would have to defer to the jury's decision on the questions of fact.

Most of the cases that you will read in law school are appellate court decisions, decisions of the state or federal intermediate court of appeals or Supreme Court. These cases, however, represent only a small, and perhaps not representative, percentage of the disputes that lawyers see during the course of the year. See Exhibit 1.2.

Thus, as you read the cases in your casebooks, remember that you are seeing only the proverbial tip of the iceberg. For a case to reach the Supreme Court, the parties must have had the financial means to pursue it, and the Court must have found that the issue raised was significant enough to grant review.

b.   *The Federal Courts*

In the federal system, most cases are heard initially in the federal district courts, the primary trial court in that system. These courts have original jurisdiction over most federal questions and have the power to review the decisions of some administrative agencies. Each state has at least one district court, and many have several. For example, Indiana has the District Court for Northern Indiana and the District Court for Southern Indiana. Cases that are not heard in the district court are usually heard in one of several specialized courts: the United States Tax Court, the United States Court of Federal Claims, or the United States Court of International Trade.

EXHIBIT 1.2	**Number of Cases That Move Through the Court System**

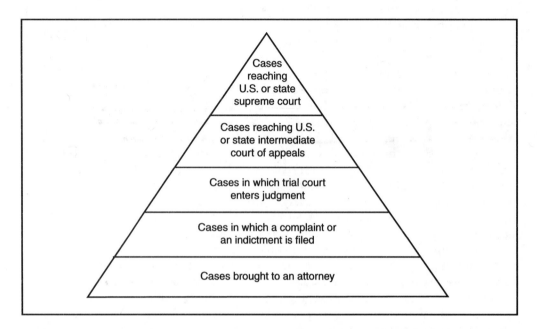

The intermediate court of appeals is the United States Court of Appeals. There are currently thirteen circuits: eleven numbered circuits, the District of Columbia Circuit, and the Federal Circuit. See Exhibit 1.3. The Federal Circuit, which was created in 1982, reviews the decisions of the United States Court of Federal Claims and the United States Court of International Trade, as well as some administrative decisions.

The highest federal court is the United States Supreme Court. Although many people believe that the Supreme Court is all-powerful, in fact it is not. As with other courts, there are limits on the Supreme Court's powers. It can play only one of two roles.

In its first role, the Supreme Court plays a role similar to that of the state supreme courts. In the federal system, it is the highest court, the court of last resort. In contrast, in its second role, it is the final arbiter of federal constitutional law, interpreting the United States Constitution and determining whether the federal government or a state has violated rights granted under the United States Constitution.

Thus, although people often assert that they will take their case all the way to the Supreme Court, they may not be able to. The Supreme Court can hear the case only if it involves a question of federal constitutional law or a federal statute. The Supreme Court does not have the power to hear cases involving only questions of state law. For example, although the United States Supreme Court has the power to determine whether a state's marriage dissolution statutes are constitutional, it does

---

| EXHIBIT 1.3 | The Thirteen Federal Judicial Circuits |

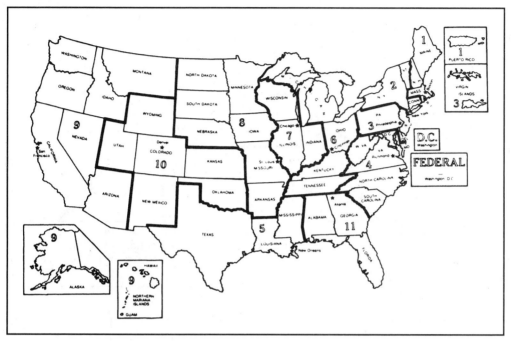

Reprinted from *Federal Reporter* (West's National Reporter System) with permission of West Group Publishing Company.

not have the power to hear purely factual questions, such as whether it would be in the best interests of a child for custody to be granted to the father or whether child support should be set at $300.00 rather than $400.00 per month.

Each year the United States Supreme Court receives more than 7,000 requests for review (writs of certiorari). Of the approximately 100 cases that it actually hears, the overwhelming majority are appeals from the federal courts.

Exhibit 1.4 illustrates the relationships among the various federal courts.

Because the United States District Court and Court of Appeals hear so many cases, not all of their decisions are published. When they are published, district court opinions are published in either the *Federal Supplement* or *Federal Rules Decisions,* and current Court of Appeals decisions are published in *Federal Reporter, Third Series.* (Decisions from the specialized courts are published in specialized reporters.)

All United States Supreme Court decisions are published. The official reporter is *United States Reports,* and the two unofficial reporters are *West's Supreme Court Reporter* and *United States Supreme Court Reports, Lawyer's Edition.*

EXHIBIT 1.4   **The Federal Court System**

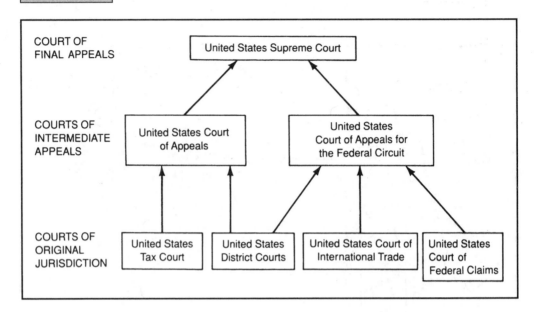

c. State Courts

A number of courts operate within the states. At the lowest level are courts of limited jurisdiction. These courts can hear only certain types of cases or cases involving only limited amounts of money. Municipal or city courts are courts of limited jurisdiction, as are county or district courts and small claims courts.

At the next level are courts of general jurisdiction. These courts have the power to review the decisions of courts of limited jurisdiction and original jurisdiction over claims arising under state law, whether it be under the state constitution, state statutes, or state common law.

About three-quarters of the states now have an intermediate court of appeals. These courts hear appeals as of right from the state courts of general jurisdiction, and the bulk of their caseload is criminal appeals. Because of the size of their workload, many of these courts have several divisions or districts.

Every state has a state supreme court. These courts review the decisions of the state trial courts and courts of appeals and are the final arbiters of questions of state constitutional, statutory, and common law.

Decisions of state trial courts are not usually published. In addition, because of the volume, not all decisions of intermediate state courts of appeals are published. Those that are, and all decisions of the state supreme court, appear in one of West Publishing Company's regional reporters and the state's official reporter, if one exists.

Exhibit 1.5 illustrates the typical relationship among the various state courts.

EXHIBIT 1.5   **The State Court System**

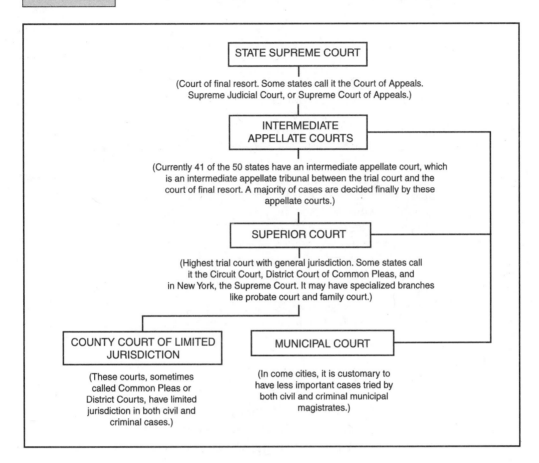

d.   Other Courts

There are also several other court systems. As sovereign entities, many Native American tribes have their own judicial systems, as does the United States military.

§1.2   THE RELATIONSHIP BETWEEN THE FEDERAL AND STATE GOVERNMENTS

It is not enough, however, to look at our system of government from only the perspective of its three branches. To understand the system, you must also understand the relationship between the federal and state governments.

§1.2.1　A Short History

Like most things, our system of government is the product of our history. From the early 1600s until 1781, the "United States" were not united. Instead, the "country" was composed of independent colonies, all operating under different charters and each having its own laws and legal system. Although the colonies traded with each other, the relationship among the colonies was no closer than the relationship among the European countries prior to 1992. It was not until the Articles of Confederation were adopted in 1781 that the "states" ceded any of their rights to a federal government.

Even though the states ceded more rights when the Constitution became effective in 1789, they preserved most of their own law. Each state retained its own executive, its own legislature and laws, and its own court system.

Thus, our system of government is really two systems, a federal system and the fifty state systems, with the United States Constitution brokering the relationship between the two. See Exhibit 1.6.

§1.2.2　The Relationship Between Laws Enacted by Congress and Those Enacted by the State Legislatures

As citizens of the United States, we are subject to two sets of laws: federal law and the law of the state in which we are citizens (or in which we act). Most of the time, there is no conflict between these two sets of laws: Federal law governs some conduct; state law, other conduct. For example, federal law governs bankruptcy proceedings, and state law governs divorce.

Occasionally, however, both Congress and a state legislature enact laws governing the same conduct. Sometimes these laws coexist. For example, both Congress and the states have enacted drug laws. Acting under the powers granted to it under the Commerce Clause, Congress has made it illegal to import controlled substances or to transport them across state lines; the states, acting consistently with the powers reserved to them, have made the possession or sale of controlled substances within the state illegal. In such instances, citizens are subject to both laws. A defendant can be charged under federal law with transporting a drug across state lines and under state law with possession.

There are times, however, when federal and state law do not complement each other and cannot coexist. An act can be legal under federal

The Relationship Between the Federal and State Systems

law but illegal under state law. In such instances, federal law supersedes state law, provided that the federal law is constitutional. As provided in the Supremacy Clause (Article VI, clause 2), laws enacted by Congress under the powers granted to it under the Constitution are the "supreme Law of the Land; and the Judges in every State shall be bound thereby. . . ."

The answer is different when the conflicting laws are from different states. Although there are more and more uniform laws (the Uniform Child Custody Act, the Uniform Commercial Code), an activity that is legal in one state may be illegal in another state. For instance, although prostitution is legal in Nevada as a local option, it is illegal in other states.

§1.2.3   The Relationship Between Federal and State Courts

The relationship between the federal and state court systems is complex. Although each system is autonomous, in certain circumstances the state courts can hear cases brought under federal law and the federal courts can hear cases brought under state law.

For example, although the majority of cases heard in state courts are brought under state law, state courts also have jurisdiction when a case is brought under a provision of the United States Constitution, a treaty, and certain federal statutes. Similarly, although the majority of cases heard in the federal courts involve questions of federal law, the federal courts have jurisdiction over cases involving questions of state law when the parties are from different states (diversity jurisdiction).

The appellate jurisdiction of the courts is somewhat simpler. In the state system, a state's supreme, or highest, court is usually the court of last resort. The United States Supreme Court can review a state court decision only when the case involves a federal question and when there has been a final decision by the state's supreme, or highest, court. If a state has an intermediate court of appeals, that court has the power to review the decisions of the lower courts within its geographic jurisdiction.

In the federal system, the United States Supreme Court is the court of last resort, having the power to review the decisions of the lower federal courts. The United States Court of Appeals has appellate jurisdiction to review the decisions of the United States District Courts and certain administrative agencies.

§1.2.4   The Relationship Among Federal, State, and Local Prosecutors

The power to prosecute cases arising under the United States Constitution and federal statutes is vested in the Department of Justice, which is headed by the Attorney General of the United States, a presidential appointee. Assisting the United States Attorney General are the United States Attorneys for each federal judicial district. The individual United States Attorneys' offices have two divisions: a civil division and a criminal division. The civil division handles civil cases arising under federal law, and the criminal division handles cases involving alleged violations of federal criminal statutes.

At the state level, the system is slightly different. In most states, the attorney for the state is the state attorney general, usually an elected official. Working for the state attorney general are a number of assistant attorney generals. However, unlike the United States attorneys, most state attorney generals do not handle criminal cases. Their clients are the various state agencies. For example, an assistant attorney general may be assigned to the department of social and health services, the department of licensing, the consumer protection bureau, or the department of worker's compensation, providing advice to the agency and representing the agency in civil litigation.

Criminal prosecutions are handled by county and city prosecutors. Each county has its own prosecutor's office, which has both a civil and a criminal division. Attorneys working for the civil division play much the s ame role as state assistant attorney generals. They represent the county and its agencies, providing both advice and representation. In contrast, the attorneys assigned to the criminal division are responsible for prosecutions under the state's criminal code. The county prosecutor's office decides whom to charge and then tries the cases.

Like the counties, cities have their own city attorney's office, which, at least in large cities, has civil and criminal divisions. Attorneys working in the civil division advise city departments and agencies and represent the city in civil litigation; attorneys in the criminal division prosecute criminal cases brought under city ordinances. State, county, and city prosecutors do not represent federal departments or agencies, nor do they handle cases brought under federal law. See Exhibit 1.7.

§1.3   A FINAL COMMENT

Although there are numerous other ways of analyzing the United States system of government, these two perspectives—the three branches perspective and the federal-state perspective—are the foundation on which the rest of your study of law will be built. Without such a foundation, without a thorough understanding of the interrelationships among the parts of the system, many of the concepts that you will encounter in law school would be difficult to learn.

This is particularly true of legal writing. Without understanding both the role each branch plays and the relationship between state and federal government, you cannot be an effective researcher or an effective legal analyst. You must understand the United States system

EXHIBIT 1.7	Federal, State, and Local Prosecutors

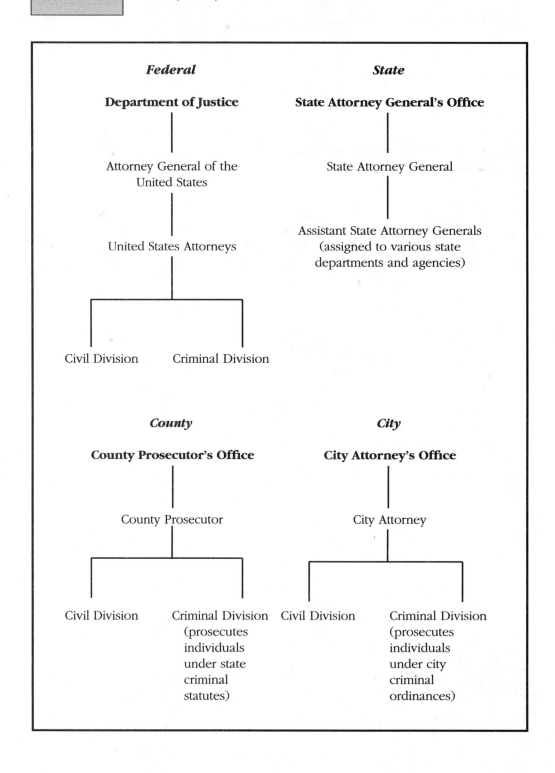

Federal

Department of Justice

Attorney General of the
United States

United States Attorneys

Civil Division   Criminal Division

State

State Attorney General's Office

State Attorney General

Assistant State Attorney Generals
(assigned to various state
departments and agencies)

County

County Prosecutor's Office

County Prosecutor

Civil Division   Criminal Division
(prosecutes
individuals
under state
criminal
statutes)

City

City Attorney's Office

City Attorney

Civil Division   Criminal Division
(prosecutes
individuals
under city
criminal
ordinances)

of government so that you can determine which sources to check. In addition, you must understand the United States system of government before you can tackle the topic of the next chapter, determining whether a particular case or statute is mandatory or persuasive authority.

Chapter 2

An Introduction to Common and Enacted Law

As you saw in Chapter 1, our system of government is complex. To some extent, each of the three branches has the power to create law. The legislative branch enacts statutes, the executive branch promulgates regulations, and the judicial branch both interprets the statutes and regulations and, in the absence of enacted law, creates its own common law rules.

concise summary

In this chapter we explore further the relationship between the three branches and the law that they create.

§2.1 COMMON LAW

Historically, most of our law was common law, or law created by the courts. Rights to property (Property), the rights of parties to enter into and enforce contracts (Contracts), and the right of an individual to recover from another for civil wrongs (Torts) were all governed by common law doctrines developed originally in England and adopted in this country by the states.

This common law relies on a system of precedent. Each case is decided not in isolation, but in light of the cases that have preceded it. In other words, instead of creating new rules for each case, the courts apply the rules announced and developed in earlier cases. The system works as follows.

Assume for the moment a blank slate. You are in a state with no statutes and no common law rules.

In the first case to come before your state's courts, Case A, a mother asks the court to grant her custody of her two children, a 2-year-old son and a 4-year-old daughter. There are no statutes or earlier cases to which the court can look for guidance. The court must make its own law. Looking at the facts of the case before it, the court must decide whether the mother should be awarded custody.

Assume that the court grants the mother's request for custody because, given the ages of the children, the court believes that it is in the children's best interest to remain with their mother. The Tender Years Doctrine is born.

Not long after, another mother requests custody of her children, a 4-year-old son and a 14-year-old daughter.

Unlike Case A, in Case B the slate is not blank. In deciding Case B, the court will be guided by the court's decision in Case A. The reasoning in Case A (that given the ages of the children it is in the children's best interest to remain with their mother) now becomes the "rule" in Case B.

Applying this rule, the court grants the mother custody of her 4-year-old son: Given his age, it is appropriate that he remain with his mother. It also grants the mother custody of her 14-year-old daughter, relying on the daughter's gender. It is most appropriate, the court reasons, that a teenage daughter remain with her mother.

In deciding the next case, Case C, the court applies the rule announced in Case A (that it is in the best interest of young children to remain with their mother) and in Case B (that it is appropriate that teenage daughters remain with their mother), granting a mother custody of 5- and 13-year-old daughters even though the mother has a history of abusing alcohol. Because the mother is not currently drinking, the court holds that it is in the girls' best interest to remain with their mother.

Thus, each case builds on past cases, the reasoning in one case becoming the rule in the next.

Case A	
The court's reasoning:	It is in the best interest of young children to remain with their mother.
Case B	
Rule that the court applies:	It is in the best interest of young children to remain with their mother (cites Case A).
Additional reasoning:	It is in the best interest of teenage daughters to remain with their mother.
Case C	
Rules that the court applies:	(1) It is in the best interest of young children to remain with their mother (cites Cases A and B).
	(2) It is in the best interest of teenage daughters to remain with their mother (cites Case B).
Additional reasoning:	It is appropriate to grant custody to mother despite her history of alcohol abuse because mother is not currently drinking.

Of course, not all of the rules announced in earlier cases are applied in subsequent cases. (If Case D involves the custody of a 1-year-old girl whose mother does not have a history of alcohol abuse, the court would apply only the rule announced in Case A; it would not need to consider the additional rules set out in Cases B and C.) Nor does each case add to the existing law. (The court could decide Case D without giving additional reasons to support its conclusion.)

In addition, in certain circumstances, the courts are not bound by rules from earlier cases. Because the law is court-made, a higher court can overrule the rules set out either in its own decisions or in the decisions of lower courts within its jurisdiction, substituting a new rule for the common law rule announced and applied in the earlier cases.

§2.2   ENACTED LAW

Although historically most of our law was common law, today much of it is enacted law. Acting under the authority granted to them, the legislative and executive branches have enacted and promulgated numerous statutes and regulations, some of which have superseded the common law. For example, state statutes have replaced common law rules governing the relationship between landlords and tenants, and the Uniform Commercial Code has replaced the common law rules governing commercial contracts.

Enacted law, however, seldom stands on its own. In the process of interpreting and applying statutes, the courts often announce new rules. Although these rules are not common law rules, they are rules nonetheless, and unless the legislature enacts legislation changing the rule, they will be followed by the courts in subsequent cases.

The relationship between common law, statutes, and cases interpreting and applying statutes becomes clearer if we look once again at the example begun in the preceding section.

This time presume that not long after the court decided Case D the state legislature enacted a statute rejecting the Tender Years Doctrine. Instead of giving preference to mothers, the statute now requires that the courts grant custody "in accordance with the best interest of the children." No longer is the mother to be given preference; instead, in determining custody, the court is to consider a number of factors including the parents' wishes; the children's wishes; the interaction and interrelationship of the child with parents and siblings; the child's adjustment to his or her home, school, and community; and the mental and physical health of all of the individuals involved.

This statute supersedes the common law doctrine set out in Cases A, B, C, and D. To the extent that these cases are inconsistent with the statute, they are no longer good law. Thus, when Case E comes before the court, the court applies the statute and not the common law doctrine.

The application of a statute is not, however, always clear. For example, in Case E the mother contends that she should be given custody not because the children are young but because she has always been their primary caretaker. Although the statute does not specifically address this argument, the court agrees with the mother, holding that because the mother has always been the primary caretaker, it would be in the children's best interest to remain with her.

Because this "rule" (that the court can consider which parent has been the primary caretaker) is not inconsistent with the statute, it can be used by the courts in subsequent cases. In deciding Case F, the court will apply not just the statute but also the rule announced in Case E. Similarly, in deciding Case G, the court will consider not only the statute but the rule in Case E and any rules announced in Case F. Just as the courts look to precedent in deciding a case involving a common law rule, they also look to precedent in deciding a case brought under a statute.

Thus, in our legal system, there are two types of law: enacted law and case law. Enacted law, when broadly defined, includes any law that has been adopted, enacted, or promulgated by either the people or a legislative body. The United States Constitution, the constitutions of each of the states, federal statutes, state statutes, city and county ordinances, and regulations promulgated by federal, state, and local agencies are all considered enacted law. In contrast, case law is law that has not been promulgated by the people or by a legislative body. It is law that has been created and announced by the courts in written opinions. See Exhibit 2.1. The trick is in knowing which law to apply.

Note: Although the terms "case law" and "common law" are sometimes used interchangeably, they are not synonyms. The term "common law" refers to law created by the courts in the absence of enacted law. For example, most of tort law and much of property law are based not on statutes but on common law doctrines created by the courts. In contrast, the term "case law" is broader. It refers to the written decisions of the courts and encompasses not only decisions announcing and applying common law, but also decisions interpreting and applying enacted law.

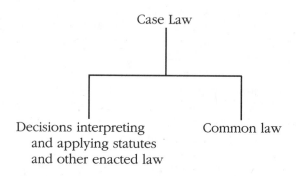

EXHIBIT 2.1	The Types of Law

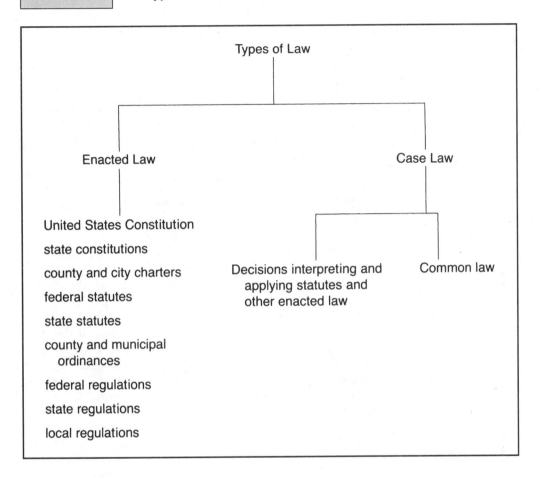

§2.3   MANDATORY VERSUS PERSUASIVE AUTHORITY

Not all enacted and common law is given equal weight. In deciding which law to apply, courts distinguish between mandatory and persuasive authority.

Mandatory authority is law that is binding on the court deciding the case. The court must apply that law. In contrast, persuasive authority is law that is not binding. Although the court may look to that law for guidance, it need not apply it.

Determining whether a particular statute or case is mandatory or persuasive authority is a two-step process. You must first determine which jurisdiction's law applies (that is, whether federal or state law applies and, if state law applies, which state's law); you must then determine which of that jurisdiction's statutes and cases are binding on the court that will be deciding the case.

§2.3.1   Which Jurisdiction's Law Applies?

Sometimes determining which jurisdiction's law applies is easy. For example, common knowledge (and common sense) tells you that federal law probably governs whether a federal PLUS loan constitutes income for federal income tax purposes. Similarly, you would probably guess that a will executed in California by a California resident would be governed by California state law. At other times, though, the determination is much more difficult. You probably would not know what jurisdiction's law governs a real estate contract between a resident of New York and a resident of Pennsylvania for a piece of property located in Florida.

Although the rules governing the determination of which jurisdiction's law applies are beyond the scope of this book (they are studied in Civil Procedure, Federal Courts, and Conflicts), keep two things in mind.

First, remember that in our legal system, federal law almost always preempts state law. Consequently, if there is both a federal and a state statute on the same topic, the federal statute will preempt the state statute to the extent that the two are inconsistent. For example, if a federal statute makes it illegal to discriminate in the renting of an apartment on the basis of familial status but under a state statute such discrimination is lawful, the federal statute governs—it is illegal to discriminate on the basis of familial status. There are a few instances, however, when a state constitutional provision or a state statute will govern: If the state constitution gives a criminal defendant more rights than does the federal constitution, the state constitution applies. States can grant an individual more protection. They cannot, however, take away or restrict rights granted by the federal constitution or a federal statute.

Second, although legal scholars still debate whether there is a federal common law, in the federal system there is not the same body of common law as there is in the states. Unlike the state systems, in the federal system, there are no common law rules governing adverse possession or intentional torts such as assault and battery, false imprisonment, or the intentional infliction of emotional distress. Thus, if the cause of action is based on a common law doctrine, the case is probably governed by state and not federal law.

§2.3.2   What "Law" Will Be Binding on the Court?

Within each jurisdiction, the authorities are ranked. The United States Constitution is the highest authority, binding both state and federal courts. Under the Constitution is other state and federal law. See Exhibit 2.2.

In the federal system, the highest authority is the Constitution. Under the Constitution are the federal statutes and regulations, and under the federal statutes and regulations are the cases interpreting and applying them.

EXHIBIT 2.2	Ranking of Authorities

United States Constitution

State Constitution
Cannot take away rights granted by the United States Constitution

Federal Statutes
Cannot take away rights granted by the United States Constitution; in addition, Congress can only enact laws that are consistent with the grant of power given to Congress under the Constitution.

State Statutes
Cannot take away rights granted by the state constitution; in addition, a state legislature can only enact laws that are consistent with the power retained by the states under the United States Constitution and power granted to that particular state legislature by that state's constitution.

United States Supreme Court
Bound by the United States Constitution and United States Code insofar as the Code is constitutional. Not bound by its own prior decisions, decisions of state courts, or decisions of lower courts.

State Supreme Court
Bound by the United States Constitution and the state's constitution, decisions of the United States Supreme Court interpreting the United States Constitution or relating to a dispute involving that state, and state statutes insofar as those statutes are constitutional. Not bound by its own prior decisions, decisions of federal courts not related to federal constitutional questions or involving the state, the decisions of other states, or decisions of lower courts within the same state.

(continued on next page)

In the state system, the ranking is similar. The highest authority is the state constitution, followed by (1) state statutes and regulations and the cases interpreting and applying those statutes and regulations and (2) the state's common law.

In addition, the cases themselves are ranked. In both the federal and state systems, decisions of the United States Supreme Court carry the most weight: When deciding a case involving the same law and sim-

---

| EXHIBIT 2.2 | *(continued)* |

United States Court of Appeals
(13 circuits)
Bound by United States Constitution, United States Code, and United States Supreme Court decisions. Not bound by decisions issued by the United States District Court, nor is any given circuit bound by its own prior decisions or the decisions of another circuit.

State Court of Appeals
Bound by the United States Constitution and state constitutions, decisions of the state supreme courts and and the United States Supreme Court relating to federal constitutional questions. Not bound by its own prior decisions, decisions by the courts of any other state, or by the decisions of any lower court within the same state.

United States District Courts
(These are the trial courts in the federal system.) Each court is bound by the United States Constitution, the United States Code, and decisions of the United States Supreme Court and the Court of Appeals for the circuit in which the district court is located. The opinions of the district court may or may not be published, and, although they have some persuasive authority, no court is bound by them.

State Trial Courts
Courts bound by the United States Constitution and state constitutions, state statutes, decisions of the United States Supreme Court relating to federal constitutional issues, and decisions of the state supreme court and state court of appeals for the geographic area in which the trial court is located. In most states decisions of the trial courts are not published. Whether or not such decisions are published, no court is bound by them.

---

ilar facts, both the courts of appeals and the trial courts are bound by the decisions of the supreme, or highest, state courts. Decisions of intermediate courts of appeals come next; the trial courts under the jurisdiction of the intermediate court of appeals are bound by the court of appeals' decisions. At the bottom are the trial courts. Trial court decisions are binding only on the parties involved in the particular case.

Statutes and cases are also ranked by date. More recent statutes supersede earlier versions, and more recent common law rules supersede early rules by the same level court. Courts are bound by the highest court's most recent decision. For example, if there is a 1967 state intermediate court of appeals decision that makes an activity legal and a 1986 state supreme court decision that makes it illegal, in the absence of a statute, the 1986 supreme court decision governs. The 1986 decision would be mandatory authority, and all of the courts within that jurisdiction would be bound by that decision.

Chapter 3

Reading and Analyzing Statutes and Cases

When someone says the word "lawyer," what images come to mind? Do you see a well-dressed individual cross-examining a witness? Making an impassioned argument to a jury? Hugging his or her client when the jury returns the verdict in their favor?

Although some lawyers do these things, these are more the images of TV lawyering than they are real lawyering. Real lawyers spend much of their time reading and writing. Consider the following quote from an associate at a major law firm.

> My view of lawyering has changed dramatically since I came to law school. In my first year of law school, I saw myself as a trial lawyer. I thought that most of my time would be spent either preparing for trial or in trial. The truth of the matter is that I have been inside the courthouse only three or four times during the last year and that was to look through court files. Instead, most of my time is spent reading and preparing documents, doing legal research, and writing memos and briefs. Don't get me wrong. The work that I do is extremely interesting. It is just that I never saw myself spending seven or eight hours a day reading and writing.
>
> —Second-year associate at a large law firm

The way in which lawyers read is not, however, the way in which most individuals read. Part of learning how to think like a lawyer is learning how to read like a lawyer.

In this chapter, we describe some of the strategies that lawyers use in reading statutes and cases. Then, in Chapters 5 and 6, we show you how to apply these strategies in reading specific statutes and cases.

§3.1   GOOD LAWYERS ARE GOOD READERS

Good lawyers are good readers. When they read a document, statute, or case, they read exactly what is on the page. They do not skip words, read in words, or misread words. In addition, they have good vocabularies. They recognize and understand most of the words they read, and the ones they do not recognize or understand they look up.

Poor reading skills can significantly affect your ability to understand what it is you are reading. For instance, in the following example, which is taken from the transcript of a law student reading a case aloud, Jackie, a first year student, mispronounced and apparently did not recognize the word "palatial."

EXAMPLE   TRANSCRIPT OF A STUDENT, JACKIE, READING CASE ALOUD

"Some months prior to the alleged imprisonment, the plaintiff, while in Jaffa, announced her intention to leave the sect. The defendant, with the help of the plaintiff's husband, persuaded the plaintiff to return to the United States aboard the sect's platial [sic] yacht, *The Kingdom*."

James, another student who read the same case, misread the following sentence. The first example shows how the sentence appears in the casebook. The second example shows how James read it when he read the sentence aloud.

EXAMPLE   SENTENCE AS IT APPEARS IN THE CASE BOOK

According to the uncontradicted evidence, at no time did anyone physically restrain the plaintiff except for the defendant's refusal once the plaintiff announced her decision to quit the yacht to let the plaintiff use a small boat to take herself, her children and her belongings ashore.

EXAMPLE   HOW JAMES READ THE SENTENCE

"According to the uncontradicted evidence, at no time did anyone physically restrain the plaintiff except for the defendant's [pause] defendant's refusal once [pause] defendant's refusal once [pause] the plaintiff announced her decision to the quit the yacht to let the plaintiff use a small boat to take herself, her children, and her belongings ashore."

When questioned about what the court was saying in this sentence, James stated that the defendant had, on one occasion, refused to let the plaintiff take the boat. In fact, the court says that the refusal came once the plaintiff announced her decision to quit the yacht.

Although at first these errors may seem insignificant, in each instance they resulted in the student misunderstanding the case and, thus, the rules and the court's reasoning. In addition, in both instances, the errors were a harbinger of things to come. Both students ended up doing poorly on their exams. At the end of the first year, Jackie was in the bottom 20 percent of her class, and James had flunked out.

To determine whether you may be misreading cases, make two copies of one of the cases in your casebook. Keep one copy for yourself, and give the other one to a trusted classmate or teaching assistant. Then read aloud from your copy while your partner follows along on his or her copy, highlighting any words or phrases that you misread and any words that you mispronounce or do not appear to understand. After you have finished your reading of the case, compare your understanding of the case with your partner's. Did you both read the case in essentially the same way? If your partner noted more than one or two problems or if your understanding of the case is substantially different from your partner's understanding of it, try the following. First, try reading more slowly. You may be trying to read the material too quickly. Second, take the time to look up any words that you are not sure you understand. Third, if the problems appear to be serious, ask your school's learning center if it can provide you with a more thorough evaluation of your reading skills.

§3.2   GOOD LEGAL READERS READ AND REREAD MATERIAL UNTIL THEY ARE SURE THEY UNDERSTAND IT

While in some types of reading you can skip sections you do not completely understand, such a strategy does not work when you are doing legal reading. If the document, statute, or case is one that is relevant to your problem, you need to read and reread it until you are sure you understand it.

The following example shows how William stayed with a case until he was sure he understood it. The material in the regular typeface is the text of the case. The material in italics is what William said after he had read that section of the text.

> **EXAMPLE**

WHITTAKER V. SANFORD

110 Me. 77, 88 S. 399 (1912)

SAVAGE, J. Action for false imprisonment. The plaintiff recovered a verdict for $1,100. The case comes up on defendant's exceptions and a motion for a new trial.

So the defendant is the appellant and is appealing the verdict of $1,100.

The plaintiff had been a member of a religious sect which had colonies in Maine and in Jaffa, Syria, and of which the defendant was a leader. Some months prior to the alleged imprisonment, the plaintiff, while in Jaffa, announced her intention to leave the sect.

I need to reread this again. [Rereads sentence.] So just prior to the alleged imprisonment the plaintiff was in Jaffa and expressed an intention to leave the sect. At this point, I am a bit confused about who the parties are. I need to reread this to make sure that I have the facts straight. [Rereads from the beginning.] OK. This is an action for false imprisonment. The plaintiff recovered a verdict for $1,100. The case came up on the defendant's exceptions. The plaintiff is a member of the sect and the defendant is the head of the sect, so Whittaker is the member of the sect and Sanford is its leader.

Although it took William more time to read the case than it took some of the other students, the payoff was substantial. Although his undergraduate GPA and LSAT placed William in the bottom 10 percent of the entering class, at the end of his first year, his law school GPA placed him in the top 10 percent.

There are several things you can do to make sure you understand the cases you are reading. First, see if you can diagram the action. At the trial court level, who sued whom and what was the cause of action? Who "won" at trial, who filed the appeal, and what is the issue on appeal?

Second, do not underestimate the value of preparing your own case briefs. While it may be faster and easier to highlight sections of a statute or case, highlighting does not ensure that you understand the material you are reading. In fact, there is some evidence that students who highlight remember less than students who do not. In highlighting a section, some students focus their attention on the process of highlighting and not on the material they are highlighting. As a result, when they are asked to recall what it is they just highlighted, they are unable to do so.

Finally, after reading a section, test yourself to make sure you understood what it is you have just read. After you have finished reading a statute or case, turn the statute or case over and summarize what it said. If you cannot do this, you need to go back and reread the material until you can.

§3.3   GOOD LEGAL READERS ENGAGE IN BOTH ANALYSIS AND SYNTHESIS

In addition to reading accurately and until they understand the materials, good legal readers analyze and synthesize the material they read. Analysis is the process of taking a statute or case apart. In reading statutes, you analyze each section and subsection, making sure you understand each. In reading cases, you identify the issue that was before the court, the rule or rules the court applied in deciding that issue, the facts the court considered in applying those rules, and the court's reasoning or rationale. When you "brief" a statute or case, you are engaging in analysis.

In contrast, synthesis is the process of putting the pieces together. You take each of the statutory sections and cases you have read and try to make sense of them. Are they consistent? What are the steps in the analysis? How do they fit into your existing conceptual frameworks? When you create a decision tree like the one set out on page 77 (in Chapter 5) or in a course outline, you are engaging in synthesis.

The following example shows how a law professor engaged in both analysis and synthesis. Note both how she analyzes the case she is currently reading and how she tries to reconcile what the court says in that case with the Restatement section that set out the elements of false imprisonment. The text is set out in regular type and the professor's comments are in italics.

EXAMPLE

There was evidence that the plaintiff had been ashore a number of times, had been on numerous outings, and had been treated as a guest during her stay aboard the yacht. According to the uncontradicted evidence, at no time did anyone physically restrain the plaintiff except for the defendant's refusal, once the plaintiff announced her decision to quit the yacht, to let the plaintiff use a small boat to take herself, her children, and her belongings ashore.

I'm sort of getting a visual image of the boat that she was in and out of . . . uhm . . . the plaintiff had been ashore. I'm thinking about the elements that I just read [a reference to the Restatement section that had been set out immediately before the case] *and I'm trying to see how, I guess, frankly how I would decide the case on a certain level before I even want to know what Judge Savage thought.* [Pause.] *I need to look at the Restatement section.* [She looks back at the Restatement section.] *Is the defendant acting to or with intent to confine the plaintiff? She got off the boat. That kind of bothers me. That results directly or indirectly in confinement. Maybe that's relevant here. The other is conscious of the confinement or is harmed by it. Given the facts, that bothers me too.*

Doing analysis and synthesis is both time-consuming and hard work. You are no longer reading just for information. Instead, as you are reading, you are either placing new information into existing conceptual frameworks or constructing completely new frameworks.

If you are like most law students, at some point you will argue that law school would be a lot easier if your professors put the pieces together for you, if they just gave you their conceptual frameworks. If you had come to law school just to learn the law, you would be right. It would be easier for both you and your professors if they just gave you the law. You would, however, need to come back to law school each time a statute was amended or a new case came out so that your professors could tell you how the change affected "the law."

Although you will learn some law while you are in law school, the real reason you came to law school was to learn how to think like a lawyer. Thus, the primary skills you will need to teach yourself while you are in law school are how to do legal analysis and synthesis. You need to be able to look at a statute and a group of cases and determine what the law is and how it might be applied in a particular situation.

§3.4   GOOD LEGAL READERS PLACE THE STATUTES AND CASES THEY READ INTO THEIR HISTORICAL, SOCIAL, ECONOMIC, POLITICAL, AND LEGAL CONTEXTS

Good legal readers understand that statutes are usually enacted to solve a problem or to promote certain interests and that judicial decisions reflect, at least in part, the time and place in which they were written. As a consequence, in reading statutes and cases, good legal readers place them in their historical, social, economic, political, and legal contexts. They note the date that the statute was enacted and amended and the year in which the case was decided. They think about the social and economic conditions during those periods and about the political issues that were in the headlines when the statute was enacted or the case was decided. Finally, they place the case in its larger legal context. They determine how the particular issue fits into the broader area of law, they note whether the decision is from an intermediate court of appeals or the highest court in the jurisdiction, and they read the court's decision in light of the standard of review the court applied. Was the court deciding the issue *de novo,* or was it simply looking to see whether there was sufficient evidence to support the jury's verdict?

For example, in the case described earlier in this chapter, the professor placed the case in its historical, social, and political context. She noted that the case was an old one: It was decided by the Supreme Court of Maine in 1912. In addition, she noted that in 1912 $1,100 was a substantial sum of money. She also considered the social climate in 1912: the role of women and their rights and the public's attitudes about "religious cults." She knew that in 1912 women had far fewer rights. It was often the husband who determined where the couple lived and what religion they practiced. What she did not know is how religious cults were viewed. In 1912 did people view religious cults in the same way most people view them today? Were cults seen as a problem? How did these factors influence the court's decision and the way the judge wrote his opinion?

You need to think about the cases you read in similar ways. When you are reading cases, pay close attention to the dates of the decisions and the courts that issued them. If you read the cases in chronological order, can you discern a trend? Over the last fifty, twenty-five, or five years, have the rules or the way the courts apply those rules changed? If the answer is yes, what social, economic, or political events might account for those changes? In contrast, if you arrange the decisions by jurisdiction, does a pattern appear? For example, do industrial states tend to take one approach and more rural states another? Are some jurisdictions more conservative while others more liberal? If you read between the lines, what do you think motivated the judges and persuaded them to decide the cases in one way rather than another?

§3.5   GOOD LEGAL READERS "JUDGE" THE STATUTES AND CASES THEY READ

As a beginning law student, you may be tempted to accept as true everything that you read. Who are you to judge the soundness of a Supreme Court justice's analysis or Congress's choice of a particular word or phrase? Do not give in to the temptation to passively accept everything you read. If you are going to be a good legal reader, you need to question and evaluate everything.

In judging the cases you read, make sure you do more than evaluate the facts. Although in the following example William engages in some evaluation, it is the evaluation of a nonlawyer. He evaluates the witness's testimony, not the court's choice of rule, application of the rules to the facts, or reasoning. Once again, the text of the case is set out using a regular typeface and William's comments are in italics.

EXAMPLE

There was evidence that the plaintiff had been ashore a number of times, had been on numerous outings, and had been treated as a guest during her stay aboard the yacht.

So at this point I'm getting a picture of what happened. . . . I'm not sure though. There is evidence that the plaintiff had been ashore, so at this point I'm thinking was she really held against her will? So I have doubts, doubts about the plaintiff's story at this point.

According to the uncontradicted evidence, at no time did anyone physically restrain the plaintiff except for the defendant's refusal, once the plaintiff announced her decision to quit the yacht, to let the plaintiff use a small boat to take herself, her children, and her belongings ashore.

Well . . . the defendant by this point isn't really stopping the plaintiff from leaving.

Throughout the entire episode the plaintiff's husband was with her and repeatedly tried to persuade her to change her mind and remain with the sect.

At this point, mentally, I think, . . . I don't think the plaintiff's story doesn't hold water. . . . That's what I am thinking. Because her husband was there so maybe you, there's in my mind that her story doesn't hold water. So I am thinking at this point that the court might end up reversing her position.

In contrast, the professor evaluated the court's conclusion and reasoning. After she finished reading the case, the professor made the following comments. Note how she talks about the elements of the tort and how she poses a hypothetical.

EXAMPLE

I'm not sure that the plaintiff proved all of the elements of false imprisonment. For example, I'm not sure that the plaintiff proved that the defendant intended to confine the plaintiff. If I remember correctly, [pause] on a number of occasions he allowed her to go ashore. He just wouldn't let her use the small boat to take her children and their things ashore. It would have been interesting to know what would have happened if a boat had come to get the plaintiff. Would the defendant have let her go? If he would have, there wouldn't have been false imprisonment. [Pause.] The facts may, however, support a finding that the defendant's actions resulted in confinement. In those days, the plaintiff may not have had a way to contact anyone on shore to ask them to come get her. Although the court may have reached the right result, I wish Judge Savage had done more analysis. [Pause.] I get the feeling that he had made up his mind, maybe he didn't like cults, and then just tried to justify his conclusion.

§3.6   GOOD LEGAL READERS READ FOR A SPECIFIC PURPOSE

The reading you do for your law school classes is very different from the reading you will do in practice. In law school, you read so that you will be prepared for class. Consider the following comment made by James.

EXAMPLE

When I read cases, I usually read them not for briefing cases per se, but more out of fear of being called on in class. I don't want to look like a fool so I just want to know the basic principles.

In contrast, in practice you will read for a specific purpose. For example, you will read to keep up to date in an area of law, to find the answer to a question that a client has posed, to find statutes or cases to support your client's position, or to find holes in your opponent's arguments.

In reading the statutes and cases for your legal writing assignments, read not as a student but as a lawyer. Initially, read to find out what the law is. Analyze the statutes and cases you have found and then put the pieces together. Then read the cases as the parties and the court would read them. Begin by putting yourself in your client's position. How can your client use the statutes and cases to support its position? Then reread the statutes and cases. How can the other side use the same statutes and cases to support its position? Finally, put yourself in the court's position. If you were the judge, how would you read the statutes and cases?

§3.7   GOOD LEGAL READERS UNDERSTAND THAT STATUTES AND CASES CAN BE READ IN MORE THAN ONE WAY

Different people have different beliefs about text. While some people believe there is a right way to read each statute or case, others believe that most statutes and cases can be read in more than one way. For those in the first group, the meaning of a particular text is fixed. For those in the second group, the meaning of a particular text is "constructed" by juries and judges and the attorneys who talk to them.

As a general rule, the students who seem to have the easiest time in their first year of law school are those who believe that statutes and cases can be read in more than one way, that the meaning of a particular text is socially constructed. These students have an easier time seeing how each side might interpret a particular statute and stating a rule so that it favors their client's position. When they talk about a court's holding, they refer to it as "a holding," not "*the* holding."

If you are a student who believes that meaning is fixed, be aware of how your belief system is affecting the way in which you read statutes and cases and the way in which you make arguments. In reading a case, can you see how both the plaintiff and the defendant might be able to use the same case to support their arguments? In making arguments, are you able to see what the other side might argue and how you might be able to respond to those arguments? Are you spending too much time looking for the correct answer and not enough time creating that answer? In contrast, if you are a student who believes that meaning is socially constructed, be careful that you do not become cynical or only a "hired gun." Although there may be many ways of reading a particular statute or case, not all of those readings will lead to a just result.

Reading and thinking like a lawyer are not skills that you can learn overnight. There are no crash courses, short cuts, or magic wands. Instead, you will learn to read and think like a lawyer through trial and error and by observing how real lawyers, not TV lawyers, read and think about statutes and cases.

Part II

Objective Memoranda and Client Letters

It is the side of lawyering that is seldom portrayed in novels or TV dramas. It is, however, how most lawyers spend most of their time. Instead of spending their days in court, they spend their days behind their desks, researching and writing.

In this book we introduce you to two of the kinds of writing you will do as a lawyer. In Chapters 4, 5, and 6, we describe objective writing, and in Chapter 7, advisory writing. In particular, we walk you through the process of writing two types of "documents": an objective in-house memorandum and a client letter.

Chapter 4

The Objective Memorandum: Its Purpose, Audience, and Format

If you work as a legal intern after your first year of law school, you will probably spend most of your time researching and writing objective memoranda, also known as office memos. An attorney will ask you to research a question, you will research it, and then you will present your research and analysis to the attorney in a written memo. The attorney who assigned the project will then read through your memo and, using the information contained in it, advise a client, negotiate with an opposing party, or prepare a brief or oral argument.

Thus, office memos are in-house memoranda that have as their primary audience attorneys in the office and that have as their primary purpose providing those attorneys with information. In addition, sometimes a copy of the memo is sent directly to the client, who will read it to determine what his or her options are.

Although the format of a memo will vary from law firm to law firm, most attorneys want the following sections: a heading, a statement of facts, a formal statement of the issue, a brief answer, a discussion section, and a formal conclusion.

elements of a memo

Set out below are two memos written by first-year law students. As you read through them, ask yourself the following questions.

- What types of information are contained in the memos?
- In what order is that information presented?
- In presenting the information, what role did the students assume? Did they simply play the role of a "reporter," summarizing what they had found, or did they do more?

- What types of authority did the students cite? How did they use those authorities?
- Are the memos well written? Why or why not?

EXAMPLE 1

To: Connie Krontz

From: Thomas McMurty

Date: September 28, 2002

Re: Beaver Custom Carpets, File No. 02-478

Whether oral contract for three rugs is enforceable under Colorado's UCC Statute of Frauds exception for specially manufactured goods when the rugs have the Reutlinger family flower woven into them at one-foot intervals.

Statement of Facts

Our client, Beaver Custom Carpets (BCC), a Colorado corporation doing business in Colorado, wants to know whether it can enforce an oral contract for three rugs that were manufactured to the buyers' specifications.

The buyers, Mr. and Mrs. McKibbin, first contacted BCC in June of this year, asking whether BCC could replicate the original rugs in the Reutlinger Mansion, which Mr. and Mrs. McKibbin were refurbishing and turning into a bed and breakfast. Around the perimeter of each rug was a twelve-inch maroon strip; in the center was beige carpet with the Reutlinger family flower woven into the carpet at one-foot intervals.

After examining a picture of the rugs, BCC called its manufacturer. The manufacturer told BCC's sales representative that it could produce the rugs. Although the looms would have to be specially set, standard dyes could be used. On June 19, the sales representative sent the McKibbins a proposal setting out the specifications and the price, $16,875.

On June 29, Mrs. McKibbin called the sales representative and told him that she and her husband wanted to purchase the rugs. The next day, the salesperson ordered the rugs from the manufacturer. A written contract was not sent to the McKibbins.

On August 4, Mrs. McKibbin called BCC and told the sales representative that because her husband had fallen from the roof of the mansion, they were canceling their order. BCC called its manufacturer the same day. Unfortunately, the rugs had already been completed, and BCC was forced to accept delivery of the rugs at a cost of $13,500.

On August 15, BCC sent the McKibbins a bill for the proposal price of the rugs. Last week, BCC received a letter from the McKibbins' attorney stating that because the contract was not in writing, it was not enforceable under the UCC Statute of Frauds.

BCC sold the rugs to a wholesaler on September 1 for $10,000. BCC has done business with this wholesaler on one prior occasion. Similar rugs are not available from other carpet stores.

BCC is a specialty carpet firm that specializes in custom work. It has been in business for only one year and is in financial trouble.

Issue

Under Colorado's UCC Statute of Frauds exception for specially manufactured goods, Colo. Rev. Stat. § 4-2-201(3)(a), is an oral contract for the sale of rugs enforceable when (1) the rugs were manufactured to the buyers' specifications, (2) the same rugs are not available at other outlets, (3) the buyers told the seller that they did not want the rugs after the rugs had been completed, and (4) the seller sold the rugs to a wholesaler with whom it had done business on one prior occasion?

[handwritten: what is the applicable Law?]

Brief Answer

Probably. Although the formal requirements of the Statute of Frauds are not met, the contract is probably enforceable under the exception for specially manufactured goods: To produce the rugs, the manufacturer had to specially set its looms, and the rugs were sold not to a retail customer but to a wholesaler at a loss.

Discussion

Specially manufactured goods are exempt from the writing requirement because the very nature of the goods serves as a reliable indication that a contract was indeed formed. When the goods conform to the special needs of a particular buyer and are not, therefore, suitable for sale to others, not only is the likelihood of a perjured claim diminished, but denying enforcement of such a contract would impose a substantial hardship on the aggrieved party. *See Colorado Carpet Installation, Inc. v. Palermo, 668 P.2d 1384, 1390 (Colo. 1983). Accord Impossible Electronics Techniques, Inc. v. Wackenhut Protective Systems, Inc.,* 669 F.2d 1026, 1037 (5th Cir. 1982).

Thus, even if the formal requirements of the UCC Statute of Frauds are not met, a contract is enforceable if the goods were specially manufactured. The applicable portion of the Colorado statute reads as follows.

(3) A contract which does not satisfy the requirements of subsection (1) but which is valid in other respects is enforceable

(a) if the goods are to be specially manufactured for the buyer and are not suitable for sale to others in the ordinary course of the seller's business and the seller, before notice of repudiation is received and under circumstances which reasonably indicate that the goods are for the buyer, has made either a substantial beginning of their manufacture or commitments for their procurement. . . .

Colo. Rev. Stat. § 4-2-201(3)(a).

In our case, two of the elements are not likely to be in dispute. The rugs had been completed before notice of repudiation was received, and the flower woven into the rugs indicates that the rugs were made for the McKibbins. Two elements will, however, be in dispute. The parties will disagree about whether the rugs were specially manufactured and about whether BCC was able to resell the rugs in the ordinary course of its business.

Specially Manufactured for the Buyer

Although the term "specially manufactured" is not defined in the statute, the Colorado Supreme Court has held that it refers to the nature of the goods and not to whether the goods were made in the usual course of the seller's business. *Colorado Carpet Installation, Inc. v. Palermo,* 668 P.2d 1384, 1390 (Colo. 1983).

In the only Colorado case discussing the exception for specially manufactured goods, the Colorado Supreme Court held that carpeting that was available from other carpet outlets and that had not been cut to unusual shapes or subjected to special dyeing, weaving, or other procedures was not specially manufactured. *Id.* In contrast, in a Virginia case, the Virginia Supreme Court held that wrapping material imprinted with the buyer's name and unique artwork and cut to the buyer's specifications was "specially manufactured because the wrapping material was personalized and of little value to a third party." *Flowers Baking Co. of Lynchburg, Inc. v. R-P Packaging, Inc.,* 329 S.E.2d 462, 464 (Va. 1985). *Accord Smith-Scarf Paper Co. v. P.N. Hirsch & Co. Stores, Inc.,* 754 S.W.2d 928 (Mo. Ct. App. 1988) (holding that cellophane imprinted with the defendant's logo and cut to the size specified by the defendant was specially manufactured).

In the present case, BCC can argue that the rugs were specially manufactured for the buyer. Relying on the plain language of the statute, it can argue that the rugs were in fact specially manufactured: BCC had to make special arrangements with the manufacturer and, to produce the rugs, the manufacturer had to specially set its looms.

BCC can also contrast the facts in its case to the facts in *Colorado Carpet.* Unlike *Colorado Carpet,* in this case, identical rugs are not available from other carpet outlets. The rugs in question are one of a kind: They were made to fit specific rooms, and special weaving was required. The case is more like *Flowers.* Like the wrapping material, the rugs were personalized. The Reutlinger family flower is as distinctive as any company name or logo and, as a consequence, rugs with such a flower woven into them are of little value to a third party.

Finally, BCC can argue policy. In this instance, the rugs themselves are evidence that a contract was formed. BCC probably would not have produced rugs matching the original rugs in the Reutlinger Mansion had there not been a contract. In addition, if the court does not enforce the contract, BCC, a small business which is already in financial trouble, will suffer a substantial loss.

The McKibbins will argue that the rugs were not specially manufactured. Unlike *Flowers,* in this case it is only the Reutlinger family flower and not the Reutlinger name that is woven into the rugs. Furthermore, the flower is not particularly unusual; BCC was able to sell the rugs to a wholesaler with little or no difficulty.

The McKibbins' best argument is, however, a policy argument. They can argue that under the UCC, oral contacts should be the exception rather than the rule. Thus, a seller whose only business is custom or specially manufactured goods should not be exempt from the Statute of Frauds simply because its goods are specially manufactured. For, if all of such a seller's goods are custom, a written contract will never be necessary, and written contracts will become the exception and not the rule. In addition, the McKibbins can argue that a seller who deals in only custom goods is just as likely to fabricate a contract for custom goods as is a seller who deals in ready-made merchandise.

BCC can respond to such an argument by citing *Wackenhut,* a case in which the seller sold custom closed-circuit television cameras. In holding that the cameras were specially manufactured, the court said the fact that the seller is in the business of manufacturing custom-designed and custom-made goods does not necessarily preclude a finding that the goods are specially manufactured. *Id.* at 1037.

The court will probably find that the rugs were specially manufactured for the McKibbins. The rugs were not available from other outlets and, to produce the rugs, the manufacturer had to specially set its looms. Although BCC is in the business of producing custom carpets, it is not likely that it would have produced rugs with the Reutlinger family flower woven into them unless it had been requested to do so.

Not Suitable for Sale to Others in the Ordinary Course of the Seller's Business

Specific rule defined

In determining whether goods are suitable for sale to others in the ordinary course of the seller's business, the courts look first at the nature of the seller's business and then at whether the seller could reasonably be expected to find a buyer for the goods. *See Colorado Carpet Inc.,* 668 P.2d at 1391. For example, in *Colorado Carpet,* the court first identified the nature of Colorado Carpet's business, finding that its business was to purchase carpet from wholesalers and then to resell the carpet to retail purchasers at a price that included a labor charge for installation. It then looked at whether it was reasonable to expect that Colorado Carpet could resell the carpets. In holding that it was reasonable, the court considered three factors: (1) that Colorado Carpet dealt in similar carpets on a regular basis, (2) that the carpets were large enough that they could be cut to other dimensions, and (3) that Colorado Carpet had in fact been able to resell the carpets. It returned some of the carpet to the manufacturer and sold the rest to a local purchaser. *Id.* Thus, the court found that the goods were suitable for sale to another in the ordinary course of Colorado Carpet's business and that the exception for specially manufactured goods did not apply. *Id.*

Discussion

Analysis

BCC can argue that it was not able to sell the goods in the ordinary course of its business. Unlike Colorado Carpet, BCC does not deal in standard carpets in standard sizes and shapes. The individuals with whom BCC does business are looking for rugs designed to their specifications. In addition, the rugs cannot be altered to make them suitable for another customer. The rugs cannot be cut to another size or shape, and the colors and flower design cannot be changed. Finally, BCC can argue that it was not able to sell the goods to a retail customer. It had to resell them to a wholesaler.

The McKibbins will respond by arguing that BCC was able to resell the goods. While it did not resell them to a retail customer, it did resell them to a wholesale dealer with whom it had done business in the past. In addition, the facts do not indicate that BCC made any attempt to resell the rugs to a retail customer.

Because BCC's ordinary course of business is selling to retail customers and not wholesale companies, a court is likely to find that the rugs were not suitable for sale to others in the ordinary course of BCC's business. It is not reasonable to expect that BCC could find a retail customer that would want rugs in those sizes and colors and with that particular design.

Conclusion

Although the formal requirements of the UCC Statute of Frauds are not met, the contract between BCC and the McKibbins is probably enforceable under the exception for specially manufactured goods.

BCC should be able to prove the first element, that the rugs were specially manufactured for the McKibbins. The rugs were made to the McKibbins' specifications: The manufacturer specially set its looms to weave the Reutlinger family flower into the rugs.

BCC should also be able to prove the second element, that the goods are not suitable for sale to others in the ordinary course of BCC's business. BCC's ordinary course of business is selling carpets to retail customers, not wholesalers.

The third element, that there had been a substantial beginning prior to repudiation, and the fourth element, that the evidence reasonably indicates that the goods were for the McKibbins, are not likely to be in dispute. The rugs had been completed at the time Mrs. McKibbin canceled the order, and the family flower is evidence that the goods were for the McKibbins.

Because it is likely that a court would enforce the contract, we should advise BCC to pursue this action. We can either contact the McKibbins' attorney and attempt to settle the matter or file a complaint.

EXAMPLE 2

To: Margaret Anne Graham
        Senior Prosecutor, King County

From: Samuel Jones
        Assistant Deputy Prosecutor

Date: September 9, 2002

Re: Case No. 02-08-6695
        Doug Richardson, Possession of Stolen Property

Statement of Facts

You have asked me to evaluate the State's case against Doug Richardson, who has been charged with Possession of Stolen Property in the First Degree.

On April 17, 2002, the owner of the Last Chance Tavern purchased a Rocket Blaster pinball machine, serial number A47699942, for $3,900.00. On July 6, 2002, the machine was stolen from the tavern.

On August 21, 2002, the police executed a search warrant for the house located at 2204 65th Ave in Seattle, Washington. In the living room, the police located a Rocket Blaster pinball machine with the serial number A47699942. There was a 4″ x 8″ identification decal visible on the front of the pinball machine. Although some of the label had been scratched off, the letters "Prop of L st C nce Tavern" were still visible. The coin box had been disabled so that coins were not necessary to operate the machine. The police did not dust the machine for fingerprints.

At the time of the search, Richardson was the sole occupant of the residence. He told the police that he was housesitting for his friend, Stan Coming, for six weeks, beginning on July 18, 2002. Richardson told the police that although he was not paying rent, he had agreed to pay for his long distance phone calls and for the pay-for-view movies that he ordered. Richardson had a key to the residence, and the police found a number of Mr. Richardson's belongings in the house, including clothing, a radio, textbooks, class notes, and a checkbook. Richardson told the police that he had his own apartment. The police have not yet verified this fact.

In response to questions about the pinball machine, Richardson told the police that Coming had told him that he had purchased the pinball machine from a "fence."

Issue Statement

Under RCW 9A.56.150,[1] can the State prove all of the elements of Possession of Stolen Property in the First Degree when (1) the pinball machine had been purchased for $3,900 approximately four months earlier; (2) the pinball machine had the same serial number as the one stolen from the tavern; (3) the defendant had been told that the pinball machine had been purchased from a fence; and (4) the defendant had been housesitting at the house for four weeks, had clothing, books, and his checkbook at the house, and had paid his share of some of the bills?

Brief Answer

Probably not. Although the State will be able to prove that the pinball machine was stolen, that it was worth more than $1,500.00, and that Richardson knew that it was stolen, the State will not be able to prove that Richardson had either actual or constructive possession of the pinball machine. The pinball machine was not in Richardson's personal custody, and Richardson did not

---

1. Because this memo was written for a Washington attorney, the author has used the Washington citation rules.

have dominion and control over either the pinball machine or the house where it was found.

Discussion

A person is guilty of possession of stolen property in the first degree if he or she knowingly possesses stolen property valued at more than $1,500. RCW 9A.56.150. The phrase "possessing stolen property" is defined as follows:

> 'Possessing stolen property' means knowingly to receive, retain, possess, conceal, or dispose of stolen property knowing that it has been stolen and to withhold or appropriate the same to the use of any person other than the true owner or person entitled thereto.

RCW 9A.56.140(1). Therefore, to obtain a conviction, the State must prove each of the following elements: (1) that the act occurred in the State of Washington; (2) that the value of the pinball machine exceeded $1,500; (3) that the pinball machine was withheld or appropriated from the true owner—that is, that the pinball machine was "stolen"; (4) that Richardson knew that the pinball machine was stolen; and (5) that Richardson had active or constructive possession of the pinball machine. *See* WPIC 77.02.

The State can easily prove the first four elements. First, the State can prove that the pinball machine was found in a residence in Seattle, Washington; therefore, the alleged act took place in the State of Washington. Second, the State can prove that the value of the pinball machine exceeds $1,500. "'Value' means the market value of the property or services at the time and in the approximate area of the criminal act." RCW 9A.56.010(18)(a). The price paid for an item of property, if not too remote in time, is proper evidence of value. *State v. Melrose*, 2 Wn. App. 824, 827 470 P.2d 552 (1970). Because the tavern had purchased the machine for $3,900 only four months earlier, it is unlikely that Richardson will be able to demonstrate that the current value is less than $1,500.

Third, the State can prove that the pinball machine was stolen property. The serial number on the machine found at the Coming residence matches the serial number on the machine stolen from the tavern. In addition, the fact that the pinball machine was found at the Coming residence supports the conclusion that the pinball machine was being withheld or appropriated from its true owner.

Fourth, the State will be able to prove that Richardson knew the machine was stolen. Richardson has admitted that Coming told him that he had purchased the pinball machine from a fence. The State may, however, have difficulty proving that Richardson had possession.

Possession may be either actual or constructive. A defendant has actual possession when the property is in his or her personal custody. *State v. Summers*, 45 Wn. App. 761, 763, 728 P.2d 613 (1986). In this case, the State will not be able to prove that Richardson had actual possession of the pinball machine. At the time the police searched the house, Richardson was not playing or even standing near the pinball machine. In addition, the State may have trouble proving that Richardson had constructive possession.

A defendant has constructive possession of stolen property when he or she has dominion and control over the premises on which the property was located or the property. *See e.g., State v. Summers*, 45 Wn. App. at 763. In determining whether a defendant has dominion and control, the courts look at the totality of the circumstances. Mere proximity to stolen merchandise is not enough to establish dominion and control over it. *Id.*

In the cases in which the courts have found that there was sufficient evidence to support a finding of constructive possession, the defendant had been staying on the premises for more than a few days and had no other residence; had personal property on the premises; and had done some act that indicated that he had dominion and control over the property. *See e.g., State v. Weiss*, 73 Wn.2d 372, 438 P.2d 610 (1968); *State v. Collins*, 76 Wn. App. 496, 886 P.2d 243 (1995). In *Collins,* the defendant admitted staying on the premises 15 to 20 times during the prior month and having no other residence; boxes filled with the defendant's personal property were found in a hallway; and, while the police were in the house, the defendant received several phone calls. *Id.* at 499. Similarly in *Weiss,* the evidence indicated that the defendant had been staying on the premises for more than a month and had helped pay the rent; a bed belonging to the defendant was found in the house; and the defendant had invited others to spend the night. *Id.* at 374. In both cases, the courts held that the facts were sufficient to support the jury's verdict that the defendant had dominion and control over both the premises and the drugs.

In contrast, in the cases in which the courts have found that there was not sufficient evidence to support a finding of constructive possession, the defendant was only a temporary visitor and had another residence. *See e.g., State v. Callahan*, 77 Wn. 2d 27, 459 P.2d 400 (1969); *State v. Davis*, 16 Wn. App. 657, 558 P.2d 263 (1977). In *Callahan,* the defendant, Hutchinson, had been on the houseboat for only a few days, had only a limited number of personal possessions on the premises, and was not paying rent. In addition, another individual admitted that the drugs belonged to him. Based on these facts, the court held that the defendant did not have constructive possession of either the premises or the drugs, which were found on a table next to the defendant. 77 Wn.2d at 32. Likewise, in *Davis,* the court held that the defendant did not have dominion and control over either the premises or the drugs when the defendant was staying at the apartment for only the weekend while his mother entertained guests at home. Even though the defendant's clothing and sleeping bag were found in the apartment, the court held that the presence of these items was not enough to establish constructive possession. State v. Davis, 16 Wn. App at 658-659.

In this case, it is unlikely that the State can prove that Richardson had constructive possession of either the premises or the stolen pinball machine. First, the jury will probably find that Mr. Richardson was only a temporary visitor. Although Richardson had been staying on the premises for more than a few days, the facts in his case can be distinguished from the facts in *Collins* and *Weiss.* Unlike Collins and Weiss, Richardson was not paying rent, and he had another residence. The facts in this case are more like the facts in *Callahan* and *Davis.* Like the defendants in those cases, Richardson was just a temporary visitor. Just as Davis was spending the weekend at a friend's house, Richardson was staying for a relatively short period of time at a friend's house.

Second, the jury will probably find that the personal possessions that were found in the house are not sufficient to establish that Richardson had dominion and control over the premises. The State will argue that the personal possessions found on the premises indicate that Richardson was using the house as his home. When the police searched the premises, they found clothing, books, and class notes belonging to Richardson. In addition, they found Richardson's checkbook and check records that indicated that Richardson had paid a portion of the telephone and cable bills. In contrast, the defendant will argue that the personal possessions found on the premises are not sufficient to support a finding that he had constructive possession. Unlike Weiss, who had brought his bed into the house, and Collins, who had boxes of his personal possessions on the premises, Richardson had just a few items. There is no evidence that indicates that the police found personal items such as Richardson's toothbrush or razor on the premises. In fact, the evidence indicates that Richardson had even fewer personal possessions on the premises than did the defendant in *Davis.*

Third, it is unlikely that the jury will find that the other evidence is sufficient to establish that Richardson had dominion and control over the premises. Even though Richardson had a key to the premises, his possession of the key is consistent with his claim that he was only housesitting. In addition, even though Richardson paid some bills, he was only paying for his share of the phone and cable bills. There is no evidence that he paid rent or utilities.

Finally, as a matter of public policy, it is unlikely that the jury will find a person who was only housesitting guilty of possession of stolen property in the first degree. While we can argue that Richardson had an obligation to report the presence of the pinball machine to the police, it is unlikely that the jury will want to impose such a duty on housesitters. At this point, the law does not require that individuals contact the police each time they notice stolen property in another person's possession or on the individual's premises. For example, dinner guests are not required to contact the police to tell them that their host was serving dinner on stolen china, and repairpersons are not required to contact the police to tell them that they were asked to repair stolen property. Although the jury may hope that such individuals will report the presence of stolen property, it is unlikely that jurors will find that an individual is guilty of a felony if he or she does not do so.

Conclusion

It is unlikely that the State will be able to prove all five elements of Possession of Stolen Property in the First Degree. Although the State will be able to prove that the act occurred in the State of Washington, that the value of the pinball machine exceeded $1,500, that the pinball machine was stolen, and that Richardson knew that it was stolen, it will not be able to prove possession. Because Richardson was not playing or even standing near the pinball machine, the State will not be able to prove that he had actual possession. In addition, the State will not be able to prove that Richardson had constructive possession. Richardson was only a temporary visitor at the house, the police found only a few of his personal possessions on the premises, and there is no evidence that Richardson was paying rent or doing any other act that indicated that he had dominion and control over the premises. The fact that he had a key to the premises and that he paid his share of the phone and cable bills is consistent with his claim that he was housesitting. Finally, it is unlikely that a jury would convict an individual of Possession of Stolen Property in the First Degree when the individual was only housesitting for a friend.

Chapter 5

The First
Memorandum

In this chapter we show you how to write a relatively simple objective memorandum. Specifically, we show you how to locate the applicable statutes and cases; how to analyze and synthesize those statutes and cases; and how to draft, revise, and edit the statement of facts, the issue statement, the brief answer, the discussion section, and the formal conclusion. A copy of the completed memo is set out at the end of the chapter.

As you read through the chapter, keep several things in mind. First, remember that the process of researching and writing an objective memorandum is a recursive one. Thus, although we show you how to write the sections in the order that they will appear in the final draft, they do not need to be written in that order. Many attorneys write the issue statement, brief answer, or discussion section before drafting the statement of facts. Second, remember to use the other chapters in this book. Chapters 1 through 3 explain our legal system and how to read and analyze statutes and cases; Chapter 6 provides additional information about writing memos.

Finally, remember that learning to write an objective memorandum is a difficult task that can take years to master. To do a good job, you must know not only the law itself but also how attorneys and judges think and talk about that law. While we can teach you some of the standard moves, much of what you need to know can be learned only through practice. Just as it takes years to become an expert physician, musician, or athlete, it takes years to become an expert attorney.

§5.1   GETTING THE ASSIGNMENT

Imagine for a moment that you are a legal intern at a mid-sized general practice firm in Boston, Massachusetts. On your first day on the job, the attorney to whom you have been assigned hands you the following memo.

EXAMPLE

To: Legal Intern

From: Charles Maier

Date: September 1, 2002

Re: Case No. 02-478
          Eliza Johnson v. Elite Insurance

     One of our long-time clients, Elite Insurance, has been contacted by an attorney representing one of its former employees, Eliza Johnson. Elite Insurance referred the call to me, and this morning I talked with Ms. Kim, the attorney representing Ms. Johnson.

     Ms. Kim alleges that Elite Insurance violated the Electronic Communications Privacy Act of 1986 when it recorded telephone conversations between her client, Ms. Johnson, and another individual, Mark Porter. Specifically, Ms. Kim alleges that Elite Insurance violated 18 U.S.C. § 2511 when it recorded Ms. Johnson's conversations without her consent. The facts, as related to me by Ms. Kim, are as follows:

     On August 19, 2002, one of Elite Insurance's office managers, Eric Wilson, called Ms. Johnson into his office and told her that she was being fired because she had violated company policy by using the office telephones for personal business. He then disclosed the fact that he had been monitoring Ms. Johnson's phone calls for the last four or five weeks and had overheard conversations between Ms. Johnson and an individual named Mark Porter that indicated that the two were having an affair.

     Ms. Johnson did not explicitly consent, either orally or in writing, to the monitoring of her phone calls and did not know that her phone calls with Porter were being monitored. Had she known, she would not have had the same conversations.

     As of this date, Ms. Johnson has not found another position. In addition, Ms. Johnson's husband has left her and is considering filing for divorce.

I have also talked to Eric Wilson at Elite Insurance. He gave me the following information.

Mr. Wilson did, in fact, monitor and record Ms. Johnson's phone calls by attaching a recorder to an extension phone. He began recording them in mid-July and stopped a day or two before he fired Ms. Johnson.

Mr. Wilson began monitoring Ms. Johnson's phone calls because he had information that indicated that Ms. Johnson might be part of an insurance fraud scheme.

At the time that Ms. Johnson was hired in January 2000, she was told that the phones and computers should be used for business purposes only. In addition, she was told that Elite would periodically monitor her phone calls to ensure that she was providing good service.

When customers call Elite, they hear a message that tells them that their phone call may be monitored.

Mr. Wilson says that, because he is so busy, he seldom monitors his employees' phone calls. Once an employee is trained, he usually listens in only two or three times a year, usually immediately before the employee's annual performance evaluation. Although he does not tell employees which calls he will be monitoring, he usually discusses the calls with them immediately afterwards. Before the monitoring in question, Mr. Wilson had last monitored two or three of Ms. Johnson's calls in January 2002 as part of her annual performance review.

Mr. Wilson also said that despite the company policy, employees regularly use the phones for personal business—for example, to check on their children or to make doctors' appointments. As long as these calls are short, they are tolerated.

Ms. Johnson worked for Elite Insurance from January 2000 until she was terminated. Her performance evaluations were average or slightly below average. In listening to Ms. Johnson's phone calls, Mr. Wilson did not hear anything that led him to believe that Ms. Johnson was engaged in insurance fraud. He did, however, overhear conversations indicating that Ms. Johnson was having an affair.

Elite Insurance employs about 250 people in eight states. The company is doing well financially.

Although it appears that Elite Insurance did willfully use a mechanical device to intercept a wire communication, see 18 U.S.C. § 2511(1)(a), one of the exceptions may apply. I would like you to research the consent exception. I'll have someone else research the business use exception. If Ms. Johnson files suit, it would be in the United States District Court for the District of Massachusetts.

A. PREWRITING

Just as the artist begins "painting" long before paint is put on canvas, the writer begins "writing" long before the first word is put on paper. The artistic process begins with an image, an idea, or an insight that is shaped and then reworked many times before the project is finished. The writing process begins with a question that is focused and refocused through research and analysis.

In both painting and writing, the process takes place in context. The artist's work is influenced by training, by the expectations of the artistic community, and by the reactions of viewers to past works. Similarly, your work will be shaped by your knowledge of the law, the conventions governing both the format and content of a legal memorandum, and your understanding of your readers and how they will use the memo.

Thus, like the artist, you begin work with a vision, although it may be a preliminary one. Although you do not yet know what the final product will look like, you have an idea of where you want to go. You know the attorney's question, the types of information the attorney needs, and how the memo will be used. All of this information is your touchstone, your point of reference, and as such can guide most if not all of the decisions you make throughout the writing process.

§5.2   PREPARING A RESEARCH PLAN

Upon receiving a memo like the one set out above, you should do three things. First, read the memo carefully, making sure that you understand both the facts and what it is that the attorney wants you to do. Second, ask questions. For example, ask the attorney how much time you should spend on the project and when it is due. Third, prepare a research plan.

Although a research plan can be either written or "in your head," at first it is a good idea to have it in writing. The first step in preparing such a plan is to determine what law is likely to apply. You should then draft a preliminary issue statement, and a list of the sources that you plan to check and the order in which you plan to check them.

§5.2.1   Determine What Law Applies

The first step is to determine whether the issue is governed by state or federal law and by enacted or common law. In our sample case, this step is easy: Opposing counsel has told us that her client is seeking relief under a federal statute, 18 U.S.C. § 2511.

In other cases, this step may be more difficult. For example, you might not know whether a case involving employment discrimination is governed by state or federal law or whether a case involving a software license is governed by enacted or common law. In such instances, start by asking questions. For example, ask the assigning attorney whether he or she knows what law governs. Instead of thinking less of you, the attorney will think more of you. If he or she does not know, either do some general background reading to familiarize yourself with the area of law or begin your research by looking first for a federal statute, second for a state statute, and third for state common law.

§5.2.2   Draft a Preliminary Issue Statement

Good research begins with a good preliminary issue statement. Although you will not be able to draft the final version of the issue statement until after you have completed your research, by drafting a preliminary one now, you force yourself to focus. What is it that you have been asked to research?

The issue can usually be stated broadly or narrowly, or it can find its focus somewhere in between.

EXAMPLES

1. Does one of the exceptions to 18 U.S.C. § 2511 apply?
2. Did Ms. Johnson explicitly consent to the monitoring of her phone calls?
3. Under the Electronic Communications Privacy Act, did Eliza Johnson consent to the monitoring of her phone calls when, at the time she was hired, she was told that the phones should be used for business purposes only and that her phone calls would be periodically monitored to ensure good customer service?

The first statement of the question is too broad. The attorney did not ask you to research all of the exceptions; he asked you to research only the consent exception. In contrast, the second question is too narrow because it asks only about explicit consent. As you will see when we look at the cases, consent may be either explicit or implied. The last question issue is the best; it is neither too broad nor too narrow, and it identifies the facts that are likely to be important in deciding whether Ms. Johnson consented.

§5.2.3   Select the Sources You Want to Check

Finally, you need to decide which sources to check and the order in which you want to check them.

When you are asked to research a statutory question, you will usually want to start your research by locating the statute itself.[1] After you have found the statute, you will then want to locate cases that are factually similar to yours that have applied or interpreted the statute. Finally, you will want to "cite check" the cases to determine whether they are still good law and to locate additional cases that are on point. The following research plan shows the sources that you would want to look at in researching our sample problem and the order in which you would want to consult them.

Another decision you will make at the start of your research is whether to use print or electronic sources. This decision is best made by weighing several factors, including the availability of print and electronic sources, the cost of using a print source versus the cost of using an electronic source, the amount of time it will take you to use the print source versus the amount of time it will take you to use an electronic source, and the reliability and currency of each source. In our case, you decide to do some of the research using print sources and some of it using LEXIS, Loislaw, or Westlaw. Because the statutes and reporters are available in the office's library, you will do the initial research using print sources. It will be cheaper, just as fast, and just as reliable as doing the research online. In contrast, you will do your cite checking using either LEXIS or Westlaw. Like many law libraries, your firm no longer subscribes to the print version of *Shepard's*. Although more costly, the online versions of *Shepard's* and KeyCite provide more up-to-date information and are easier and more efficient to use.

EXAMPLE

SAMPLE RESEARCH PLAN

Jurisdiction: Federal

Type of Law: Enacted law

Preliminary Issue Statement:

Under the Electronic Communications Privacy Act, did Eliza Johnson consent to the monitoring of her phone calls when, at the

---

1. There are times, however, when you may want to start your research by doing some background reading in a secondary source. For example, you may want to do background reading if you do not know whether an issue is governed by federal or state law or by enacted or common law. In addition, even when you know the answers to these questions, you may want to do background reading when the problem is complex and you are unfamiliar with the area.

time she was hired, she was told that the phones should be used for business purposes only and that her phone calls would be periodically monitored to ensure good customer service?

Step 1:   Locate 18 U.S.C. § 2511.

Step 2:   Locate the version of 18 U.S.C. § 2511 in effect at the time the cause of action arose.

Step 3:   Locate that portion of 18 U.S.C. § 2511 that deals with consent and determine which elements are likely to be in dispute.

Step 4:   Look for statutory definitions.

Step 5:   Read through the notes of decisions following section 2511 and identify the cases that appear to be most useful.

Step 6:   Locate the cases in the appropriate federal reporter, and read the relevant portion(s) of each case.

Step 7:   Cite check the cases to determine (1) whether the cases are still good law and (2) whether there are any additional cases. Look up and, if appropriate, cite check any additional cases that you locate through cite checking.

Step 8:   Locate law review articles and other commentaries that might be on point.

---

§5.3   RESEARCHING THE PROBLEM

Research plan in hand, you head for the library.

Step 1:   Locate 18 U.S.C. § 2511

Federal statutes can be found in one of four print sources: the *Statutes at Large,* the *United States Code* (U.S.C.), the *United States Code Annotated* (U.S.C.A.), and the *United States Code Service* (U.S.C.S.). In addition, federal statutes are available on LEXIS, Loislaw, and Westlaw and on the Internet.

In the *Statutes at Large,* federal acts are set out in the order that they were enacted. For example, an act signed into law on January 24, 1998, precedes an act signed into law on January 25, 1998. Because the *Statutes at Large* uses a chronological rather than a topical organizational scheme, it is not usually the best source. Unless you are doing a legislative history or looking for a statute that is no longer in effect, the better source is a code.

In a code, the statutes that are currently in effect are grouped by topic. For example, all the statutes relating to the military are placed under one title, those relating to the federal tax code under another, and those relating to education or social and health services under still another. As legislation is passed relating to one of these topics, the code is revised to show the changes.

The official version of the federal code is the *United States Code,* which is published by the United States Printing Office. In it are the text of all the federal statutes, arranged by title and section numbers, and legislative history notes. There are also two unofficial versions of the code: the *United States Code Annotated* and the *United States Code Service.* Both sets have the following: the text of the United States Constitution, the text of the federal statutes currently in effect, historical notes for each statute, notes of decision, and tables of cases. In addition, the *United States Code Annotated* contains references to West's key number system and cross-references to other West materials, and the *United States Code Service* contains references to applicable A.L.R. annotations and other books in the American Jurisprudence series.

If you are using the print versions of these codes, you can locate a particular statutory section in one of three ways. If you know the number of the applicable statute, you can go directly to the volume that contains that title and section number. If you do not know the section number, you can locate that number using either the popular names table or the subject index. If you are using an online source, you can search either by typing in the statutory number or, if you do not know the number, by using the table of contents or by doing a terms and connectors search.

In our example case, you know the citation to the applicable statute. As a result, you go directly to the main volumes of the *United States Code Annotated,* locating first those volumes that contain Title 18 of the *United States Code* and then, within those volumes, the volume that contains section 2511. In the bound portion of the volume, you find excerpts from the text of the statute and, following the statute, historical notes, references to other West materials, and notes of decisions. See Exhibit 5.1.

Step 2:   Locate the Version of 18 U.S.C. § 2511 in Effect at the Time the Cause of Action Arose

The next step is to determine whether you have the version of the statute that was in effect at the time the cause of action arose. In our example case, this means that you want to make sure that you have the version of 18 U.S.C. § 2511 in effect in July and August 2002.

When using the print version of a code, locating the applicable version of a federal statute is a multistep process. First, you need to lo-

EXHIBIT 5.1   *United States Code* 18 § 2511

Ch. 119   INTERCEPTION OF COMMUNICATIONS   18 § 2511

§ 2511. Interception and disclosure of wire, oral, or electronic communications prohibited

(1) Except as otherwise specifically provided in this chapter any person who—

(a) intentionally intercepts, endeavors to intercept, or procures any other person to intercept or endeavor to intercept, any wire, oral, or electronic communication;

(b) intentionally uses, endeavors to use, or procures any other person to use or endeavor to use any electronic, mechanical, or other device to intercept any oral communication when—

(i) such device is affixed to, or otherwise transmits a signal through, a wire, cable, or other like connection used in wire communication; or

(ii) such device transmits communications by radio, or interferes with the transmission of such communication; or

(iii) such person knows, or has reason to know, that such device or any component thereof has been sent through the mail or transported in interstate or foreign commerce; or

(iv) such use or endeavor to use (A) takes place on the premises of any business or other commercial establishment the operations of which affect interstate or foreign commerce; or (B) obtains or is for the purpose of obtaining information relating to the operations of any business or other commercial establishment the operations of which affect interstate or foreign commerce; or

(v) such person acts in the District of Columbia, the Commonwealth of Puerto Rico, or any territory or possession of the United States;

(c) intentionally discloses, or endeavors to disclose, to any other person the contents of any wire, oral, or electronic communication, knowing or having reason to know that the information was obtained through the interception of a wire, oral, or electronic communication in violation of this subsection;

(d) intentionally uses, or endeavors to use, the contents of any wire, oral, or electronic communication, knowing or having reason to know that the information was obtained through the interception of a wire, oral, or electronic communication in violation of this subsection; or

(e) (i) intentionally discloses, or endeavors to disclose, to any other person the contents of any wire, oral, or electronic communication, intercepted by means authorized by sections 2511(2)(a)(ii), 2511(2)(b) to (c), 2511(2)(e), 2516, and 2518 of this

*   *   *

EXHIBIT 5.1   *(continued)*

Ch. 119   INTERCEPTION OF COMMUNICATIONS   18 § 2511

* * *

certification under this chapter, except as may otherwise be required by legal process and then only after prior notification to the Attorney General or to the principal prosecuting attorney of a State or any political subdivision of a State, as may be appropriate. Any such disclosure, shall render such person liable for the civil damages provided for in section 2520. No cause of action shall lie in any court against any provider of wire or electronic communication service, its officers, employees, or agents, landlord, custodian, or other specified person for providing information, facilities, or assistance in accordance with the terms of a court order or certification under this chapter.

(b) It shall not be unlawful under this chapter for an officer, employee, or agent of the Federal Communications Commission, in the normal course of his employment and in discharge of the monitoring responsibilities exercised by the Commission in the enforcement of chapter 5 of title 47 of the United States Code, to intercept a wire or electronic communication, or oral communication transmitted by radio, or to disclose or use the information thereby obtained.

(c) It shall not be unlawful under this chapter for a person acting under color of law to intercept a wire, oral, or electronic communication, where such person is a party to the communication or one of the parties to the communication has given prior consent to such interception.

(d) It shall not be unlawful under this chapter for a person not acting under color of law to intercept a wire, oral, or electronic communication where such person is a party to the communication or where one of the parties to the communication has given prior consent to such interception unless such communication is intercepted for the purpose of committing any criminal or tortious act in violation of the Constitution or laws of the United States or of any State.

(e) Notwithstanding any other provision of this title or section 705 or 706 of the Communications Act of 1934, it shall not be unlawful for an officer, employee, or agent of the United States in the normal course of his official duty to conduct electronic surveillance, as defined in section 101 of the Foreign Intelligence Surveillance Act of 1978, as authorized by that Act.

(f) Nothing contained in this chapter or chapter 121, or section 705 of the Communications Act of 1934, shall be deemed to affect the acquisition by the United States Government of foreign intelligence information from international or foreign communications, or foreign intelligence activities conducted in accordance with otherwise applicable Federal law involving a foreign electronic communica-

EXHIBIT 5.1   *(continued)*

CRIMES AND CRIMINAL PROCEDURE

18 § 2511
Note 5

Where telephone company maintained test-board where trouble reports from customers were handled and use of board by employees was monitored by supervisors for purpose of service quality control checks and, in plaintiff employee's case, for purpose of preventing his persistent use of testboard phone for personal calls, against which he had been warned several times, company's legitimate interest in maintaining quality control and availability of lines brought its monitoring activities within exception from prohibition against interception of wire communications, contained in this section. Simmons v. Southwestern Bell Tel. Co., W.D.Okla. 1978, 452 F.Supp. 392, affirmed 611 F.2d 342.

Homeowners could not amend trespass complaint to allege violation of wiretapping statutes by television broadcaster, where broadcaster's employee purportedly entered home as veterinary student and secretly videotaped events in home which were subsequently broadcast, as broadcaster intercepted communication for commercial purposes, not purpose of committing tortious act or trespass. Copeland v. Hubbard Broadcasting, Inc., Minn.App.1995, 526 N.W.2d 402, review denied.

3e. Willfully

For purposes of provision of statute making it crime to willfully intercept any wire or oral communication, person acts "willfully" if he knowingly or recklessly disregards known legal duty. Farroni v. Farroni, C.A.6 (Ohio) 1988, 862 F.2d 109.

Civil liability for allegedly unlawful wiretapping required proof of criminal willfulness; "willfully" within meaning of criminal prohibition against interception of wire or oral communication required employee in civil action to show intentional or reckless disregard of legal obligations by employer. Malouche v. JH Management Co., Inc., C.A.4 (S.C.) 1988, 839 F.2d 1024.

Term "willfully" as used in this section has the same meaning whether liability is imposed criminally or civilly; thus, neither civil nor criminal liability can be established against any defendant without showing that he acted with intentional or reckless disregard of his legal obligations. Citron v. Citron, C.A.2 (N.Y.) 1983, 722 F.2d 14, certiorari denied 104 S.Ct. 2350, 466 U.S. 973, 80 L.Ed.2d 823.

Wife's allegation that husband, caused electronic recording device to be installed on her phone and took tape recordings of conversation between wife and third parties was sufficient to raise question as to whether husband acted intentionally or in reckless disregard of his legal obligations and thus sufficiently pleaded "willfulness" of husband's conduct to survive motion to dismiss action pursuant to electronic surveillance provisions of Omnibus Crime Control and Safe Streets Act, where complaint alleged that husband played tapes thus obtained for persons other than his attorney. Nations v. Nations, W.D.Ark.1987, 670 F.Supp. 1432.

Civil action under federal statutes prohibiting illegal wiretaps or other electronic surveillance could be brought against media defendants who, although they did not participate in illegal surveillance, allegedly knew that recorded conversations they were given had been illegally obtained. Natoli v. Sullivan, N.Y.Sup.1993, 606 N.Y.S.2d 504, 159 Misc.2d 681, affirmed 616 N.Y.S.2d 318, 206 A.D.2d 841, leave to appeal denied.

3f. Intent

Criminal and civil liability is imposed under federal-wiretapping statute upon proof that defendant intentionally intercepted oral communications at issue, without showing of disregard of known legal duty, at least to those communications to which he was not party. Earley v. Smoot, D.Md.1994, 846 F.Supp. 451.

Husband's record of telephone conversations of his wife violated federal wiretapping law, even though husband claimed that he was not aware that interception was illegal; law required only that act of recording be intentional, without regard to motive. Young v. Young, Mich.App. 1995, 536 N.W.2d 254, 211 Mich.App. 446.

3g. Knowledge

Attorney for fire insurer was not liable in damages to insureds, under federal wiretap statute, for having made use of allegedly illegally obtained tape recording in attempt to establish that insureds had committed fraud in connection with their claim; attorney had no knowledge of facts tending to show that tape recording was illegally obtained and federal court presiding over insurance claim had allowed recording into evidence. Hamed v. Pfeifer, Ind.App. 3 Dist. 1995, 647 N.E.2d 669.

4. Discovery

In civil action for allegedly intercepting, tape recording, and threatening to disclose contents of plaintiffs' personal telephone conversations in violation of this chapter, admission by one defendant to intercepting and recording some of plaintiffs' telephone conversations did not establish the illegality of the interception and recording so as to prohibit, under this section, disclosure of recordings to defendants' attorney, as it could not be determined whether he might effectively invoke a statutory exception to the recording, such as consent. McQuade v. Michael Gassner Mechanical & Elec. Contractors, Inc., D.C.Conn.1984, 587 F.Supp. 1183.

5. Consent

U. S. v. Merritts, E.D.Ill.1975, 387 F.Supp. 807, [main volume] reversed 527 F.2d 713.

Pretrial detainee impliedly consented to audiotaping of his telephone calls from detention center, and, thus, consent exception applied under provision of Title III of Omnibus Crime Control and Safe Streets Act prohibiting intentional use of any electronic, mechanical, or other device to intercept any oral communication; detainee signed consent form and was given prison manual a few days after his arrival, and detention center posted signs above telephones warning of monitoring and taping. U.S. v. Van Poyck, C.A.9 (Cal.) 1996, 77 F.3d 285, certiorari denied 117 S.Ct. 276.

Consent to have telephone communications intercepted should not be casually inferred, but rather surrounding circumstances must convincingly show that party knew about and consented to interception in spite lack of formal notice or deficient formal notice, in determining whether

EXHIBIT 5.1 *(continued)*

intercepted telephone conversations are admissible. U.S. v. Lanoue, C.A.1 (R.I.) 1995, 71 F.3d 966.

Employer's interception of employee telephone calls did not come within consent exception to federal and Maine wiretapping laws; although intercepted corporate officer was told that employee calls would be monitored, officer was not told of manner in which monitoring was conducted or that he himself would be monitored. Williams v. Poulos, C.A.1 (Me.) 1993, 11 F.3d 271.

"Consent to use" defense did not apply to defendant who represented husband in divorce action and who allegedly improperly used wife's recorded telephone conversations in connection with divorce action. U.S. v. Wuliger, C.A.6 (Ohio) 1992, 981 F.2d 1497, rehearing denied 999 F.2d 1090, certiorari denied 114 S.Ct. 1298, 510 U.S. 1191, 127 L.Ed.2d 647, rehearing denied 114 S.Ct. 1872, 128 L.Ed.2d 492.

Employee's consent to tape recording of intercepted telephone calls could not be implied, so as to exempt employer from liability for violating wire and electronic communications interception provisions of the Omnibus Crime Control and Safe Streets Act, merely because employer warned employee that calls may be monitored to cut down on personal use of telephone, or because extension telephone was located in owners' residence. Deal v. Spears, C.A.8 (Ark.) 1992, 980 F.2d 1153.

District court, ruling on suppression motion, did not clearly err in its factual finding that police informant's consent to recording of his telephone conversation with drug supplier was not coerced; police officer denied threatening informant with prosecution of his girlfriend, and DEA agent's testimony furnished evidence that informant cooperated out of desire for leniency for himself. U.S. v. Wake, C.A.5 (Tex.) 1991, 948 F.2d 1422, certiorari denied 112 S.Ct. 2944, 504 U.S. 975, 119 L.Ed.2d 569.

Consent required for admissibility of tape recording is question of fact to be determined from totality of circumstances, and court need not submit consent issue to jury after making initial determination of admissibility. U.S. v. Gomez, C.A.5 (Tex.) 1991, 947 F.2d 737, certiorari denied 112 S.Ct. 1504, 503 U.S. 947, 117 L.Ed.2d 642.

Although right at stake in an exclusionary hearing to prevent admission of conversations recorded in violation of federal wiretapping restrictions is statutory, not constitutional, Fourth Amendment precedents determine whether party to communication consented to an interception within meaning of statute. U.S. v. Antoon, C.A.3 (Pa.) 1991, 933 F.2d 200, rehearing denied, certiorari denied 112 S.Ct. 300, 502 U.S. 907, 116 L.Ed.2d 243.

Where Government made recording of conversation between defendant and government informant with consent and cooperation of informant, there was no need to inform defendant or to obtain court order. U.S. v. Barone, C.A.2 (N.Y.) 1990, 913 F.2d 46.

Tenant consented to his landlady's recording of his telephone calls and, therefore, her interception of calls did not violate federal wiretap-

ping statute; landlady repeatedly informed tenant that all of her incoming calls were being monitored and that blanket admonishment left no room for tenant to wonder whether his calls would be intercepted. Griggs-Ryan v. Smith, C.A.1 (Me.) 1990, 904 F.2d 112.

Absent evidence that arrestee who agreed to telephone defendant knew that call was being monitored, Government failed to carry burden of establishing consent to taping of call, as required for admission of tape under federal wiretap statute. U.S. v. Gomez, C.A.5 (Tex.) 1990, 900 F.2d 43, rehearing denied.

Electronic surveillance of attorney did not violate federal communications interception statute where one of parties to conversation had consented to interception; accordingly, police officers could not be held liable in civil rights action brought by attorney arising out of interception. Lewellen v. Raff, C.A.8 (Ark.) 1988, 843 F.2d 1103, rehearing denied 851 F.2d 1108, certiorari denied 109 S.Ct. 1171, 489 U.S. 1083, 103 L.Ed.2d 229.

Inmates impliedly consented to interception of their telephone calls by using prison telephones when they were on notice of the prison's interception policy from at least four sources. U.S. v. Amen, C.A.2 (N.Y.) 1987, 831 F.2d 373, certiorari denied 108 S.Ct. 1573, 485 U.S. 1021, 99 L.Ed.2d 889.

Where defendant knew that third party would monitor his phone calls by listening in periodically and agreed to let her do so and did not object when she broke in and participated in conversations, he did not consent only to "mechanical" interceptions of his calls, but also gave her right to record calls. U.S. v. Tzakis, C.A.2 (N.Y.) 1984, 736 F.2d 867.

Government agent, a party to conversation between agent and defendant, testified that he gave his voluntary consent to have the conversation monitored, and therefore tape-recorded conversation was admissible pursuant to this section. U.S. v. Boley, C.A.10 (Okla.) 1984, 730 F.2d 1326.

Communication is not unlawfully intercepted within meaning of this section where one of parties to conversation is acting under color of law or has given prior consent to interception; this section permits introduction of consensual recordings and thus controls over conflicting state eavesdropping regulations. U.S. v. McNulty, C.A.10 (Colo.) 1983, 729 F.2d 1243.

Employee's knowledge of employer's capability of monitoring her private telephone conversations, by itself, could not be considered implied consent to such monitoring. Watkins v. L.M. Berry & Co., C.A.11 (Ala.) 1983, 704 F.2d 577.

Where paid informer gave his consent before recording conversations in which he was involved, the conversations were free from warrant requirement. U.S. v. Davanzo, C.A.11 (Fla.) 1983, 699 F.2d 1097.

Trial court properly admitted tapes of defendant's telephone conversations, where the tapes were made with the consent of the other party to the conversations. U.S. v. Jones, C.A.5 (La.) 1982, 693 F.2d 343.

Conspirator, who requested private detective to install electronic equipment on him in order cate the statute in the bound portion of the code. Second, if your cause of action arose after the dates covered in the bound volume, you need to check the pocket part at the back of the bound volume to determine whether an amended version of your statutory section appears there. Third, if your cause of action arose after the dates covered in the pocket part, you need to check the quarterly and monthly print supplements that are usually shelved at the end of the code to determine whether an amended version of your statute appears there. Finally, if you need even more current information, you need to check an online source, for example, LEXIS, Loislaw, or Westlaw.

When using an online source, there are fewer sources to check: You will usually need to use only the online source. Note, however, that while it may be easier to find the most current version of a statute using an online source, it can be difficult, if not impossible, to find an older version. For example, if your cause of action arose in 2000 and the statute was amended in 2002, you may not be able to find the 2000 version of the statute on the online source.

Step 3: Locate That Portion of 18 U.S.C. § 2511 That Deals with Consent and Determine Which Elements Are Likely to Be in Dispute

Once you have found the applicable version of 18 U.S.C. § 2511, the next step is to read through the statute, skimming the entire statute and locating the sections that discuss consent. Note that subsection (1) sets out the language that the senior attorney referred to in his memo.

> Except as otherwise specifically provided in this chapter any person who
> (a) intentionally intercepts, endeavors to intercept, or procures any other person to intercept or endeavor to intercept, any wire, oral or electronic communication . . .
> shall be punished as provided in subsection (4) or shall be subject to suit as provided in subsection (5).

Also note that two subsections discuss consent. Section (2)(c) applies when the person intercepting the communication is acting under color of law, and section (2)(d) applies when the person intercepting the communication is not acting under color of law.

> Subsection (2)(c):
> It shall not be unlawful under this chapter for a person acting under color of law to intercept a wire, oral, or electronic communication, where such person is a party to the communication or where one of the parties to the communication has given prior consent to such interception.

Subsection (2)(d):

It shall not be unlawful under this chapter for a person not acting under color of law to intercept a wire, oral, or electronic communication where such person is a party to the communication or where one of the parties to the communication has given prior consent to such interception unless such communication is intercepted for the purpose of committing a criminal or tortuous act in violation of the Constitution or law of the United States or of any State.

In our case, subsection 2(d) appears to be the applicable section. The supervising attorney's memo does not contain any facts that indicate that either Mr. Wilson or Elite Insurance was acting under color of law, that is, there is no evidence that either Mr. Wilson or Elite Insurance was a government employee or agent or was acting under the direction of a government employee or agent.

The next step is to reread the statute, looking carefully at the language. In doing so, note that the subsection sets out both an exception and an exception to the exception and that both the exception and the exception to the exception have several parts or "elements."

Exception

It shall not be unlawful under this chapter

(1) for a person not acting under color of law
(2) to intercept a wire, oral, or electronic communication
(3) where such person is a party to the communication
    or where one of the parties to the communication has given prior consent to such interception.

Exception to the Exception

unless

(1) such communication
(2) is intercepted
(3) for the purpose of committing any criminal or tortuous act in violation of the Constitution or laws of the United States or of any State.

In our case, the first element of the exception should not be in dispute. As discussed earlier, there is no evidence that either Mr. Wilson or Elite Insurance was acting under color of law. In addition, the second element does not appear to be in dispute. More likely than not a phone call is a wire communication, and a communication was intercepted when Elite Insurance recorded Ms. Johnson's phone conversations. It is, however, likely that the third element will be in dispute. Elite will argue that there was prior consent, and Ms. Johnson will argue that there was no prior consent.

If Elite is able to prove all of the elements of the exception, it seems unlikely that Ms. Johnson would argue the exception to the exception. She does not want to contest the fact that there was a communication or that that communication was intercepted. In addition, there does not seem to be any evidence that the communication was intercepted for the purpose of committing a criminal or tortuous act.

Thus, it appears that only one element, prior consent, is likely to be in dispute.

Step 4:   Look for Statutory Definitions

In interpreting a statute, courts look first to the definitions set out in the act. In enacting the statute, did the enacting body, that is, Congress or the state legislature, define the terms that it used?

Definitions can be located in one of several ways. In text versions, they can be located using the table of contents at the beginning of the act or the cross-references following the text of the statute; with online services, they can be located using the table of contents or a terms and connectors search.

In our case, definitions are set out in 18 U.S.C. § 2510. Although this section does not define the terms "consent" or "prior consent," it does define "communication," "intercept," and "electronic, mechanical, or other device." Thus, you should read these definitions, checking to make sure that those elements are not likely to be in dispute. A reading of these definitions confirms our earlier decisions. "Telephone call" seems to fall within the definition of "wire communication," and a call is intercepted when it is recorded.

Step 5:   Read Through the Notes of Decisions Following the Statute, Identifying the Cases That Appear to Be Most Useful

The next step is to look for a case that has defined or interpreted the phrase "prior consent." Although there are a number of ways to locate cases interpreting or applying a statute, one of the easiest and most efficient is to use the notes of decisions that follow the text of the statute in an annotated code. These notes, or "annotations," are written by attorneys who work for the company that publishes the set in which the notes appear. The attorneys read the opinions and then prepare a note for each point of law set out in the case. If a case sets out one point of law, the attorney prepares one note; if the case contains twenty points, the attorney prepares twenty notes.

These notes are then placed at the beginning of the cases as head-notes and under the applicable statute. For example, notes relating to 18 U.S.C. § 2511 are placed in the notes of decisions following 18 U.S.C. § 2511, and notes relating to 18 U.S.C. § 2510 are placed in the notes of decisions following 18 U.S.C. § 2510. If a case sets out only one point of law relating to a particular statute, then that case will be referred to only once in the notes following that statute. If, however, the case sets out several points of law relating to the statute, there will be several notes, all referring to the same case, in the notes of decisions section.

If there are only a few notes of decisions for a particular statutory section, those notes will be organized by only court and date. Notes from decisions issued by higher courts will appear before notes from decisions of lower courts, and notes from more recent opinions will appear before notes from older decisions. If, however, there are a number of notes of decisions under a particular statutory section, those notes of decisions will be organized by topic, and a list of the topics with their corresponding section numbers will precede the notes themselves. Then, within each topic, the notes from higher court opinions will precede notes from lower court opinions, and the notes from more recent cases will precede the notes from older cases.

In our example problem, there are five pages of notes under the subheading for consent. See Exhibit 5.1. Although you could locate and read all of the cases listed under the consent subheading, it is usually better to be more selective, initially locating the four or five "best" cases. The question, of course, is how to determine which cases are best.

While the process of selecting cases is somewhat subjective, there are guidelines that you should follow. First, as a general rule, select cases that are mandatory authority over cases that are only persuasive authority. For instance, in our example case, select United States Supreme Court and, because Massachusetts is in the First Circuit, First Circuit Court of Appeals cases over cases from other circuits and cases from the district courts. Second, as a general rule, select more recent cases over older cases. For example, if there are ten or fifteen First Circuit cases, select the more recent ones over older ones. Similarly, if you are selecting among cases that are only persuasive authority, you will usually want to select more recent cases over older cases.[2]

Third, select cases that appear to set out the types of information that you are looking for over cases that are more general or that discuss another point. For example, if you are looking for what constitutes implied consent, select a case that specifically mentions implied consent

---

2. The information that you need to determine whether a case is mandatory or persuasive, that is, the name of the court and the date of the decision can usually be found either at the beginning or end of the annotation. For more on mandatory and persuasive authority, see Chapter 2.

over a case that discusses consent in more general terms. Finally, select cases that are more factually similar over cases that are less factually similar. Thus, in our case, select cases involving the monitoring of phone calls by individuals not acting under color of law over cases involving the monitoring of phone calls by government employees or agents, cases involving employers and employees over cases involving family members, and cases that involve the interception of wire communications over cases that involve the interception of electronic communications.

Step 6:   Locate the Cases in the Appropriate Federal Reporter and Read the Relevant Portion(s) of Each

Cases are published in sets of books called reporters, each of which contains opinions from a particular court or group of courts. For example, the *United States Reporter* (U.S.), *Supreme Court Reporter* (S. Ct.), and *United States Supreme Court Reports, Lawyers' Edition* (L.Ed.), contains only opinions from the United States Supreme Court. Similarly, the *Federal Reporter* (F., F.2d, or F.3d) publishes only opinions from the United States Court of Appeals. In contrast, the *Pacific Reporter* (P., P.2d, or P.3d) has intermediate court of appeals and supreme court opinions from fifteen different states. In each set, the opinions are set out in the order in which they were issued, not by topic or, if a reporter contains the opinions of more than one court, by court.

For some reporters, for example, the *United States Reporter,* there is only one series. For other reporters, however, there is more than one. For instance, the *Federal Reporter* has three series: *Federal Reporter* (F.), *Federal Reporter, Second Series* (F.2d), and *Federal Reporter, Third Series* (F.3d). The *Federal Reporter* has 300 volumes and opinions issued between 1789 and 1924; the *Federal Reporter, Second Series,* has 1000 volumes and opinions issued between 1924 and 1993; and the *Federal Reporter, Third Series,* has opinions from 1993 to present.

To locate a particular case you need its citation.[3] In the following citation, the first set of numbers following the case gives you the volume number, the letters the reporter, and second set of numbers the page on which the opinion begins.

Williams v. Poulos,	11	F.3d	271.
case name	volume	name of reporter	first page of opinion

---

3. Although typically the citations set out in the annotations are not in the proper form, they do give you the information you need to locate a case.

Once you have found several potentially applicable cases, the next step is to read them. As a general rule, you will want to begin by reading the synopsis and headnotes that precede the text of each decision. Although they are not part of the court's decision and cannot be cited as authority, they can help you determine whether the case might be useful.

If after reading the synopsis and headnotes you determine that a case is not useful, discard it, writing in your research notes that you looked at the case but did not find it useful. If, however, the case appears to be useful, read the opinion itself. When the opinion is short (three to five pages), you will usually want to read all of it. If it is longer, begin by reading the portions that (1) set out the issue or issues, (2) summarize the facts, and (3) discuss the relevant points of law.

In doing this reading, look for a number of different things. First, make sure that the opinion is "on point." For example, does it discuss the section of the statute that you are researching? Second, make sure that you understand the question before the court. Was the court determining whether there was consent, or was it deciding only a procedural issue, such as whether the trial court erred in granting the defendant's motion for summary judgment?

Also determine how you might be able to use the case. Is this a case that you can cite as authority for the general rule? If not, is it a case that you or the other side might be able to use in your arguments? Finally, look at the statutes, cases, and secondary authorities that the court cites. If any of them look promising, copy the citations and look them up later.

The following example shows what went through the mind of an experienced legal researcher as she read *Williams v. Poulos*. The first column is the section of the court's opinion in *Williams v. Poulos* that discusses consent. The second column is our experienced legal researcher's thoughts.

Text of Opinion	**What Researcher Was Thinking As She Read**
Williams v. Poulos 11 F.3d 271 (1st Cir. 1993)	OK, this case is mandatory authority and it is relatively recent.
[First part of opinion not set out.]	[The researcher began by reading the syllabus set out at the beginning and by noting that the Court of Appeals affirmed the trial court's decision. She then read through the headnotes, locating the one that discussed consent. She then turned to that part of the opinion.]
[6] Both the federal and Maine acts specifically exempt from their prohibitions the interception of telephone calls where	I wonder if there is a Massachusetts statute on point? If there is, why hasn't Johnson's attorney said anything about

one or more of the conversants has consented to or, in the case of the Maine act, previously authorized the interception. *See* 18 U.S.C. § 2511(2)(d) and 15 M.R.S.A.§ 709(4)(C).

As we have made clear, consent under Title III need not be explicit; instead it can be implied. *See Griggs-Ryan v. Smith,* 904 F.2d 112, 116 (1st Cir. 1990).

Implied consent is not, however, constructive consent. *Id.* "Rather, implied consent is 'consent in fact' which is inferred 'from surrounding circumstances indicating that the party *knowingly agreed* to the surveillance.'" *Id.* at 116-17 (quoting *United States v. Amen,* 831 F.2d 373, 378 (2d Cir. 1987), *cert. denied,* 485 U.S. 1021, 108 S.Ct. 1573, 99 L.Ed.2d 889 (1988) (brackets omitted). In light of the prophylactic purpose of Title II, implied consent should not be casually inferred. *See id.* at 117.

Here the record reflects and the district court found that Ralph Dyer was told of the "monitoring" of CAR employee telephone calls. The record is not clear, however, as to whether Dyer was informed (1) of the manner—i.e., the intercepting and recording of telephone conversations—in which this monitoring was conducted; and (2) that he himself would be subjected to such monitoring. There was testimony tending to indicate that he was so informed, which the district judge apparently chose not to credit, and testimony tending to indicate that he was not.

it? Although I don't need to worry about it now, I should make the attorney aware that the plaintiff might also be able to bring suit under a state statute.

Good. This is a case that discusses the section of the statute applicable to our case.

It looks like there are two types of consent: explicit and implied. I probably should take a look at *Griggs-Ryan:* it is cited as authority for the rule and is mandatory authority.

I wonder what the court means by "constructive consent"? How is constructive consent different from implied consent? I'd better look for a definition of that term.

This may be a problem. It appears that to establish consent, we will need to prove that Ms. Johnson knowingly agreed to the surveillance. I wonder if telling her that her phone calls might be recorded is going to be enough or whether she needed to sign something? Because the court is relying so heavily on *Griggs-Ryan,* I need to make sure that I read it.

It seems as if the court may be setting out a two-part test: The employee must be told how his or her calls will be monitored and the employee must specifically know that his or her calls are being monitored. If this is the test, we may be OK. Although we'll have to check it out, my guess is that Ms. Johnson probably knew how the monitoring occurred. In addition, it seems as if she was specifically told that her calls might be monitored.

What was the testimony? I need to go back and read the first part of the opinion to find out what evidence was presented at trial.

In our view, the latter testimony, far from incredible, was highly plausible. Thus, there is no basis for us to conclude that the district court clearly erred in finding that Dyer was not told of the manner in which the monitoring was conducted and that he himself was to be monitored. *Cf. Rodriguez-Morales,* 931 F.2d at 982 (district court's finding should not be disturbed where there are two possible views of the evidence). And without at least this minimal knowledge on the part of Dyer, we do not see how his consent in fact to the monitoring could be inferred from this record. *Cf. Griggs-Ryan,* 904 F.2d 177 (implied consent inferred where defendant was informed (1) that all incoming calls, (2) on a particular line, (3) would be tape recorded.) Accordingly, we reject the contention that the court erred in finding that defendants are not protected by the consent exception.

OK, the court is not reviewing the issue de novo. It's just looking to see whether the evidence is sufficient to support the jury's verdict. Because it's only cited for the standard of review, I probably don't need to look at *Rodriguez.*

I really need to look at *Griggs-Ryan.* Although we might be able to get past this court's test, I'm not sure that we can get past the *Griggs-Ryan* test. Which is the right test? We can argue the test set out here, but I'm sure that Ms. Johnson will argue that it's the test set out in *Griggs-Ryan.* I need to check for some more cases. Probably the easiest thing to do at this point is to cite check *Williams v. Poulos* looking for cases that refer to headnote 6.

If the first four or five cases that you select answer the question you were asked to research, you do not need to look for more cases. If, however, these cases do not answer the question, you need to do additional research. At this point you have a number of options: (1) You can go back to the notes of decisions, identifying and then looking up the next best four or five cases; (2) you can look up cases that were cited in the cases you have already read, for example, the *Griggs-Ryan* case; or (3) you can run a search in an online database.

Step 7: Cite Check to Determine (1) Whether the Cases That You Plan to Use Are Still Good Law and (2) Whether There Are Any Additional Cases

Attorneys cite check cases for two reasons: to determine whether a particular case is still "good law" and to determine whether there are any other, more recent cases that are on point. Although it is still possible to do cite checking using the print version of *Shepard's,* most attorneys do their cite checking online using either the electronic version of *Shepard's* or KeyCite. The online information is usually more current than the printed information, and it takes less time to cite check online.

To check a cite using *Shepard's,* simply click on the "Check Citation" icon on the top toolbar. If you only want to know whether the case is good law, that is, whether it has been reversed or overruled, click on "*Shepard's* for Validation." If, however, you want to know both whether the case is still good law and whether there are any other, more recent cases, click on "*Shepard's* for Research."

For the purposes of this chapter, presume that when you clicked on "*Shepard's* for Research," you found the following information for *Williams v. Poulos.*

EXAMPLE

Copyright ©2001 SHEPARD'S—102 Citing references
Williams v. Poulos, 11 F.3d 271, 1993 U.S. App. LEXIS 32270 (1st Cir. Me. 1993)

SHEPARD'S® Signal: Caution: Possible negative treatment
Restrictions: *Unrestricted*
FOCUS® Terms: *No FOCUS terms*
Print Format: *FULL*
Citing Ref. Signal: *Hidden*

Prior History

Williams v. Poulos, 801 F. Supp. 867, 1992 U.S. Dist. LEXIS 14462
    (D. Me. 1992)
Affirmed by (Citation you entered):
Williams v. Poulos, 11 F.3d 271, 1993 U.S. App. LEXIS 32270 (1st
    Cir. Me. 1993)

Subsequent Appellate History (2 citing references)

Summary opinion at:
Williams v. Poulos, 22 Mass. Law. Weekly 729, 14 R.I. Law Weekly
    682 (1st Cir. Dec. 14, 1993)
Costs and fees proceeding at:
Williams v. Poulos, 1995 U.S. App. LEXIS 10667 (1st Cir. Me. May
    12, 1995)

Citing Decisions (77 citing decisions)

First Circuit—Court of Appeals

Cited by:

Haemonetics Corp. v. Dupre (In re Dupre), 2000 U.S. App. LEXIS
20898 (1st Cir. Mass. July 3, 2000)
> **Cited by:**
> 2000 U.S. App. LEXIS 20898

Cited by:

Miller v. United States Trustee (In re Independent Eng'g Co.), 197
F.3d 13, 1999 U.S. App. LEXIS 31558, 35 Bankr. Ct. Dec.
(LRP) 72, Bankr. L. Rep. (CCH) P78070 (1st Cir. 1999)
> **Cited by:**
> 197 F.3d 13 p.16

Cited by:

Desilets v. Wal-Mart Stores, Inc., 171 F.3d 711, 1999 U.S. App.
LEXIS 5629, 14 I.E.R. Cas. (BNA) 1642, 137 Lab. Cas.
(CCH) P58598 (1st Cir. N.H. 1999)
> **Cited by:**
> 171 F.3d 711 p.714

Cited by:

*National Educ. Ass'n-Rhode Island by Scigulinsky v. Retirement
Bd. of the R.I. Employees' Retirement Sys.*, 172 F.3d 22,
1999 U.S. App. LEXIS 5220, 23 Employee Benefits Cas.
(BNA) 1261, 160 L.R.R.M. (BNA) 3012 (1st Cir. R.I. 1999)
> **Cited by:**
> 172 F.3d 22 p.26

Cited by:

Appleyard v. Douglass, 1999 U.S. App. LEXIS 4023 (1st Cir. Mass.
Mar. 10, 1999)
> **Cited by:**
> 1999 U.S. App. LEXIS 4023

Cited by:

United States v. Nicholas, 133 F.3d 133, 1998 U.S. App. LEXIS
486 (1st Cir. Mass. 1998)
> **Cited by:**
> 133 F.3d 133 p.136

[Note: The rest of the citations have not been included.]

In the above example, cases are listed under three headings: Prior
History, Subsequent Appellate History, and Citing Decisions. The first
entry under Prior History is a reference to an earlier decision in the
same case. Before the case was decided by the First Circuit Court of Appeals, the case was heard and decided by the United States District
Court; its opinion was published and can be found in volume 801 of the

Federal Supplement at page 867. The second entry under Prior History is a reference to our case. The entries under Subsequent Appellate History are a citation to a source in which *Williams v. Poulos* was summarized and to the First Circuit's decision reviewing the District Court's decision on attorneys' fees and costs.

The 77 entries under Citing Decisions are citations to cases in which other courts have cited *Williams v. Poulos.* The citations are listed by court (for example, the decisions from the First Circuit Court of Appeals are listed in one subsection) and, within each subsection, in reverse chronological order. Some of the citations are to published decisions, and some are to unpublished decisions, that is, decisions that appear only on LEXIS, Loislaw, or Westlaw.

For each citing decision, there is a word describing how the citing court treated *Williams*. For example, did the court simply cite to *Williams,* or did it follow the rule set out in *Williams,* explain the rule set out in *Williams,* or criticize the rule set out in *Williams?*

Although you could look at each of the 77 citing decisions, doing so is not very efficient. Many of the cases that have cited to *Williams* have done so for a different point of law than the one in which we are interested. The better strategy is to identify the headnote or headnotes in *Williams* that set out the points of law in which you are interested and then to determine which cases have cited to *Williams* for those points. To do this using *Shepard's,* click on "custom restrictions" and then on headnote 6, the headnote in *Williams* that discusses implied consent.

When you do this, you will find that there is only one case that has cited *Williams* for the point of law set out in headnote 6: *Gilday v. Dubois,* 124 F.3d 277, 297 (1st Cir. 1997).

Thus, shepardizing *Williams* tells you that it is still good law. The case was not reversed by the United States Supreme Court or overruled in a subsequent decision. In fact, it has been distinguished by only one court and that was for a different point of law. In addition, shepardizing leads you to another case that you can use in your memo.

Step 8:   Locate Law Review Articles or Other Commentaries That Might Be on Point

Although this final step is not essential, it is often useful. A law review article can help you make sense of the statutory language and cases that you have found; it can help you identify arguments that each side might make; and it can provide you with a check on your research, alerting you to an important case that you may have missed.

Just as there are a number of ways to locate statutes and cases, there are a number of ways to locate law review articles: (1) You can locate articles using a print index, for example, the print version of the *Index to Legal Periodicals*; (2) you can use LEXIS, Loislaw, or Westlaw, doing either full text searches or searches in one of the available indexes; or (3) you can look up the law review articles listed in annotated and coded *Shepard's* or KeyCite, or in the cases themselves.

In our example case, we decide to look up the law review article we found when we shepardized *Williams v. Poulos.* Because the firm's library does not have the Northwestern University Law Review, we look first for it on Northwestern University's Law Review's home page. Not finding it there, we then locate it on Westlaw using the Find command.

§5.4   KNOWING WHEN TO STOP

By now you have probably spent at least several hours in the library locating and reading the applicable statutes and cases. Are you doing something wrong?

The answer is, probably not. Whether you do your research in print sources or online, it takes time. It takes time to locate the statutes and cases, and it takes even more time to read, analyze, and synthesize them. There will also be times when you take a wrong turn and spend time tracking down and reading statutes and cases that turn out not to be useful. Within limits, this is a normal part of the research process.

You do, however, need to make sure that you do not over-research an issue. Once you have found the applicable tests and rules, the cases that illustrate how those tests and rules have been applied in similar cases, and done your cite checking, stop. If, during the writing process, you determine that you need to do additional research, you can go back and do it then.

§5.5   KEEPING TRACK OF WHAT
YOU HAVE FOUND

In doing legal research, you must have a system. You must know where you have already looked and what it is you have found, and you must keep track of which statutes and cases you have and have not cite checked. In addition, you must think as you research. Although it may seem easier to photocopy everything and then read it, it isn't. Read as you go, analyzing each piece and trying to put the pieces together. You won't know what else you need until you know what you already have.

One way of keeping yourself organized is to develop a structured note-taking system. For example, many researchers find it helpful to create a sheet for each element, such as the one set out in Exhibit 5.2. Other researchers start a notebook with tabs. They set out cases that

EXHIBIT 5.2

Research Notes

Element in Dispute
Prior Consent

I. Rule or test that court applies in determining whether element is met:

Cites:

II. Analogous Cases

First Case:

Second Case:

Third Case:

III. Arguments that we can make:

IV. Arguments that the other side is likely to make:

provide the general rule under one tab, the cases that set out or discuss the first element under a second tab, cases that set out or discuss the second element under the third tab and so on. (Note: if you use this system, you will often need to make more than one copy of a decision.) Still other researchers create their own computerized filing system.

Whichever method you use, make it a practice to write down the full citation for each case and to list the statutes and cases you have cite checked. You will need this information when you write your memo.

§5.6   Understanding What You Have Found

At this point, you may feel overwhelmed. You have spent hours in the library, and your desk is stacked with notes and photocopies or you have dozens of computer files. The question is, now what? Is it time to start drafting the memo? The answer is, not yet. Before you begin drafting, you must put the pieces together.

Begin by creating a decision tree such as the one in Exhibit 5.3, which outlines the steps that the court would go through in deciding the issue.

Then, pull the cases that discuss each of the disputed elements. For the first disputed element, divide the cases into two stacks. In the first stack, put all of the cases in which the court held that the element was met. In the second stack, put all of the cases in which the court held that the element was not met.

Now look at the first stack. When you look the courts' discussions of the first disputed element, can you discern a common thread? For example, do all of the cases have a particular set of facts in common? In the alternative, can you see a trend? In recent years, have the courts tended to construe this element more narrowly? More broadly? In deciding this element, do the courts tend to find for the State? For the employer? For the tenant? For the consumer? Did one division or circuit tend to interpret this element in one way while other circuits or divisions tended to interpret it in another way?

While sometimes it is easy to identify the common threads, at other times it is more difficult. In these situations, it often helps to create a chart. For example, in our sample problem, you might create charts like those in Exhibit 5.4 and Exhibit 5.5.

As you examine the charts, you begin to identify some common threads. First, in each of the cases, the courts applied essentially the same rules. Second, in the cases in which the courts found consent, the plaintiffs had been told that all of their phone calls were being monitored. In contrast, in the cases in which the courts held that there was no consent, either the plaintiffs had not been told that their calls would be monitored or the plaintiffs did not know that all of their calls would be monitored.

EXHIBIT 5.3

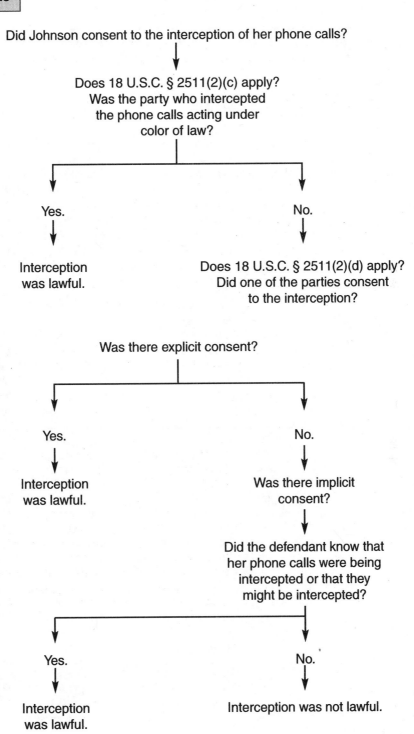

EXHIBIT 5.4

Consent: Cases in Which the Courts Held That the Plaintiff Had Consented to the Interception of His or Her Phone Calls

Case Name	Year	Court	Rules	Key Facts	Court's Reasoning
Griggs-Ryan v. Smith	1990	First Circuit Court of Appeals	Consent may be explicit or implied. No all-purpose definition of implied consent. "Implied consent is 'consent in fact,' which is inferred from surrounding circumstances indicating that the party knowingly agreed to the surveillance." pp. 116-117. Implied consent should not be causally inferred.	Action under § 2511(2)(d). Landlady repeatedly told tenant that all incoming phone calls would be monitored. All of the tenant's incoming calls were monitored.	The court upheld the trial court's decision granting defendant's motion for summary judgment. The plaintiff did not put forth any evidence indicating that he had some plausible reason for believing that fewer than all his calls were being monitored.
Gilday v. Dubois	1997	First Circuit Court of Appeals	Implied consent may be "inferred from . . . language or acts which tend to prove . . . that a party knows of, or assents to, encroachments on the routine expectation that conversations are private." p. 297 (citing Griggs-Ryan) "[A] reviewing court must inquire into the dimensions of the consent and then ascertain whether the interception exceeded those boundaries." *Id.*	Action under § 2511(2)(c). Before making phone calls, prisoners and the persons they were calling heard a recorded message that told them that, except for approved calls to attorneys, the entire contents of their calls would be intercepted and recorded.	The court affirmed the trial court's granting of summary judgment. The court held that there was consent because the prisoner knew that all of his conversations were being monitored.

EXHIBIT 5.5

Consent: Cases in Which the Courts Held That the Plaintiff Had Not Consented to the Interception of His or Her Phone Calls					
Case Name	*Year*	*Court*	*Rules*	*Key Facts*	*Court's Reasoning*
Campiti v. Walonis	1979	First Circuit Court of Appeals	Court does not set out rules.	Action under § 2511(2)(c). Police officer used an extension phone to listen to phone calls between two inmates. An officer placed the calls for the inmates, and the inmates knew that prison officials sometimes listened in on phone calls.	The court held that there was sufficient evidence to support the trial court's finding that the inmate had not consented to the interception of his phone calls. The prison had argued that the inmate should have known that that his calls might be monitored.
Williams v. Poulos	1993	First Circuit Court of Appeals	"Implied consent is 'consent in fact,' which may be inferred from surrounding circumstances indicating the party knowingly agreed to the surveillance. Implied consent should not be casually implied." p. 117	Action under § 2511(2)(d). Employer installed monitoring system to reduce its telephone bill and decrease employee theft. Managers were told that all phone calls were subject to to random monitoring and that they should inform those under them of this fact. The plaintiff was told about the monitoring system when he assumed the position of CEO and Chairman of the Board.	The court affirmed the trial court's granting of an injunction on the grounds that the plaintiff was not informed (1) of the manner in which the calls would be monitored and (2) that his calls would be monitored.

EXHIBIT 5.5	*(continued)*

Consent: Cases in Which the Courts Held That the Plaintiff Had Not Consented to the Interception of His or Her Phone Calls

Case Name	Year	Court	Rules	Key Facts	Court's Reasoning
Deal v. Spears	1992	Eighth Circuit Court of Appeals	Consent is not to be "cavalierly implied." p. 1157. Knowledge that employer is capable of monitoring calls is not enough.	Action under § 2511(2)(d). Employers warned employees that they might monitor phone calls to reduce the number of personal phone calls. In fact, employers also hoped to gain information about a burglary that they believed had been an inside job.	Court held that, as a matter of law, the plaintiff had not consented to the monitoring of her phone calls. The employers had told the employee that they might monitor her phone calls, not that they were monitoring them. Fact that employers hoped to catch employee talking about the burglary indicates that employers believed that employee did not know that her phone calls were being monitored.

B.   DRAFTING

With the prewriting stage behind you, it is now time to put pen to paper or fingers to keyboard.

As you begin writing, keep several things in mind. First, remember your audience. In writing an objective memorandum, you are not writing for the other side or even a judge. Your primary audience is an attorney in your firm.

Second, remember how the attorney will use the memo. Your purpose is not to persuade; it is to give the attorney the information that he or she needs to evaluate the case objectively and advise the client. Consequently, in writing the memo, you must present the law objectively. This is not the time to omit or even de-emphasize unfavorable cases or facts. If the attorney is to evaluate your case accurately, you must present both the favorable and unfavorable information.

Third, remember that unlike briefs, there are no court rules specifying the format of an objective memorandum. There are only conventions. Although these conventions are useful for both the writer and the reader, once you understand them, you should feel free to break them when appropriate. When a convention does not serve its purpose, do not use it.

Finally, and perhaps most importantly, remember that writing a memo is a recursive process. Writing is not just putting completely formed ideas on paper; it is a process of discovery. As a result, as you write you will begin thinking about the problem in new ways, which may require doing more research or rethinking your analysis or synthesis of the law.

Similarly, because the process is recursive, there is no right order in which to write the various sections. While some writers draft the sections in the order in which they appear in the memo, others begin with the brief answer, the discussion section, or even the conclusion. Because each section is connected to the others, wherever you start, you will have to go back to that section at the end, revising it in light of what you wrote in the other sections.

§5.7   DRAFTING THE HEADING

The heading is the easiest section to write. It consists of only four entries: the name of the person to whom the memo is addressed, the name of the person who wrote the memo, the date, and an entry identifying the client and the issue or issues discussed in the memo. Although the first three entries are self-explanatory, the fourth needs some explanation.

In some firms, the memo is filed only in the client's file. For such firms, the "Re:" entry can be quite general.

EXAMPLE 1

To: Charles Maier

From: Legal Intern

Date: September 8, 2002

Re: Eliza Johnson v. Elite Insurance, File No. 02-478

In other firms, the memo is filed not only in the client's file but also in a "memo bank," that is, a computer or paper file in which all memos are filed by topic. In these offices, the "Re:" section serves two purposes. Within the client's file, it distinguishes the memo from any other memos that may have been or will be written, and in the memo bank, it provides either the database for a word search or topic categories under which the memo will be filed. To serve this last purpose, the heading should include the key terms.

EXAMPLE 2

To: Charles Maier

From: Legal Intern

Date: September 8, 2002

Re: Eliza Johnson v. Elite Insurance, File No. 02-478
        18 U.S.C. § 2511: Consent to intercept or monitor phone
        calls.

---

§5.8   Drafting the Statement of Facts

Just as every case starts with a story, so does every memo. Before you set out the issues, the law, and the arguments, tell the attorney who did what when.

§5.8.1   Decide What Facts to Include

In a typical statement of facts, there are three types of facts: the legally significant facts, the emotionally significant facts, and the background facts. In addition, the writer usually identifies those facts that are unknown.

a.   Legally Significant Facts

A legally significant fact is a fact that a court would consider in deciding whether a statute or rule is applicable or in applying that statute or rule. In our example case, a court would find legally significant those facts that the court would consider in determining whether Ms. Johnson consented to the interception of her phone calls, for example, the fact that Elite had told Ms. Johnson it was Elite's policy to monitor all of an employee's phone calls during his or her one-month training period. In contrast, the facts related to the number of people employed by Elite would not be legally significant. They are not facts that the court would consider in deciding whether all of the elements were met.

Either of two techniques can be used to determine whether a fact is legally significant. The first technique, which is used before the discussion section has been written, is to prepare a two-column chart. In the first column, list the elements, and in the second, the facts that the court would consider in deciding whether those elements are met. Facts that are not listed next to an element are not legally significant.

EXAMPLE

Element	Facts the court would consider in deciding whether element is met
Prior Consent	Employees were told that phones should be used for business purposes only.
	Employees were told that all of their phone calls would be monitored during their one-month training period and periodically after that to ensure that employees were providing good service to customers.
	Clients calling the office heard a message saying that their phone calls might be monitored to ensure good service.
	Elite seldom monitored employee calls. After the training period, employee calls were monitored only two or three times a year, usually immediately before the employee's annual performance review.
	Employees were not told in advance that their calls would be monitored.

The second technique is used after the discussion section has been completed. To ensure that you have included all of the legally significant facts in your statement of facts, go through your discussion section, listing each fact that you used in setting out each side's arguments; then check this list against your fact statement. If you used a fact in the arguments, that fact is legally significant and should be included in the statement of facts. (Remember, writing a memo is a recursive process. Even though you may write the statement of facts first, you will need to revise it after you have completed the discussion section.)

b.   *Emotionally Significant Facts*

An emotionally significant fact is one that, while not legally significant, may affect the way the judge or jury decides the case.

In our example case, several facts could be considered emotionally significant. For example, although it is not legally significant that Ms. Johnson was having an affair, this fact, if admitted, might influence a jury. The jury might see the case differently if it knew that Ms. Johnson was talking to a lover rather than a sick child. Similarly, although it is not legally significant that Ms. Johnson's husband has filed for divorce, this fact might affect the way the judge or jury views the case. As a consequence, the attorney needs to consider these facts in evaluating the case.

c.   *Background Facts*

In addition to including the legally and emotionally significant facts, also include those facts that are needed to tell the story and that provide the context for the legally and emotionally significant facts. For example, in our example case, the fact that Ms. Johnson began working for Elite Insurance in January 2000 is neither legally nor emotionally significant. You would, however, want to include this fact because it helps tell the story.

d.   *Unknown Facts*

Sometimes you are not given all of the facts needed to analyze an issue. For instance, because the attorney did not know the law, he or she did not ask the right questions, or the documents containing the unknown facts are in the possession of the opposing party. If the unknown facts go to the heart of the issue, try to obtain them before writing the memo. For example, if Mr. Maier had not told you whether Elite had told Ms. Johnson about its monitoring policy, you should try to obtain this information. It would be hard to analyze the case without this information. In contrast, if the unknown facts are less important, go ahead and write the memo, but tell the attorney, either in the statement of facts or in the discussion section, what facts are unknown.

EXAMPLE

Mr. Wilson intercepted the phone calls by attaching a tape recorder to an extension phone. At this point, we do not know whether, when she answered the phone, Ms. Johnson heard the message warning incoming callers that their calls might be monitored.

§5.8.2   Select an Organizational Scheme

As a general rule, begin your statement of facts with an introductory paragraph that identifies the parties and the cause of action. Then present the facts using one of three organizational schemes: a chronological organizational scheme, a topical organizational scheme, or a combination of the two, for example, a scheme in which you organize the facts by topic and then, within each topic, present the facts in chronological order.

The facts themselves usually dictate which organizational scheme will work best. If the case involves a series of events related by date, then the facts should be presented chronologically. If, however, there are a number of facts that are not related by date (for example, the description of several different pieces of property) or a number of unrelated events that occurred during the same time period (for example, four unrelated crimes committed by the defendant over the same two-day period), the facts should be organized by topic.

In our example case, the facts can be presented using either a scheme that is primarily chronological or a scheme that is primarily topical.

EXAMPLE	CHRONOLOGICAL ORGANIZATION

Statement of Facts

Elite Insurance has contacted our office asking whether it violated the Electronic Communications Privacy Act when it intercepted Eliza Johnson's phone calls without her explicit consent.

Ms. Johnson began working for Elite Insurance in January 2000. When she was hired, Ms. Johnson was told that the phones and computers should be used for business purposes only. In addition, she was told that it was Elite's policy to monitor all of an employee's phone calls during his or her one-month training period and to periodically monitor them after that time to ensure that employees were providing good service to Elite's clients. In accordance with this policy, clients calling the office heard a message saying that their phone calls might be monitored to ensure good service.

In fact, Elite seldom intercepts its employees' calls. According to Eric Wilson, the office supervisor, once the training period ends, employee calls are intercepted only two or three times a year, usually immediately before the employee's annual performance review. At these times, Mr. Wilson does not tell employees in advance that he will be intercepting their calls, but he usually discusses the calls with them immediately after they have been intercepted.

Because he had information indicating that Ms. Johnson might be involved in an insurance fraud scheme, Mr. Wilson began intercepting her calls in mid-July and stopped intercepting them in mid-August. At no point during this time did Mr. Wilson tell Ms. Johnson that he was intercepting her calls or discuss the calls with her. Although his intercepting did not produce any evidence that Ms. Johnson was involved in any type of illegal activity, Mr. Wilson did overhear conversations indicating that Ms. Johnson was having an affair. On August 19, 2002, Mr. Wilson fired Ms. Johnson because she had used the phones for personal business.

Mr. Wilson intercepted the phone calls by attaching a tape recorder to an extension phone. At this point, we do not know whether, when Ms. Johnson answered the phone, she heard the message warning incoming callers that their calls might be monitored. Ms. Johnson did not explicitly agree, either orally or in writing, to the interception of her calls, and she states that she did not know that her calls were being intercepted.

EXAMPLE   TOPICAL ORGANIZATION

Statement of Facts

Elite Insurance has contacted our office, asking whether it violated the Electronic Communications Privacy Act when it monitored Eliza Johnson's phone calls without her express consent.

As a matter of company policy, Elite Insurance periodically monitors its employees' phone calls to ensure that its employees are providing good service to Elite's clients. All calls are monitored during the employee's initial one-month training period. After that, employee calls are monitored two or three times a year, usually immediately before the employee's annual performance review. Individuals calling Elite hear a message telling them that their calls may be monitored.

Although Elite tells its employees that the phones and computers should be used for business purposes only, employees do use the phones for personal calls, for example, to check on a child or to make doctors' appointments. These calls are tolerated if they are short.

Elite began monitoring Ms. Johnson's calls in mid-July 2002 because it had information indicating that she might be involved in an insurance fraud scheme. It continued monitoring her calls until about mid-August, when Johnson was fired for using the phones for personal calls. Although the monitoring did not produce any evidence that Johnson was involved in an insurance fraud scheme, it did reveal that she was having an affair with another individual.

Although Mr. Wilson does not tell employees in advance that he will be intercepting their calls, he usually discusses the calls with them immediately after the calls have been intercepted. Elite intercepted Ms. Johnson's phone calls using a recorder attached to an extension phone. At this point, we do not know whether, when she answered the phone, Ms. Johnson heard the message warning incoming callers that their calls might be monitored. Ms. Johnson did not explicitly agree, either orally or in writing, to the interception of her calls, and she states that she did not know that her calls were being intercepted.

Which of the above examples works best? Why?

§5.8.3   Present the Facts Accurately and Objectively

In writing the statement of facts for an objective memorandum, you need to present the facts accurately and objectively. This means that you cannot set out facts that are not in the record, you cannot leave out facts that are legally significant, and you cannot present the facts so that they favor one side over the other.

In the following example, the author has violated all three of these "rules."

EXAMPLE

Beginning in July 2002, Elite Insurance began surreptitiously monitoring Ms. Johnson's phone calls in an attempt to find information that it could use to fire her. Although the monitoring did not produce any information indicating that Ms. Johnson was involved in an illegal activity, Elite continued monitoring all of her client calls until mid-July, when, without notice, it fired her.

The author violated the first rule when, in the first sentence, she states that Elite began monitoring Ms. Johnson's phone calls in an attempt to find information that it could use to fire her. This fact is not in the memo from Mr. Maier. The memo says only that Elite began monitoring Ms. Johnson's calls because it had information that she was involved in an insurance fraud scheme. The author violated the second rule when she fails, in the second sentence, to mention that as a result of the monitoring Elite discovered that Ms. Johnson was using the phone for personal calls, a violation of company policy. Finally, the author violated the third rule by using such words and phrases as "surreptitiously," "in an attempt," and "without notice."

In addition to stating the facts accurately and objectively, you also need to present the facts as facts, not as legal conclusions. For example, in our sample statement of facts, you cannot say that Ms. Johnson did or did not consent. Although in the context of some cases such a statement would be a statement of fact, given the issue that you have been asked to research, it is a legal conclusion.

§5.8.4   Checklist for Critiquing the Statement of Facts

A.   Content

- All of the legally significant facts have been included.
- When appropriate, emotionally significant facts have been included.
- Enough background facts have been included so that a person not familiar with the case can understand what happened.
- The unknown facts have been identified.
- The facts are presented accurately.
- The facts are presented objectively.
- The writer has not included legal conclusions in the statement of facts.

B.   Organization

- The writer has included an introductory sentence or paragraph that identifies the parties and the nature of the dispute.
- The writer has used one of the conventional organizational schemes: chronological, topical, or a combination of chronological and topical.

C.   Writing

- The attorney can understand the facts of the case after reading the statement of facts once.

- The paragraph divisions are logical, and the paragraphs are neither too long nor too short.
- Transitions and dovetailing have been used to make the connections between ideas clear.
- In most sentences, the writer has used the actor as the subject of the sentence, and the subject and verb are close together.
- The writer has varied the length of the sentences and the sentence patterns so that each sentence flows smoothly from the prior sentence.
- The writing is concise and precise.
- The writing is grammatically correct and correctly punctuated.
- The statement of facts has been proofread.

§5.9   DRAFTING THE ISSUE STATEMENT OR QUESTION PRESENTED

The issue statement, also called the question presented, establishes the memo's focus. It identifies the applicable statute or common law rule, it sets out the legal question, and it summarizes the facts that will be significant in deciding that question.

§5.9.1   Decide How Many Issue Statements You Should Have and the Order in Which They Should Be Listed

By convention, you should have the same number of issue statements as parts to the discussion section. Accordingly, if you have three issue statements—whether service of process was adequate, whether the statute of limitations has run, and whether the defendant was negligent—you should also have three parts to the discussion section, one corresponding to each of the three issues. If, however, you have only one issue statement, for example, whether Ms. Johnson consented to the monitoring of her phone calls, your discussion section will have only one part.

Convention also dictates that in a multi-issue memo you list the issues in the same order in which you discuss those issues in the discussion section. The first issue statement will correspond to the first section of the discussion section, the second will correspond to the second section, and so on.

§5.9.2   Select a Format

The two most common formats for an issue statement are the "under-does-when" format and the "whether" format. This chapter discusses the under-does-when format; the next chapter discusses the whether format.

The under-does-when format is easier to use because the format forces you to include all the essential information. After the "under," insert a reference to the applicable law; after "does," "is," "may," or a similar verb, insert the legal question, and after "when," insert the most important of the legally significant facts:

> Under *[insert reference to applicable law]*
> does/is/may *[insert legal question]*
> when *[insert most important legally significant facts]*?

a.   *Reference to Applicable Law*

If it is to provide the reader with useful information, the reference to the rule of law cannot be either too specific or too general. For example, in our sample problem a reference to just the statute would be too specific; very few attorneys would know that 18 U.S.C. § 2511(2)(b) deals with the interception of wire communications. Similarly, a reference to "federal law" is too broad; hundreds of thousands of cases are filed each year in which the issue is governed by federal law.

EXAMPLES

References that are too specific:

Under 18 U.S.C. § 2511(2)(c), . . .
Under 18 U.S.C. § 2511, . . .
Under Title 18, . . .

References that are too broad:

Under federal law, . . .
Under the applicable statute, . . .

Appropriate references:

Under the Electronic Communications Privacy Act, . . .
Under the Electronic Communications Privacy Act, 18 U.S.C. § 2511, . . .

---

b.   *The Legal Question*

After setting out the applicable law, you need to set out the question. Again, in doing so you want to make sure that your statement is neither too narrow nor too broad. If stated too narrowly, the question will not cover all of the issues and sub-issues in the discussion section; if stated too broadly, the question doesn't serve its function of focusing the reader's attention on the real issue.

EXAMPLES

Legal questions that are too narrow:

did Ms. Johnson explicitly consent to the monitoring of her phone calls . . .
did Ms. Johnson impliedly consent to the monitoring of her phone calls . . .

Legal questions that are too broad:

were Ms. Johnson's rights violated . . .
is Elite Insurance liable . . .

Legal questions that are properly framed:

did Ms. Johnson consent to the interception of her phone calls when . . .
is there prior consent to the interception of a wire communication when . . .

---

c.   *Legally Significant Facts*

In our legal system questions are always decided in the context of specific facts. As a consequence, you need to include in your issue statement those facts that the court will consider in answering the legal question.

The problem lies in deciding which facts to include. If there are only two or three facts that are legally significant, the answer is easy. Include them all. If, however, there are five, ten, or even fifteen legally significant facts, it will be difficult, if not impossible, to include them all and still write an issue statement that is readable. In these situations you need to do one of three things: Summarize the facts, categorize the facts and then list only the categories, or include only the most significant of the legally significant facts.

In the first example set out below, the issue statement is too long. As a consequence, most attorneys would not take the time to read through it. The second issue statement is much better. Although not all the legally significant facts are included, the most important ones are.

EXAMPLE 1   POOR

Under the Electronic Communications Privacy Act, 18 U.S.C. § 2511, did Ms. Johnson consent to the interception of her phone calls when (1) at the time she was hired she was told that the phone and computers should be used for business purposes only and that it was the company's policy to monitor all of an employee's phone calls during his or her one-month training period and to periodically monitor them after that to ensure good customer service; (2) in fact, after the initial training period, Elite monitored its employees' phone calls only two or three times a year, usually immediately before an employee's annual performance evaluation; (3) all incoming callers heard a message telling them that their calls were subject to monitoring; (4) because it had information indicating that Ms. Johnson might be involved in an insurance fraud scheme, Elite monitored her calls for four to five weeks using a recorder attached to an extension phone; (5) although the monitoring did not produce information indicating that Ms. Johnson was involved in an insurance fraud scheme, it did produce information indicating that Ms. Johnson was using the phones for personal calls; and (6) Ms. Johnson did not know that her calls were being monitored?

EXAMPLE 2   BETTER

Under the Electronic Communications Privacy Act, 18 U.S.C. § 2511, did Ms. Johnson consent to the interception of her phone calls when (1) she was told that her calls would be periodically monitored to ensure good customer service, but Elite seldom monitored its employees' calls and (2) Ms. Johnson did not know that her calls were being monitored?

There are several other situations that may cause problems. First, you may encounter a situation in which it is not clear which rule of law the court will apply: If the court adopts one rule, one set of facts will be significant, and if it adopts another rule, another set of facts will be significant. In such a situation, include only those facts that the court would consider significant in determining which rule to apply.

Second, you may encounter a situation in which the facts are in dispute: The plaintiff alleges that things happened one way, and the defendant alleges that they happened another way. In such situations, summarize each side's allegations. If you cannot, simply state the facts that are not disputed and indicate which facts, or categories of facts, are in dispute.

You may also be tempted to state as a fact something that is a legal conclusion. For example, the first time you write an issue statement, you may write something like the following:

> Under the Electronic Communications Privacy Act, did Ms. Johnson consent to the monitoring of her phone calls when she did not expressly or impliedly consent to such monitoring?

Common sense tells you that the answer to this question must always be no. If she did not expressly or impliedly consent, she did not consent. If your issue statement is to be meaningful, you must set out the facts that the court will consider in determining whether the test is met, not the test itself.

Finally, one of the "facts" that you will usually include in your issue statement is the identity of the client. There are two schools of thought about how this fact should be handled. One says that the issue statement should be case-specific and that the client should be referred to by name. The other says that the issue statement should be generic. Proponents of this school say that the client should not be referred to by name; instead you should determine what role the client plays and then use that label. Before writing a memo, check with your supervising attorney to determine which approach he or she would like you to take.

§5.9.3   Checklist for Critiquing the Issue Statement

A.   Content

- The reference to the rule of law is neither too broad nor too narrow.
- The legal question is properly focused.
- The most significant of the legally significant facts have been included.
- Legal conclusions have not been set out as facts.

B.   Format

- The writer has used one of the conventional formats, for example, the "under-does-when" format.

C.   Writing

- The reader can understand the issue statement after reading it once.
- The writer has used all three slots in the sentence: the opening, the middle, and the end.
- The writer has used a concrete subject and an action verb, and the subject and verb are close together.
- In presenting the facts, the writer has used parallel constructions.
- The sentence is grammatically correct and correctly punctuated.
- The issue statement has been proofread.

§5.10   DRAFTING THE BRIEF ANSWER

The brief answer serves a purpose similar to that served by the formal conclusion: It tells the attorney how you think a court will decide an issue and why. It is not, however, as detailed as the formal conclusion.

As a general rule, include a separate brief answer for each issue statement. In addition, start each of your brief answers with a one- or two-word short answer. The words that are typically used are "probably," and "probably not." After this one- or two-word answer, explain the answer in one or two sentences.

EXAMPLE

Issue

Under the Electronic Communications Privacy Act, 18 U.S.C. § 2511, did Ms. Johnson consent to the interception of her phone calls when (1) she was told that her phone calls would be periodically intercepted to ensure good customer service but Elite Insurance seldom monitored its employees' calls and (2) Ms. Johnson did not know that her calls were being monitored?

Brief Answer

Probably not. Johnson did not explicitly consent to the interception of her phone calls and, under the circumstances, the court probably will not find implied consent. Even though Elite told Johnson that her calls might be intercepted and incoming callers heard a message warning them that their calls might be monitored, Elite did not make a practice of monitoring employees' calls for extended periods of time, and Elite's own reason for intercepting the calls indicates that it did not believe that Johnson knew that her calls were being intercepted.

§5.10.1　Checklist for Critiquing the Brief Answer

A.　Content

- The writer has predicted but not guaranteed how the issue will be decided.
- The writer has briefly explained his or her prediction, for example, the writer has explained which elements will be easy to prove and which will be more difficult.

B.　Format

- A separate brief answer has been included for each issue statement.
- The answer begins with a one- or two-word short answer. This one- or two-word short answer is then followed by a one- or two-sentence explanation.

C.　Writing

- The writer can understand the brief answer after reading it once.
- The writer has used concrete subjects and action verbs, and the subjects and verbs are close together.
- When appropriate, the writer has used parallel constructions.
- The writing is grammatically correct and correctly punctuated.
- The brief answer has been proofread.

§5.11   Drafting the Discussion Section: An Introduction

In reading the discussion section, attorneys expect to see certain types of information, and they expect to see that information presented in a particular order.

These expectations are not born of whim. Instead, they are based on conventional formats, which are themselves based on the way attorneys approach legal questions. In analyzing a legal problem, the attorney begins with the law. What is the applicable statute or common law rule? The attorney then applies that law to the facts of the client's case. Are both sides likely to agree on the conclusion, or will the application of the law be in dispute?

If the application is in dispute, the attorney looks to see how the law has been applied in similar cases. Because our system is a system based on precedent, the courts usually decide like, or analogous, cases in a like manner.

The attorney then considers the arguments that each side is likely to make. What types of factual arguments or arguments based on the analogous cases are each side likely to make? Given the purpose and policies underlying the statute or rule, what type of policy arguments might each side make?

Finally, the attorney makes a prediction. Given the facts, rules, cases, and arguments, how will a court decide each element? The case?

The discussion section reflects this process. It contains the same components—rules, analogous cases, arguments, and mini-conclusions—in the same order. At its simplest, and at its best, the discussion section analyzes the problem, walking the attorney step-by-step through the law, cases, and arguments to the probable outcome.

§5.12   Drafting the Discussion Section: Selecting an Organizational Plan

Just as there are standard house plans, there are standard plans for discussion sections. While builders have blueprints for ramblers, two-story homes, and split levels, attorneys have blueprints for problems involving an analysis of elements, for problems that require the balancing of competing interests, and for issues of first impression. In this chapter we discuss one of those blueprints: the plan for an elements analysis. In the next chapter we discuss the second and third types of plans: the plan for the balancing of competing interests and the plan that is used when the issue is one of first impression.

The most frequently used blueprint is the one for a problem that involves an analysis of elements. It is used any time that the governing statute, regulation, common law rule, or court rule sets out a list of elements. For example, you will use it in analyzing the elements of a crime or intentional tort, to determine whether an individual has gained title through adverse possession, to determine whether service of process is valid, or, as in our example problem, to determine whether the requirements of a statute are met.

When the blueprint for an elements analysis is used, the discussion begins with a statement of the general rule and a list of the elements. After raising and dismissing the elements that are not in dispute, the writer discusses each of the elements that are in dispute, for each disputed element setting out the applicable rules, the analogous cases, each side's arguments, and a mini-conclusion. At its most basic, the blueprint for an elements analysis is as follows.

Elements Analysis

A. Set out the governing law: for example, the governing statute, regulation, common law rule, or court rule.
B. Raise and dismiss undisputed elements.
C. Discuss the first disputed element.
D. Discuss the second disputed element.
E. Discuss the third disputed element.

Just as a builder may need to modify a standard blueprint so that the house fits on the lot and satisfies the buyer's preferences, you may need to modify this basic blueprint so that it works for your problem and your reader. The following examples show how you might modify the plan for a problem in which there are only three elements, one of which is not in dispute and two of which are. The first example shows you how to modify the plan for an attorney who prefers the script format, and the second example shows you how to modify the plan for an attorney who prefers one of the integrated formats. (For a discussion of the script and integrated formats, see section 6.8.)

EXAMPLE 1   BLUEPRINT FOR AN ELEMENTS ANALYSIS

Version 1 (Script Format)

I. First Issue
    A. Introduce the issue and set out general rules.
    B. Raise and dismiss undisputed elements.
        1. Identify elements.
        2. Explain why each of these elements is not in dispute.

   C. Analyze the first disputed element.
      1. Set out the tests or rules that courts use in determining whether the first disputed element is met.
      2. Describe cases that illustrate how the tests or rules have been applied in factually similar situations.
      3. Set out the plaintiff's (or moving party's) assertion and arguments.
      4. Set out the defendant's (or responding party's) assertion and arguments.
      5. Predict how the court or jury is likely to decide this element.
   D. Analyze the second disputed element.
      1. Set out the tests or rules that courts use in determining whether the second disputed element is met.
      2. Describe cases that illustrate how the tests or rules have been applied in factually similar situations.
      3. Set out the plaintiff's (or moving party's) assertion and arguments.
      4. Set out the defendant's (or responding party's) assertion and arguments.
      5. Predict how the court or jury is likely to decide this element.
II. Second Issue
    [Not set out.]

EXAMPLE 2   ORGANIZATIONAL PLAN FOR AN ELEMENTS ANALYSIS

Version 2 (Integrated Format)

I. First Issue
   A. Introduce the issue and set out general rules.
   B. Raise and dismiss undisputed elements.
      1. Identify the elements.
      2. Explain why each of these elements is not in dispute.
   C. Analyze the first disputed element.
      1. Set out the tests or rules that courts use in determining whether the first disputed element is met.
      2. Describe cases that illustrate how the tests or rules have been applied in factually similar cases.
      3. Predict how the court or jury is likely to decide this element.
      4. Set out the first line of reasoning that supports your prediction. In doing so, set out and evaluate each side's arguments.

      5. Set out the second line of reasoning that supports your prediction. In doing so, set out and evaluate each side's arguments.

  D. Analyze the second disputed element.

      1. Set out the tests or rules that courts use in determining whether second disputed element is met.

      2. Describe cases that illustrate how the tests or rules have been applied in factually similar situations.

      3. Predict how the court or jury is likely to decide this element.

      4. Set out the first line of reasoning that supports your prediction. In doing so, set out and evaluate each side's arguments.

      5. Set out the second line of reasoning that supports your prediction. In doing so, set out and evaluate each side's arguments.

II. Second Issue
[Not set out.]

The next example shows how you might modify the basic blueprint so that it works for our sample problem, a problem in which there is only one undisputed element (party to the communication) and one disputed element (consent). The one disputed element has two parts, however, one of which is undisputed and one of which is in dispute.

EXAMPLE 3 **ORGANIZATIONAL SCHEME FOR SAMPLE PROBLEM**

A. Introduce the issue and set out the general rule.
      Introduce 18 U.S.C. § 2511 and set out applicable portions.

B. Discuss the element not in dispute.
      Explain why the element "party to the communication" is not in dispute.

C. Discuss the element in dispute.
      Explain that consent may be explicit or implied but not constructive.

      1. Explicit consent (not in dispute)
         a. Rules
         b. Application of rules

      2. Implied consent (in dispute)
         a. Rules
         b. Descriptions of analogous cases
         c. Ms. Johnson's arguments
         d. Elite Insurance's arguments
         e. Mini-conclusion

§5.12.1   Present the General Rule

Because all legal analysis begins with a rule, which is then applied to the facts of a particular case, you will usually begin the discussion section by setting out the general rule.

OUTLINE OF DISCUSSION SECTION

I. First Issue
    Statement of the general rule

Sometimes, the general rule will be a statute or a subsection of a statute. For instance, in our sample case, the general rule could either be 18 U.S.C. § 2511 or 18 U.S.C. § 2511(2)(d), depending on where we decide to start the discussion. At other times, the general rule may be a constitutional provision, for example, the Fourth Amendment; a common law rule, for example, the test for adverse possession; or a court rule, for example, Civil Rule 56, the rule that governs motions for summary judgment. This chapter discusses the first situation, in which the general rule is a statute. The next chapter discusses the other situations.

a.   Single Statutory Section

When the rule is a single statutory section, introduce the statute and then quote the relevant portions. In the following examples, the first example is poor because the writer has not introduced the statute. She has simply begun the discussion by setting out the text of the statute. The second example is much better. The writer has placed the statute in context, telling the attorney what to look for.

EXAMPLE 1   STATUTE NOT INTRODUCED

(3)   A contract which does not satisfy the requirements of subsection (1) but which is valid in other respects is enforceable
    (a)   if the goods are to be specially manufactured for the buyer and are not suitable for sale to others in the ordinary course of the seller's business and the seller, before notice of repudiation is received and under

circumstances which reasonably indicate that the goods are for the buyer, has made either a substantial beginning of their manufacture or commitments for their procurement; . . .

Colo. Rev. Stat. § 4-2-201(3)(a).

EXAMPLE 2   STATUTE INTRODUCED

Even if the formal requirements of the UCC Statute of Frauds are not met, a contract is enforceable if the goods were specially manufactured. The applicable portion of the statute reads as follows:

(3)   A contract which does not satisfy the requirements of subsection (1) but which is valid in other respects is enforceable
     (a)   if the goods are to be specially manufactured for the buyer and are not suitable for sale to others in the ordinary course of the seller's business and the seller, before notice of repudiation is received and under circumstances which reasonably indicate that the goods are for the buyer, has made either a substantial beginning of their manufacture or commitments for their procurement; . . .

Colo. Rev. Stat. § 4-2-201(3)(a).

---

b.   Multiple Statutory Sections

The approach is similar when there is more than one applicable statutory section: Introduce the statutes and then quote the relevant portions, starting with the more general sections and ending with the more specific. Think of your general rule section as an inverted pyramid: broadest rules first, narrower rules next, specific rules and exceptions last. See section 3.2 in *Just Writing*.

In the following example, the writer has made two mistakes. First, the introductions are weak. The writer identifies the sections but does not place those sections in a larger context, tell the attorney what to look for in reading the statutory sections, or explain how the sections are related. Second, instead of setting out the general rules before the more specific rules, the writer has set out the sections in the order that they appeared in the code.

EXAMPLE   **WEAK INTRODUCTIONS AND GENERAL RULES NOT PRESENTED BEFORE MORE SPECIFIC RULES**

Section 9A.40.010 reads as follows:

(1) "Restrain" means to restrict a person's movements without consent and without legal authority in a manner which interferes substantially with his liberty.

(2) "Abduct" means to restrain a person by either (a) secreting or holding him in a place where he is not likely to be found, or (b) using or threatening to use deadly force.

Section 9A.40.030 states that

(1) A person is guilty of kidnapping in the second degree if he intentionally abducts another person under circumstances not amounting to kidnapping in the first degree.

The following example is much better. The introductions establish a context and explain the relationships among the sections, and the more general rules are set out before the more specific ones.

EXAMPLE   **STRONGER INTRODUCTIONS AND MORE GENERAL RULES SET OUT BEFORE MORE SPECIFIC RULES**

A person is guilty of kidnapping in the second degree if "he intentionally abducts another person under circumstances not amounting to kidnapping in the first degree." RCW 9A.40.030(1). The term "abducts" is defined in RCW 9A.40.010(2):

(2) "Abduct" means to restrain a person by either (a) secreting or holding him in a place where he is not likely to be found, or (b) using or threatening to use deadly force.

"Restrain" is defined in RCW 9A.40.010(1).

(1) "Restrain" means to restrict a person's movements without consent and without legal authority in a manner which interferes substantially with his liberty.

---

c. Statutes Plus Cases

In some problems you will have to present not only the statute but also rules from cases that have interpreted the statute. In these situations, quote the statute and then set out the rules from the cases.

EXAMPLE

Section 402 sets out the standard that the trial court must use in awarding child custody:

Section 402: Best Interest of Child

The court shall determine custody in accordance with the best interest of the child after considering all relevant factors including:

(1) the wishes of the child's parent or parents as to his custody;

(2) the wishes of the child as to his custodian;

(3) the interaction and interrelationship of the child with his parent or parents, his siblings, and any other person who may significantly affect the child's best interest;

(4) the child's adjustment to his home, school, and community; and

(5) the mental and physical health of all individuals involved.

The court shall not consider conduct of a proposed custodian that does not affect his relationship to the child.

Because this statute supersedes the common law, there is no longer a presumption that the custody of young children should be awarded to the mother. *In re Marriage of Huen*, 56 Wn.2d 487, 534 P.2d 1985 (1986). The Supreme Court has, however, held that if the child is too young to express his or her preference, the best interests of the child mandate that the trial court award custody of the child to the primary caregiver absent a finding that the caregiver is unfit to have custody. *Id.*

In our case about intercepted phone calls, we need to use a variation of one of the basic patterns. Although ultimately we will discuss a single statutory section, subsection 2511(2)(d), we need to let the attorney know how we decided that that subsection was the applicable section.

EXAMPLE

Discussion

18 U.S.C. § 2511 sets out two consent exceptions. Subsection 2511(2)(c) applies when the party intercepting the communication was acting under color of law, and subsection 2511(2)(d) applies when the party intercepting the communication was not acting under color of law. Because there is no evidence that Elite Insurance was acting under color of law when it intercepted Ms. Johnson's phone calls, the applicable subsection is 2511(2)(d), which reads as follows:

> (d)   It shall not be unlawful under this chapter for a person not acting under color of law to intercept a wire or oral communication where such a person is a party to the communication or where one of the parties to the communication has given prior consent to such interception. . . .

The applicable language of this subsection is "where one of the parties to the communication has given prior consent to such interception."

---

§5.13   DRAFTING THE DISCUSSION SECTION: RAISING AND DISMISSING THE UNDISPUTED ELEMENTS

Although sometimes you will want to discuss the elements in order, integrating your discussion of undisputed and disputed elements, or put your discussion of the undisputed elements at the very end of your discussion section, most of the time you will want to raise and dismiss them at the very beginning.

OUTLINE OF DISCUSSION SECTION

I.   First Issue
    A.   Introduce issue and set out general rules
    B.   Raise and dismiss those elements that are not in dispute
       1.   Identify elements that are not in dispute
       2.   Explain why elements are not in dispute

In raising and dismissing the undisputed elements, do three things: identify the elements that are not in dispute, briefly explain why those elements are not in dispute, and provide a transition to the discussion of the disputed elements. In the first of the following examples, the writer has identified the undisputed element but has not set out the facts that support her conclusion or provided a transition to the next part of the discussion. In contrast, in the second example, the writer has done all three things.

EXAMPLE 1   WRITER IDENTIFIES ELEMENT BUT DOES NOT EXPLAIN CONCLUSION OR PROVIDE TRANSITION TO NEXT PART OF DISCUSSION

In our case, both sides will agree that the first element, that the person giving consent be a party to the communication, is not in dispute.

| EXAMPLE 2 | WRITER IDENTIFIES ELEMENT, SETS OUT FACTS THAT SUPPORT CONCLUSION, AND PROVIDES TRANSITION TO NEXT PART OF DISCUSSION |

In our case, both sides will agree that the first element, that the person giving consent be a party to the communication, is not in dispute. In each of the phone calls at issue, Johnson was one of the parties involved in the call. Thus, the only element that is in dispute is whether Johnson gave prior consent.

§5.14   DRAFTING THE DISCUSSION SECTION: DISCUSSING THE DISPUTED ELEMENTS

After dismissing the elements that are not in dispute, you need to move to what is the heart of the discussion, the discussion of the element or elements that are in dispute. In discussing these elements, you need to provide the attorney with four types of information: (1) the rule or test that the court will apply in deciding whether the element is met; (2) if cases are available, descriptions of cases that illustrate how the rules have been applied in analogous cases; (3) each side's arguments; and (4) your prediction about how the court is likely to decide the element. Although there are a number of different ways in which this information can be presented, this chapter presents them in the order discussed above: rules first, analogous cases second, arguments third, and prediction last.

OUTLINE OF DISCUSSION SECTION

I. First Issue
    A. Introduce issue and set out general rules
    B. Raise and dismiss those elements that are not in dispute
        1. Identify elements that are not in dispute
        2. Explain why elements are not in dispute
    C. Discuss first disputed element
        1. Identify element
        2. Set out specific rules and tests
        3. Describe analogous cases
        4. Set out each side's arguments
        5. Predict how court is likely to decide element
    D. Discuss second disputed element
        1. Identify element
        2. Set out specific rules and tests
        3. Describe analogous cases
        4. Set out each side's arguments
        5. Predict how court is likely to decide element

§5.14.1   Set Out the Specific Rule

In addition to setting out the general rules, you also need to set out the specific rules for each element. Although sometimes these specific rules are set out in the statute, more often than not they are not. If there is a rule or test, it is one that the courts have developed in applying the statute. For instance, in our example case, the statute does not set out the rule or test that the courts should apply in determining whether there is prior consent. The statute only says that there must be prior consent. The courts have, however, created rules. For example, as we discovered during our research, prior consent may be either explicit or implied but not constructive.

In setting out specific rules, keep the following in mind. First, set out only those rules and tests that are applicable to the particular element you are discussing. Second, set out the more general rules before more specific rules or exceptions. See sections 5.12.1 and 3.3 in *Just Writing*. Finally, let content dictate organization. Instead of trying to fit the rules into a prescribed organizational scheme, let the rules themselves determine the organization.

What this means in the context of our example case is that we begin our discussion of consent with what is the most general rule, the rule that consent may be explicit or implied but not constructive. We then divide our discussion into two parts. In the first part, we raise and dismiss explicit consent, briefly explaining why there was no explicit consent in our case. In the second part, we discuss implied consent, setting out the rules and tests that the courts apply in determining whether there is implied consent, describing the analogous cases, setting out each side's arguments, and making our prediction.

EXAMPLE

Specific rule for consent

The courts have construed the phrase "prior consent" to include explicit and implied consent but not constructive consent. *See Williams v. Poulos*, 11 F.3d 271, 281 (1st Cir. 1993); *Griggs-Ryan v. Smith*, 904 F.2d 112, 119 (1st Cir. 1990). In our case, there was no explicit consent. Although Ms. Johnson was told that calls were monitored, she did not explicitly agree to the interception of her calls. There may, however, have been implied consent.

Raise and dismiss explicit consent

Transition

The courts have repeatedly held that consent should not be "cavalierly" implied. *Deal v. Spears*, 980 F.2d 1153, 1159 (8th Cir. 1992); *Watkins v. L.M. Berry & Co.*, 704 F.2d 577, 581 (11th Cir. 1983). Instead, implied consent should be

Specific rules for implied consent

found only when the circumstances indicate that an individual knowingly agreed to the interception of his or her communications. *Williams v. Poulos*, 11 F.3d at 281; *Griggs-Ryan*, 904 F.2d at 117.	More general rule set out before more specific rule

§5.14.2   Describe the Analogous Cases

If the application of a particular rule to a particular set of facts is clear, analogous case descriptions are not needed. Just set out the rule and then apply that rule to your facts. If, however, the application is not clear, descriptions of analogous cases will help the attorney understand how the rule might be applied in the client's case.

a.   Selecting Analogous Cases

In selecting analogous cases, try to select at least one case in which the court found that the element was met and one case in which the court held that it was not. In addition, select the cases you know you would want to use in arguing your position to the court and the cases you believe the other side is most likely to rely on in making its arguments. Do not make the mistake of including just the cases that support your client's position. The attorney also needs to know about the other side's cases.

Sometimes there are only one or two cases from which to choose. In such circumstances, present those cases, letting the attorney know that they were the only cases on point. At other times, there will be dozens or maybe even hundreds of cases. In these instances, be selective. Using the same criteria you used in doing your research, select cases from your jurisdiction over cases from other jurisdictions, cases from higher courts over cases from lower courts, more recent cases over older cases, and more factually analogous cases over less factually analogous cases.

Also keep in mind that you may use different cases to illustrate different points. For example, when several elements are in dispute, you may use one set of cases in conjunction with one of the disputed elements and a different set of cases in conjunction with another disputed element.

b.   Presenting the Analogous Cases

As a general rule, start your descriptions of the analogous cases with a sentence that sets out the rule, principle, or point you are using the cases to illustrate. For example, if you are using the cases to illustrate the types of fact situations in which the courts have found that a particular element is met, you could fill in the blanks in the following sentence.

EXAMPLE

In the cases in which the courts have held [identify the element that is met], the plaintiff/defendant [describe the common facts].

EXAMPLES

1. In the cases in which the courts have held that the plaintiff consented to the interception, the defendant had told the plaintiff that all of his or her phone calls would be intercepted.

2. In the cases in which the courts have held that the defendant had constructive possession, the defendant had been staying on the premises for more than a few days, personal possessions belonging to the defendant were found on the premises, and the defendant did some act that indicated that he had dominion and control over the premises.

In contrast, if you are using the cases to illustrate a trend, make that point in your introductory sentence.

EXAMPLES

1. Although historically the courts construed the rule narrowly, in more recent cases they have construed it more broadly.

2. In most of the cases, the courts have denied the defendants' motion for summary judgment.

After setting out the rule, principle, or point that you are using the cases to illustrate, set out your descriptions of the cases. In doing so, include only the information that is relevant to the rule, principle, or point that you are using the cases to illustrate.

In reading the following example, note how the writer begins each paragraph by setting out the principle she is using the cases to illustrate. Also note that her case descriptions are relatively short. Instead of "briefing" each case, she has set out only the information that is relevant to the point that she is using the cases to illustrate.

EXAMPLE

Sentence setting out principle writer is using the cases to illustrate

Transition and then description of first analogous case

In the cases in which the courts have held that the plaintiff consented to the interception, the defendant had told the plaintiff that all of his or her phone calls would be intercepted. For example, in *Griggs-Ryan v. Smith*, the defendant, the plaintiff's landlady, had repeatedly told the plaintiff that she monitored all incoming phone calls. 904 F.2d at 117. Similarly, in *Gilday v. Dubois*, 124 F.3d

277, 279 (1st Cir. 1997) each time that inmates made a phone call they heard a recorded message that told them that their phone call was being intercepted and monitored. In each case, the First Circuit held that these facts were sufficient to support the trial court's order granting the defendants' motion for summary judgment.

In contrast, the courts have repeatedly held that the consent requirement is not met if the individual knew only that his or her phone calls might be monitored. For example, in *Campiti v. Walonis*, 611 F.2d 387 (1st Cir. 1979) the First Circuit affirmed the trial court's decision that there was no consent despite the defendant's argument that the plaintiff, a prisoner, should have known that his phone calls might be monitored. Similarly, in *Williams v. Poulos*, the First Circuit affirmed the granting of an injunction because there was no evidence in the record indicating that the plaintiff, a CEO, knew that his phone calls were being monitored. 11 F.3d at 281.

In addition, the courts have held that the plaintiff did not consent to the interception of his or her phone calls when the defendant's statements or actions indicated that the defendant did not believe that the plaintiff knew that his or her phone calls were being intercepted. For instance, in *Deal v. Spears*, the Spears, Deal's employers, installed a recording device on an extension phone in the hopes of catching Deal in an unguarded admission. When turned on, the recorder automatically recorded all conversations with no indication to the parties using the phone that their conversations were being recorded. 980 F.2d at 1155-1156. The Eighth Circuit Court of Appeals affirmed the district court's determination that there was no consent because (1) the Spears only told Deal that they might intercept her phone calls, not that they were intercepting the calls, and (2) the facts indicated that the Spears believed that Deal did not know that her phone calls were being intercepted. *Id.* at 1157.

Margin notes:

Transition and then description of second analogous case

Sentence setting out principle writer is using the cases to illustrate

Transition and then description of first analogous case

Transition and then description of second analogous case

Sentence setting out principle writer is using the cases to illustrate

Transition and then description an analogous case

c. Presenting Each Side's Arguments

It is at this point in writing the memo that your role changes dramatically. No longer are you just a "reporter" telling the attorney what you found in doing your research. If you are going to do a good job presenting each side's arguments, you must become an advocate, using all of your training and resources to construct the arguments each side is likely to make. You must think like the plaintiff's attorney and then like the defendant's attorney.

Although there is no easy way to come up with each side's arguments, the following three strategies can be useful.

Strategy No. 1: Consider the Standard Moves

Like other disciplines, law has its own set of "standard moves." For example, attorneys make four basic types of arguments: factual arguments, in which the attorney applies the plain language of the statute or rule to his or her facts; analogous case arguments, in which the attorney compares and contrasts his or her facts to the facts in the analogous cases; policy arguments, in which the attorney argues that a particular policy dictates that the court reach a particular result; and legislative history arguments, in which the attorney argues that Congress or a state legislative body intended that a statute have a particular effect or be interpreted in a particular way. Thus, one way to determine what each side might argue is to run through these standard moves, completing a chart like the one set out below.

	Plaintiff's argument	*Defendant's argument*	*Plaintiff's rebuttal*
Factual argument			
Analogous case arguments			
Policy arguments			
Legislative history arguments			

**Strategy No. 2:   Look at the Principles You Set Out in the
                     Sentences Introducing Your Descriptions of the
                     Analogous Cases**

As a general rule, there should be a direct connection between the principles you set out in introducing the analogous cases and the assertions and arguments each side will make.

EXAMPLES

Sentence introducing first set of analogous cases:

> In the cases in which the courts have held that the plaintiff consented to the interception, the defendant had told the plaintiff that all of his or her phone calls would be intercepted.

Plaintiff's assertion and argument:

> In this case, there is no consent because Johnson was not told that all of her phone calls would be monitored. She was only told that her calls would be monitored periodically.

Sentence introducing second set of analogous cases:

> In contrast, the courts have repeatedly held that the consent requirement is not met if the individual only knew that his or her phone calls might be monitored.

Plaintiff's assertion and argument:

> In this case, there is no consent because Johnson only knew that her calls might be monitored. She did not know that these particular calls were being monitored.

**Strategy No. 3:   Look at the Arguments the Parties Made in
                     Analogous Cases**

Although constructing each side's arguments is always a creative act, you just need to improve the wheel, not reinvent it. To come up with what the parties might argue in your case, look at what the parties argued in similar cases. For example, Elite Insurance can probably make the same argument the defendant made in *Campiti v. Walonis*: Given the circumstances, Ms. Johnson should have known that her calls would be monitored. Similarly, Ms. Johnson can make the same argument that the plaintiff made in *Campiti:* Such a rule would distort the plain language of the statute.

At least initially, write down all of the arguments that come to mind.

Possible Plaintiff's Arguments	*Possible Defendant's Arguments*
• Given Elite's past practices, Ms. Johnson did not expect that her calls would be monitored in July and August. In the past, they had been monitored only in January, immediately before her annual performance review.	• Ms. Johnson was told that her calls would be monitored periodically and they were, in fact, monitored periodically.
• The recording was not sufficient to put Ms. Johnson on notice. It was heard by incoming callers, not by Ms. Johnson.	• Even though Ms. Johnson may not have heard the message telling incoming callers that the conversations might be monitored, she knew about the message.
• This case is like *Deal v. Spears*. Like the defendant in that case, Elite was trying to prove that Ms. Johnson was involved in an illegal activity. Thus, it is not reasonable to assume Elite thought Ms. Johnson knew her calls were being recorded.	• As a matter of public policy, employers should not have to tell employees that they are going to intercept a particular call or set of calls. If this type of specific notice is required, employers will not be able to adequately monitor their employees' phone calls.
• This case may also be like *Williams v. Poulos* and *Campiti v. Walonis*. It is not clear from the facts whether Ms. Johnson knew how her calls were being recorded.	• Our case is different from *Campiti* and *Williams*. In those cases, the plaintiffs were never specifically told their calls would be monitored. Here, Ms. Johnson was told her calls would be subject to monitoring.
• Unlike the earlier instances when Ms. Johnson's calls were monitored, this time her supervisor did not talk to her immediately after the call.	• Our case is similar to *Griggs-Ryan*. As in that case, in our case the defendant did what it said it would do. In *Griggs-Ryan* that was to monitor all calls, and in our case it was to monitor calls periodically.
• If Ms. Johnson did consent, she consented to the monitoring of her calls to see if she was providing good customer service. She did not consent to the monitoring of calls that were clearly personal in nature or to monitoring designed to catch her in an illegal act.	

Then, after creating your list, go back through the list and cross off those arguments that don't pass the "giggle" test (a court would laugh if you made the argument) and organize the arguments. Does the plaintiff have just one assertion that it can support in one or more ways, or does it have several alternative arguments? Similarly, does the defendant have just one assertion, or are there several different arguments that it can make? For each "line of argument," set out the assertion and then the facts, cases, and policies that support that argument.

Ms. Johnson's Arguments	*Elite's Arguments*

First Line of Argument:

No implied consent. The circumstances do not indicate that Ms. Johnson "knowingly agreed" to the interception of her phone calls.

- Like the plaintiffs in *Williams v. Poulos*, and *Campiti v. Walonis*, Ms. Johnson did not know that her calls were being intercepted.
- In addition, given Elite's common practices, Ms. Johnson did not expect that her calls would be monitored in July and August. She expected them to be monitored only in January, at the time of her annual performance review, and she expected that her supervisor would talk to her about a call immediately after the call was made.
- The facts also indicate that Elite did not believe that Johnson knew that her calls were being intercepted. Like the defendant in *Deal v. Spears*, Elite hoped to uncover evidence indicating that Johnson was involved in an illegal activity.

Second Line of Argument:

Even if Ms. Johnson did consent to some monitoring of her calls, she only consented to limited monitoring.

- Ms. Johnson was told only that her calls would be monitored to determine whether she was providing good customer service.

After determining what arguments each side is likely to make, decide how you want to present those arguments. Although you have a number of options, in this chapter we present only one: the script format. Like a playwright writing the script for a mock argument to a court, when you use this format, you set out the moving party's arguments first, the responding party's arguments next, and the moving party's rebuttal, if any, last.

The following example shows how to set out each side's arguments using this format. Note that in setting out each side's arguments, the writer has started by setting out the party's assertion. She then sets out her support for that assertion.

EXAMPLE

First Draft of Each Side's Arguments

Ms. Johnson's first assertion	Ms. Johnson will argue that the consent element is not met because she did not know that her phone calls were being intercepted. Like the plaintiffs in *Campiti*, *Williams*, and *Deal*, who did not know that their calls were being intercepted,
Use of cases and facts to support first assertion	Ms. Johnson did not know that Elite was intercepting her calls. In the past, her phone calls had been monitored only in January, immediately before her annual performance review, and her supervisor had intercepted only two or three of her calls and had talked to her about those calls immediately afterwards. In addition, the facts indicate that Elite did not believe that Ms. Johnson knew that her calls were being intercepted. Just as the Spears in *Deal v. Spears* hoped to catch Deal in an admission tying her to a burglary, Elite hoped to catch Ms. Johnson in an admission tying her to an insurance fraud scheme.
Ms. Johnson's second assertion	In the alternative, Ms. Johnson can argue that even if she did consent to the monitoring of her phone calls to determine whether she was providing good customer service, she did not consent to the monitoring of her personal calls.
Elite's first assertion	In contrast, Elite will argue that the consent element is met because Ms. John-

son had been told that her phone calls would be monitored periodically. Elite will begin by distinguishing *Campiti* and *Williams*. Unlike *Campiti*, in which the prisoners were never told that their calls would be intercepted, and *Williams*, in which the CEO was never told that his calls might be intercepted, in our case Ms. Johnson was told about the company's monitoring policy. In addition, Elite can distinguish *Deal*. Unlike Deal, who never knew that any of her calls were being intercepted, Ms. Johnson knew that her calls had been intercepted in the past and that they were subject to being intercepted in the future. In fact, this case is more like *Griggs-Ryan*, the case in which the landlady repeatedly told her tenants that all incoming calls would be intercepted, than it is any of the other cases. Just as the tenants in *Griggs-Ryan* received regular reminders about their landlady's policy, so did Ms. Johnson: the message that incoming callers received telling them that their calls were subject to monitoring should have provided Ms. Johnson with a daily reminder about Elite's monitoring policy.

Elite distinguishes Ms. Johnson's cases.

In addition, Elite can argue that, as a matter of public policy, employers with monitoring policies like Elite's should be able to intercept employee phone calls without explicitly telling them that a particular call or set of calls will be intercepted. Because employees are likely to act differently when they know a particular call is being intercepted, employers will not be able to effectively monitor the type of service their employees are providing or determine whether an employee is violating a company policy or is engaged in fraud if they must tell an employee that a particular call or set of calls is being intercepted.

Elite's second assertion

Ms. Johnson is likely to respond to these arguments in two ways. First, it is not

Ms. Johnson's rebuttal

clear whether she heard the message that incoming callers heard. As a result, although the message may have put incoming callers on notice, it did not put her on notice, particularly given what she knew about Elite's actual practices. Second, the statute specifically requires that an individual give prior consent. Thus, even though an employer may have an interest in intercepting an employee's phone call, that interest is not recognized under the statute.

§5.14.3   Predict How the Court Will Decide the Element

The final piece of information you need to include is your prediction about how a court would decide the element. Is it more likely that it will find the element is met or more likely that it will find the element is not met?

In writing this section, you must once again change roles. Instead of playing the role of reporter describing the rules and analogous cases or an advocate making each side's arguments, you must play the role of judge. You must put yourself in the position of the particular court that would decide the issue—the trial court, appellate court, state court, federal court—and decide how that court is likely to rule.

At least initially, you may be uncomfortable making such predictions. How can a first-year law student predict how the court might rule? The good news is that with time, and experience, you will get better and better at predicting how a court will rule. In the meantime, read the statutes and cases carefully and critically evaluate each side's arguments. Careful reading and careful consideration of arguments, plus common sense, will all help you make reliable predictions. Remember too that you are predicting, not guaranteeing, an outcome.

In setting out your conclusion, do two things: Set out your prediction, and briefly explain why you believe the court will decide the element as you have predicted. In the first example, the writer has set out his prediction but not his reasoning. In the second, the writer has set out both his prediction and his reasoning.

EXAMPLE 1   **WRITER HAS SET OUT HIS PREDICTION BUT NOT HIS REASONING**

A court will probably find that there was no implied consent because the test for implied consent is not met.

EXAMPLE 2   **WRITER HAS SET OUT BOTH HIS PREDICTION AND HIS REASONING**

A court will probably find that there was no implied consent because Ms. Johnson did not knowingly agree to the interception of her calls. Although Elite told Ms. Johnson that her calls were subject to periodic monitoring, the interceptions that took place were not consistent with prior company practices. In addition, Elite's own reasons for monitoring Ms. Johnson's calls indicate that it did not believe that Ms. Johnson knew her calls were being intercepted.

---

§5.15   AVOIDING THE COMMON PROBLEMS

Although the path to writing a good discussion section is filled with pitfalls, if you know what to look for, you can avoid most of them.

§5.15.1   Speak for Yourself

At first, you may be tempted to string together a series of quotations. Particularly when you are not sure you understand the law, it can seem easier to quote than to put the rules into your own words.

However, quoting almost always creates more problems than it solves. To write a good memo, you must understand not only each rule but also how the rules fit together and how they will be applied to the facts of your case. Thus, although quotations may get you past the rule section, they cannot help you write the descriptions of analogous cases, each side's arguments, or your prediction.

Overquoting can also cause writing problems. In quoting, you inevitably run into problems with verb tenses and pronouns. In setting out the rules, one judge uses the past tense and another the present tense, and instead of using the proper noun, a judge will use a pronoun that does not have, at least in the quoted language, a referent. In addition, each judge usually has his or her own writing style and, when you combine them, your own writing becomes a mishmash of styles.

Because of these problems, use quotations sparingly. Quote statutes but little else. See section 6.2.3 in *Just Writing*.

§5.15.2   Lay It Out

Most attorneys are bright. Given all the pieces of a puzzle and enough time, they can put the puzzle together. A discussion section is not, however, a puzzle. Attorneys reading a memo do not want you to hand them the pieces in a box; they want you to hand them the completed puzzle. It is you, not they, who should be doing the work.

Study the following examples.

EXAMPLE 1   PIECES JUST HANDED TO THE ATTORNEY IN A BOX

In *Campiti*, *Williams*, and *Deal*, the defendants did not know their calls were being monitored. Johnson did not know her calls were being intercepted. In *Deal v. Spears*, the defendants taped the plaintiff's calls in the hope of connecting her to a burglary. Elite taped Ms. Johnson's calls in the hope of finding out whether she was involved in an insurance fraud scheme. In the past, Elite had taped Ms. Johnson's calls only as part of her annual performance review. This time the taping occurred in July and August. In the past, when Ms. Johnson's supervisor intercepted her calls, he talked to her immediately after listening in on a call.

Even the brightest attorney would have difficulty understanding this first example. Although the writer has given the attorney all of the pieces, the pieces are not sorted or connected.

EXAMPLE 2   PIECES SORTED BUT NOT CONNECTED

Like the plaintiffs in *Campiti*, *Williams*, and *Deal*, Ms. Johnson did not know her calls were being intercepted. The taping occurred well past the end of her initial one-month training period and was done in July and August rather than in January as part of her annual performance review. Her supervisor did not talk to her about the calls immediately after recording them. He taped calls for almost six weeks before telling her that her calls were being intercepted. As in *Deal v. Spears*, in this case, Elite's motive for recording the calls indicates that it did not believe that Ms. Johnson knew that her calls were being recorded. Just as the Spears hoped to catch Deal in an admission tying her to a robbery, Elite hoped to catch Ms. Johnson in an admission tying her to an insurance fraud scheme.

In this second example, the writer has sorted and ordered the pieces. Although the resulting text is more understandable, because the pieces are not connected, the attorney still has to work to figure out how they go together.

EXAMPLE 3   PIECES PUT TOGETHER

Ms. Johnson will argue that the consent element is not met because she did not know that her phone calls were being intercepted. Like the plaintiffs in *Campiti*, *Williams*, and *Deal*, who did not know their calls were being intercepted, Ms. Johnson did not know that Elite was intercepting her calls. In the past, her phone calls had been monitored only in January, immediately before her annual performance review, and her supervisor had intercepted only two or three of her calls and had talked to her about those calls immediately afterwards. In addition, the facts indicate that Elite did not believe that Johnson knew her calls were being intercepted. Just as the Spears hoped to catch Deal in an admission tying her to a burglary, Elite hoped to catch Ms. Johnson in an admission tying her to an insurance fraud scheme.

This example is much better than the previous two. By adding topic sentences and transitions, the writer has made the connections between ideas explicit. For more on topic sentences and transitions see sections 3.5 and 4.1 in *Just Writing*.

§5.15.3　Show How You Reached Your Conclusions

After you have spent days researching and thinking about a problem, the answer often seems obvious. The client has a cause of action or it does not; the element is met or it is not. Because the answer is so clear, when it comes time to write the discussion section, the natural tendency is to jump from the rule directly to the conclusion.

You must not do this. Although attorneys are interested in your conclusions, they are more interested in how you reached those conclusions. They want you to think through the problem for them, rehearsing and evaluating each side's arguments.

The following examples illustrate the difference between analysis that is conclusory and analysis that gives attorneys what they need.

EXAMPLE 1

Ms. Johnson will argue that the consent element is not met because she did not know that her phone calls were being intercepted. In contrast, Elite will argue that Ms. Johnson did consent because she knew about its monitoring policy. The court will probably find that there was prior consent.

In Example 1, the analysis is conclusory. The writer simply sets out each side's assertions and her conclusion. Without knowing what the arguments are, the attorneys have no basis for evaluating either the assertions or the conclusion.

EXAMPLE 2

Ms. Johnson will argue that the consent element is not met because our case is more like *Campiti*, *Williams*, and *Deal* than *Griggs-Ryan v. Smith*. Elite will respond by distinguishing *Campiti*, *Williams*, and *Deal* and by showing how this case is more like *Griggs-Ryan v. Smith*. The court will probably find that this case is more like *Griggs-Ryan v. Smith* than it is *Campiti*, *Williams*, and *Deal* and find that the consent element is met.

Example 2 is only marginally better. It is not enough to tell the attorney which cases each side will use. You must show the attorney how the two sides will use the cases.

EXAMPLE 3

Like the plaintiffs in *Campiti*, *Williams*, and *Deal*, who did not know that their calls were being intercepted, Ms. Johnson did not know that Elite was monitoring her calls. In the past, her phone calls had been monitored only in January, immediately before her annual performance review, and her supervisor had monitored only two or three of her calls and had talked to her about those calls immediately afterwards. In addition, as in *Deal*, in our case Elite monitored Ms. Johnson's calls to try to obtain evidence that she was involved in an illegal activity.

Example 3 is better than the first two. In addition to identifying the cases, the writer has used them, comparing the facts in the analogous cases with the facts in the client's case. The writer has not, however, explained why the factual similarities and differences are significant. Why is it significant that, like the plaintiffs in *Campiti*, *Williams*, and *Deal*, Johnson did not know that her calls were being monitored? Similarly, why is it significant that in both *Deal* and our case the defendant was trying to determine whether the plaintiff was involved in an illegal activity?

EXAMPLE 4

Ms. Johnson will argue that the consent element is not met because she did not know that her calls were being intercepted. Like the plaintiffs in *Campiti*, *Williams*, and *Deal*, who did not know that their calls were being monitored, Ms. Johnson did not know that

Elite was intercepting her calls. In the past, Ms. Johnson's phone calls had been monitored only in January, immediately before her annual performance review, and her supervisor had intercepted only two or three of her calls and had talked to her about those calls immediately afterwards. In addition, the facts indicate Elite did not believe Ms. Johnson knew her calls were being intercepted. Just as the Spears in *Deal v. Spears* hoped to catch Deal in an admission tying her to a burglary, Elite hoped to catch Ms. Johnson in an admission tying her to an insurance fraud scheme.

This last example is an example of a good argument. The writer begins by setting out his first assertion, which is tied to the legal test. He then uses the analogous cases and the facts from his case to support that assertion. He then sets out a second assertion, once again using the cases and facts to support that assertion.

§5.15.4   Use Terms Consistently

In some types of writing, elegant variation—that is, the frequent use of synonyms—is desirable. While novelists and poets frequently vary the words they use, at different times calling the lake a shimmering pond, a foreboding sea, or environmental waste, lawyers do not. In law, a lake is a lake. If you use a different word, the attorney or the court will assume that you mean something different.

This means that as a writer, you need to find the right word and then use that word throughout the discussion. For example, you should not use words like "element" and "factor" interchangeably. Use "element" when you are talking about a series of requirements that must be met. "To convict the defendant of murder in the first degree, the State must prove each of the elements of the crime." In contrast, use "factor" when you are talking about the factors that a court may consider in deciding an issue. "In deciding which parent should be granted custody, the court may consider such factors as the parents' wishes, the child's wishes, the child's relationship with his or her parents and siblings, the child's adjustment to his or her school and community, and the mental and physical health of the parties."

In addition, use the words "found," "ruled," and "held" carefully. As a general rule, use the word "found" when you are talking about findings of fact. "The jury found that the pinball machine was worth more than $1,500." Use the word "ruled" when describing a court's decision on an objection or a motion. "The court ruled that the evidence was admissible." Finally, as a general rule, use the word "held" to describe an appellate court's decision. "The appellate court held that the trial court had not erred in granting the plaintiff's motion for summary judgment."

§5.15.5   See More Than the Obvious

Finally, look beyond the obvious. The difference between an acceptable memo and one that wins praise is sophisticated analysis. The exceptional intern is one who sees, and then presents, arguments that other interns, and other attorneys, do not see. For instance, in our example case, the intern who would win praise is the one who recognized that it is not just Ms. Johnson who could give consent. Mr. Porter was also a party to the communication and, if he called Ms. Johnson, he would have heard the message telling him that the calls were subject to monitoring.

§5.15.6   Checklist for Critiquing the Discussion Section

A.   Content

General Rule Section

- The writer has included a sentence or paragraph introducing the issue and the governing statute or common law rule.
- The writer has set out the general rule, quoting the applicable statutory sections or quoting or paraphrasing the common law rule.
- The writer has not included rules or information that the attorney does not need.
- The rules are stated accurately and objectively.
- For each rule stated, the writer has included a citation to authority.

Discussion of Each Element

- For each element, the writer has set out the applicable definitions, tests, and rules.
- When an element is undisputed, the writer has raised and dismissed it.
- When an element is in dispute, the writer has included descriptions of analogous cases.
- Before describing the analogous cases, the writer has set out the rule, principle, or point that he or she is using the cases to illustrate.
- In describing analogous cases, the writer has set out only that information that is needed to illustrate the rule, principle, or point.
- The descriptions of the analogous cases are accurate.
- The writer has set out each side's assertions and the arguments that he or she will make in supporting those assertions.
- The analysis is not conclusory: The writer has explained why the plain language supports the conclusion, why the factual similarities between the analogous cases and the client's case

are significant, and why it would be consistent with the policies underlying the statute or rule to decide the case in a particular way.

- The analysis is sophisticated: The writer has addressed more than the obvious arguments.
- The writer has included mini-conclusions in which he or she predicts how each element will be decided and gives reasons to support those predictions.
- In setting out the rules, analogous cases, arguments, and mini-conclusions, the writer has used the language of the law.

B.   Large-Scale Organization

- The writer has presented the information in the order in which the attorney expects to see it. For example, the writer begins by setting out the general rules and then walks the attorney through each of the elements, setting out the specific rules, describing the cases that illustrate how those rules have been applied in similar cases, setting out each side's arguments, and predicting how the jury or court is likely to decide each element.

C.   Writing

- The attorney can understand the discussion section after reading it once.
- The paragraph divisions are logical, and the paragraphs are neither too long nor too short.
- Signposts, topic sentences, transitions, and dovetailing have been used to make clear the connections between ideas.
- In most sentences, the writer has used the actor as the subject of the sentence, and the subject and verb are close together.
- The writer has varied the length of the sentences and the sentence patterns so that each sentence flows smoothly from the prior sentence.
- The writing is concise and precise.
- The writing is grammatically correct and correctly punctuated.
- The discussion section has been proofread.

§5.16   DRAFTING THE FORMAL CONCLUSION

In a one-issue memo, the formal conclusion is used to summarize your analysis of that one issue. For example, in our example case, the conclusion is used to tell the attorney why you believe the consent exception applies or does not apply. Begin by setting out your conclusion. Then briefly summarize your reasoning.

EXAMPLE **CONCLUSION**

A court will probably find that Elite intentionally intercepted Johnson's telephone calls without her prior consent. Ms. Johnson did not explicitly agree to the interception of her calls, and the facts do not indicate that Johnson knowingly agreed to such interceptions. Although Elite told Ms. Johnson that her calls were subject to periodic monitoring, the monitoring that took place was not consistent with prior company practices: (1) the monitoring occurred not in January at the time of Ms. Johnson's annual performance review but in July and August; (2) instead of monitoring only two or three calls, Elite monitored calls for four or five weeks; and (3) instead of talking to Ms. Johnson about a call immediately after the call, Elite only talked to her about the calls when it fired her.

In addition, even if Ms. Johnson did consent to the monitoring of her calls to determine whether she was providing good customer service, she did not consent to the monitoring of personal calls, which, although against company policy, were tolerated. Even though the court is likely to find that Ms. Johnson did not consent to the interception, we may be able to establish that the other party to the communication, Mr. Porter, consented to the monitoring of any calls that he may have made to Ms. Johnson. Although establishing Porter's consent may not eliminate Elite's liability, it may lessen it.

While some attorneys will want you to stop at this point, others will want you to go one step further and advise the attorney about what you think should be done next. What should the attorney tell the client? What action should the attorney take next? Is this the type of case that the firm should, or wants to, handle? When you are asked to include this type of information in your conclusion, add a paragraph like the following.

EXAMPLE

Because it does not appear that the consent exception applies, I recommend that we try to settle this case unless another exception applies.

§5.16.1   Checklist for Critiquing Conclusion

A.   Content

- In a one-issue memorandum, the conclusion is used to predict how the issue will be decided and to summarize the reasons supporting that prediction.
- When appropriate, the writer includes not only the conclusion but also strategic advice.

B.   Organization

- The information is organized logically.

C.   Writing

- The attorney can understand the conclusion after reading it once.
- The paragraph divisions are logical, and the paragraphs are neither too long nor too short.
- Signposts, topic sentences, transitions, and dovetailing have been used to make clear the connections between ideas.
- In most sentences, the writer has used the actor as the subject of the sentence, and the subject and verb are close together.
- The writer has varied the length of the sentences and the sentence patterns so that each sentence flows smoothly from the prior sentence.
- The writing is concise and precise.
- The writing is grammatically correct and correctly punctuated.
- The conclusion has been proofread.

C.   REVISING

Revising is the process of "re-visioning" what you have drafted. You step back from your draft and look at it through the eyes of your reader. Have you given the attorney all of the information that he or she needs? Have you presented that information in the order that the attorney expects to see it?

During the revising stage, you need to be willing to make major changes. If in revising your draft, you realize that you did not need to include one part of your discussion, delete that part, no matter how many hours you spent drafting it. Similarly, if in revising your draft, you realize that you did not research or discuss a major point, go back and do that research, analysis, and writing. Finally, if in revising your draft you realize that your organizational scheme just doesn't work, you need to be willing to start over, reorganizing one section or even your entire memo.

As a general rule, writers do a better job revising when they print out their draft and lay out the pages side by side. Problems that were not apparent when you looked at your draft screen by screen will become apparent when you look at the draft in printed form.

§5.17   CHECKING CONTENT

In revising a draft, look first at its content. If there are problems with content, solving those problems must be your first priority.

§5.17.1   Have You Given the Attorneys the Information They Need?

In checking content, the first question to ask yourself is whether you have given the attorneys the information they requested. Did you research the assigned issue or issues? Did you locate all of the applicable statutes and cases? Did you identify and present the arguments that each side is likely to make? Did you evaluate those arguments and predict how the court is likely to rule?

In our example problem, the intern has given the attorney the information that he requested. The research is complete: The intern found not only the applicable statute but also the key cases. The discussion also begins at the right place. Because the attorney only asked about the exception, the intern did not discuss the underlying offense. The discussion also stops where it should. The attorney did not ask for a discussion of damages. The assignment was to determine whether the exception applied.

Last but not least, the intern included all of the pieces. She included both the general and specific rules and, when appropriate, descriptions of analogous cases. In addition, she applied those rules and cases to the facts of the client's case, anticipating the arguments that each side was likely to make and then evaluating those arguments and predicting how the court was likely to rule.

Thus, when the intern asks herself whether she has given the attorney the information he needs, the answer is yes. She knew the law, and in presenting that law, she used good judgment.

§5.17.2   Is the Information Presented Accurately?

In law, small errors can have serious consequences. The failure to cite check to make sure that a case is still good law, an omitted "not," or an "or" that should have been an "and" can make the difference between winning and losing, between competent lawyering and malpractice.

As a consequence, in writing the memo, you must exercise great care. Because the attorney is relying on you, your research must be thorough. You need to make sure that you have located the applicable statutes and cases and that you have checked to make sure that those statutes and cases are still good law. In addition, you need to make sure your analysis is sound. Did you read the statutes and cases carefully? Is the way in which you have put the pieces together sound? Finally, you need to make sure you have presented the statutes and cases accurately and fairly. Did you correctly identify the issue in the analogous case? Did you take a rule out of context? Did you misrepresent the facts or omit a key fact? Unless the attorney reads the statutes and cases you cite, he may not see an error until it is too late.

In the following example, the intern has made a number of mistakes. If you were the attorney, would you see them?

EXAMPLE

Consent will be implied only when the individual knowingly agrees to the interception of his or her phone calls. *Williams v. Poulos*, 11 F.3d 271, 281 (8th Cir. 1993); *Griggs-Ryan v. Smith*, 904 F.2d 112, 119 (1st Cir. 1990). Thus, while the court found that there was implied consent in *Griggs-Ryan*, a case in which the plaintiff's landlady repeatedly told the plaintiff that she monitored all incoming calls, the court found that there was no implied consent in *Deal v. Spears*, 980 F.2d 1153 (8th Cir. 1992), a case in which the plaintiff's employers only told the plaintiff that they might intercept her calls.

The first mistake is in the first sentence: The writer has not stated the rule accurately. The rule is not that consent will be implied only when the individual knowingly agrees to the interception of his or her phone calls. Instead, the rule is that consent is implied only when the circumstances indicate that an individual knowingly agreed to the interception of his or her calls. The second error is in the citation to *Williams v. Poulos*. The case is a First Circuit, not an Eighth Circuit, authority. The last mistake is in the description of *Griggs-Ryan*. The issue in that case was not whether there was implied consent but whether the trial court's granting of summary judgment was proper. Thus, it is wrong to say that the court found that there was implied consent.

§5.17.3   Is the Information Well Organized?

The next step is to check the discussion section's large-scale organization. Has the information been presented in the order that the attorney expects to see it?

One way to check large-scale organization is to prepare an after-the-fact outline. This is done either by labeling the subject matter of each paragraph and then listing those labels in outline form or by summarizing what each paragraph says. See section 1.4.2 in *Just Writing*.

The following example shows how the first type of after-the-fact outline is done using an excerpt from the discussion section from the example problem.

Step 1: Identify the Subject Matter of Each Paragraph

EXAMPLE   **FIRST DRAFT OF DISCUSSION SECTION**

Discussion

Introduction

18 U.S.C. § 2511 sets out two consent exceptions. Subsection 2511(2)(c) applies when the party intercepting the communication was acting under color of law, and subsection 2511(2)(d) applies when the party intercepting the communication was not acting under color of law. Because there is no evidence that Elite Insurance was acting under color of law when it intercepted Ms. Johnson's phone calls, the applicable subsection is 2511(2)(d), which reads as follows:

Tells the attorney that there are two consent exceptions and identifies the one that is applicable in this case

Sets out the text of the applicable statutory subsection

(d) It shall not be unlawful under this chapter for a person not acting under color of law to intercept a wire or oral communication where such a person is a party to the communication or where one of the parties to the communication has given prior consent to such interception. . . .

The applicable language of this subsection is "where one of the parties to the communication has given prior consent to such interception."

	Identifies the key language

In our case, both sides will agree that the first element, that the person giving consent be a party to the communication, is not in dispute. In each of the phone calls at issue, Ms. Johnson was one of the parties involved in the call. Thus, the only element in dispute is whether Ms. Johnson gave prior consent.

Undisputed Element

Explains why the first element is not in dispute

The courts have construed the phrase "prior consent" to include explicit and implied consent but not constructive consent. *See Williams v. Poulos*, 11 F.3d 271, 281 (1st Cir. 1993); *Griggs-Ryan v. Smith*, 904 F.2d 112, 119 (1st Cir. 1990). In our case, there was no explicit consent. Although Ms. Johnson was told that calls were intercepted, she did not explicitly agree to the interception of her calls. There may, however, have been implied consent.

Disputed Element

Specific rules for prior consent

Raises and dismisses explicit consent

Introduces discussion of implied consent

In deciding whether there is implied consent, the courts have stated that such consent should not be cavalierly implied. *Deal v. Spears*, 980 F.2d 1153, 1157 (8th Cir. 1992); *Watkins v. L.M. Berry & Co.*, 704 F.2d 577, 581 (11th Cir. 1983). Instead, implied consent should be found only when the circumstances indicate that an individual knowingly agreed to the interception of his or her communications. *Williams v. Poulos*, 11 F.3d at 281; *Griggs-Ryan v. Smith*, 904 F.2d at 117.

Sets out specific rules for implied consent

In the cases in which the courts have held that the plaintiff consented to the interception, the defendant had told the plaintiff that all of his or her phone calls would be intercepted. For example, in *Griggs-Ryan v. Smith*, the defendant, the plaintiff's landlady, had repeatedly told the plaintiff that she monitored all incoming phone calls. Similarly, in *Gilday v. Dubois*, 124 F.3d 277, 297 (1st

Descriptions of analogous cases

Sets out cases that illustrate the types of fact

situations in which the courts have found that the plaintiff consented to the interception of his or her phone calls

Cir. 1997), each time inmates made a phone call they heard a recorded message that told them their phone call was being intercepted and monitored. In each case, the First Circuit held that these facts were sufficient to support the trial court's order granting the defendants' motion for summary judgment.

Sets out cases that illustrate one type of fact situation in which the courts have found that the plaintiff did not consent to the interception of his or her phone calls

In contrast, the courts have repeatedly held that the consent requirement is not met if the individual knew only that his or her phone calls might be monitored. For example, in *Campiti v. Walonis*, 611 F.2d 387 (1st Cir. 1979), the First Circuit affirmed the trial court's decision that there was no consent despite the defendant's argument that the plaintiff, a prisoner, should have known that his phone calls might be monitored. *Id.* at 389. Similarly, in *Williams v. Poulos*, the First Circuit affirmed the granting of an injunction because there was no evidence in the record indicating that the plaintiff, a CEO, knew that his phone calls were being monitored. 11 F.3d at 281.

Sets out a case that illustrates another type of fact situation in which the courts have found that the plaintiff did not consent to the interception of his or her phone calls

In addition, the courts have held that the plaintiff did not consent to the interception of his or her phone calls when the defendant's statements or actions indicated that the defendant did not believe that the plaintiff knew his or her phone calls were being intercepted. For instance, in *Deal v. Spears*, the Spears, Deal's employers, installed a recording device on an extension phone in the hopes of catching Deal in an unguarded admission. When turned on, the recorder automatically recorded all conversations made on either the store phone or the extension with no indication to the parties using the phone that their conversations were being recorded. 980 F.2d at 1155-1156. The Eighth Circuit Court of Appeals affirmed the district court's determination that there was no consent because (1) the Spears told Deal only that they might intercept her phone calls, not that they were intercepting the calls and (2) the facts indicated that the

Spears believed that Deal did not know that her phone calls were being intercepted. *Id.* at 1157.

Step 2:   Put the Labels in Outline Form and Compare the After-the-Fact Outline with the Original Outline

---

EXAMPLE

Original Outline

I. First Issue
    A. Introduction
        Introduces 18 U.S.C. § 2511
        and sets out applicable
        portions.

    B. Undisputed Element
        Introduces element.
        Sets out applicable rules.
        Explains why element is not
        in dispute.

    C. Disputed Element
        Tells attorney that consent
        may be explicit or implied
        but not constructive.
        1. Explicit consent (not in
           dispute)
           a. Sets out rules
           b. Applies rules
        2. Implied consent (in dispute)
           a. Sets out rules
           b. Describes analogous cases

After-the-Fact Outline

I. First Issue
    A. Introduction
        Tells the attorney that there
        are two consent exceptions and
        identifies the one that is
        applicable in this case.
        Sets out the text of the applicable
        statutory subsection.
        Identifies the key language.

    B. Undisputed Element
        Explains why the first element is
        not in dispute.

    C. Disputed Element
        1. Specific rules for prior consent.
           Raises and dismisses explicit
           consent.
           Introduces discussion of implied
           consent.
           Sets out specific rules for
           implied consent.
        2. *Descriptions of analogous cases*
           Sets out cases that illustrate
           the types of fact situations
           in which the courts have
           found that the plaintiff consented to the interception of
           his or her phone calls.
           Sets out cases that
           illustrate one type of fact
           situation in which the courts
           have found that the plaintiff
           did not consent to the
           interception of his or her
           phone calls.

Step 3:   Make the Changes

After comparing the two outlines, the next step is to decide what changes are needed. Sometimes this means changing the draft so that it matches the original outline; at other times it means deciding that the draft is better than the original outline. The goal, however, remains the same: to present the information in a manner that meets the attorney's expectations as a reader.

§5.17.4   Are the Connections Explicit?

Having revised for content and organization, you now need to look at your use of roadmaps, signposts, topic sentences, and transitions.

a.   Roadmaps

A roadmap is just what the term implies: a "map" providing the reader with an overview of the document. In some instances, you will need to include a separate roadmap in which you outline the steps in the analysis. At other times, the general rules will act as an outline.

EXAMPLE 1   SEPARATE ROADMAP OUTLINING THE STEPS IN THE ANALYSIS

In deciding whether the contract is enforceable, the court must first determine whether the formal requirements of the Statute of Frauds are met. If they are, the contract is enforceable; if they are not, the contract is not enforceable unless one of the exceptions, for example, the exception for specially manufactured goods, applies.

EXAMPLE 2   RULE SECTION THAT ACTS AS ROADMAP

The courts have construed the phrase "prior consent" to include explicit and implied consent but not constructive consent. *See Williams v. Poulos*, 11 F.3d 271, 281 (1st Cir. 1993); *Griggs-Ryan v. Smith*, 904 F.2d 112, 119 (1st Cir. 1990). In our case, there was no explicit consent. Although Ms. Johnson was told that calls were monitored periodically, she did not explicitly agree to the interception of her calls. There may, however, have been implied consent.

Note that in both examples, the roadmaps are substantive in nature. Instead of saying, "First I will discuss this and then I will discuss that," the writers have outlined the court's decisionmaking process. See section 2.2.1 in *Just Writing*.

b. Signposts, Topic Sentences, and Transitions

Signposts, topic sentences, and transitions serve the same function that directional signs serve on a freeway. They tell the attorneys where they are, what to expect, and how the pieces are connected. See sections 2.2.2 and 3.5 in *Just Writing*. While these directional signs may not be particularly important in some types of writing, they are essential in legal writing. Without them, the connections between paragraphs and between sentences are not clear and the attorney will have trouble following the analysis.

Compare Example 1 below, in which the writer has not included topic sentences, signposts, or transitions with Example 2. In Example 2, the topic sentence, signposts, and transitions are in boldface type.

**EXAMPLE 1 NO TOPIC SENTENCES, SIGNPOSTS,
       OR TRANSITIONS**

Elite did not tell Ms. Johnson that all of her phone calls were being monitored. Elite only told Ms. Johnson that her calls would be monitored periodically. Like the plaintiffs in *Campiti* and *Williams*, Ms. Johnson did not know that her calls were being monitored. In the past, her phone calls had been monitored only in January, immediately before her annual performance review, and her supervisor had intercepted only two or three of her calls and had talked to her about those calls immediately afterwards. Elite's statements and actions indicate that Elite did not believe that Ms. Johnson knew that her calls were being intercepted. Just as the Spears hoped to catch Deal in an admission tying her to a burglary, Elite hoped to catch Ms. Johnson in an admission tying her to an insurance fraud scheme. Even if she did consent to the monitoring of her phone calls to determine whether she was providing good customer service, Ms. Johnson did not consent to the monitoring of her personal calls. Elite should have stopped recording any personal calls of hers as soon as it recognized that the call was a personal call.

> **EXAMPLE 2**   TOPIC SENTENCES, SIGNPOSTS, AND TRANSITIONS ADDED

Ms. Johnson can make four arguments. First, she can argue that the consent element is not met because Elite did not tell her that all of her phone calls were being monitored. Elite only told Ms. Johnson that her calls would be monitored periodically. **Second, Ms. Johnson can argue that,** like the plaintiffs in *Campiti* and *Williams*, she did not know that her calls were being monitored. In the past, her phone calls had been monitored only in January, immediately before her annual performance review, and her supervisor had intercepted only two or three of her calls and had talked to her about those calls immediately afterwards. **Third, Ms. Johnson can argue that** Elite's statements and actions indicate that Elite did not believe that Ms. Johnson knew that her calls were being intercepted. Just as the Spears hoped to catch Deal in an admission tying her to a burglary, Elite hoped to catch Ms. Johnson in an admission tying her to an insurance fraud scheme. **Finally, Ms. Johnson can argue that** even if she did consent to the monitoring of her phone calls to determine whether she was providing good customer service, she did not consent to the monitoring of her personal calls. **Thus,** Elite should have stopped recording any personal calls of hers as soon as it recognized that the call was a personal call.

---

c. Dovetailing

Another technique that you can use to make the connections between ideas clear is dovetailing. You use dovetailing when you refer back to a point made in the prior sentence or paragraph. In the following example, the writer has used dovetailing to make clear the connections between the first and second sentences.

> **EXAMPLE 1**

Sentence 1	*Sentence 2*
In January 2000 Elite Insurance **hired Ms. Johnson.**	**At the time she was hired,** Ms. Johnson was told that the phones and computers should be used for business purposes only.

While in the above example dovetailing was used to make clear the connections between sentences, in the next example it is used to make clear the connections between paragraphs. The first sentence in the second paragraph refers back to the last sentence in the first paragraph and the first sentence in the third paragraph refers back to the last sentence in the second paragraph.

EXAMPLE 2

Both sides will agree that the first element, that the person giving consent be a party to the communication, is not in dispute. In each of the phone calls at issue, Ms. Johnson was one of the parties involved in the call. **Thus, the only element in dispute is whether Ms. Johnson gave prior consent.**

The courts have construed the phrase "prior consent" to include explicit and implied consent but not constructive consent. *See Williams v. Poulos*, 11 F.3d 271, 281 (1st Cir. 1993); *Griggs-Ryan v. Smith*, 904 F.2d 112, 119 (1st Cir. 1990). In our case, there was no explicit consent. Although Ms. Johnson was told that her calls might be intercepted, she did not explicitly agree to the interception of them. **There may, however, have been implied consent.**

In deciding whether there is implied consent, the courts have stated that such consent should not be cavalierly implied. *Deal v. Spears*, 980 F.2d 1153, 1157 (8th Cir. 1992); *Watkins v. L.M. Berry & Co.*, 704 F.2d 577, 581 (11th Cir. 1983). Instead, implied consent should be found only when the circumstances indicate that an individual knowingly agreed to the interception of his or her communications. *Williams v. Poulos*, 11 F.3d at 281; *Griggs-Ryan v. Smith*, 904 F.2d at 117.

D. EDITING

The work is now almost done. When you step back from the memo and look at it through the attorney's eyes, you are pleased with its content, organization, and presentation.

The last steps in the process are editing and proofreading your work. Like the painter preparing to have his work judged by a critic, you must go back through your memo once again, correcting errors in grammar, punctuation, and usage and checking your citations. You also read your memo for style. Does each sentence flow smoothly from the prior sentence? Do the words create vivid images? Does the writing engage the reader? In sum, is the memo the work of an artisan or an artist?

§5.18   EDITING AND PROOFREADING

Although some writers mistakenly believe that revising, editing, and proofreading are all the same skill, they are not. While during the revision process you "re-vision" your creation, during the editing process you make that vision clearer, more concise, more precise, more accessible.

Proofreading is different yet again. It is the search for errors. When you proofread, you are not asking yourself, "Is there a better way of saying this?" Instead, you are looking to see if what you intended to have on the page is in fact there.

Although the lines between revising and editing and between editing and proofreading blur at times, the distinctions among these three skills are important to keep in mind, if for no other reason than to remind you that there are three distinct ways of making changes to a draft and that the best written documents undergo all three types of changes.

§5.18.1   Editing

Editing, like revising, requires that you look at your work through fresh eyes. At this stage, however, the focus is not on the larger issues of content and organization but on sentence structure, precision and conciseness, grammar, and punctuation. The goal is to produce a professional product that is easy to read and understand. In this chapter, we focus on writing effective sentences and writing correctly; in the next chapter, we focus on precision and conciseness.

a.   Writing Effective Sentences

Most writers can substantially improve their sentences by following four simple rules:

1. Use the actor as the subject of most sentences.
2. Keep the subject and verb close together.
3. Put old information at the beginning of the sentence and new information at the end.
4. Vary sentence length and pattern.

Rule 1   Use the Actor as the Subject of Most Sentences

By using the actor as the subject of most of your sentences, you can eliminate many of the constructions that make legal writing hard to understand: overuse of the passive voice, most nominalizations, expletive constructions, and many misplaced modifiers.

1. Passive Constructions

In a passive construction, the actor appears in the object rather than the subject slot of the sentence, or it is not named at all. For example, in the following sentence, although the jury is the actor, the word "jury" is used as the object of the preposition "by" rather than as the subject.

EXAMPLE 1   PASSIVE VOICE

A verdict was reached by the jury.

In the following example, the actor, "jury," is not named at all.

EXAMPLE 2   PASSIVE VOICE

A verdict was reached.

To use the active voice, simply identify the actor (in this case, the jury) and use it as the subject of the sentence.

EXAMPLE   ACTIVE VOICE

The jury reached a verdict.

Now read each of the following sentences, marking the subject and verb and deciding whether the writer used the actor as the subject of the sentence. If the writer did not use the actor as the subject of the sentence, decide whether the sentence should be rewritten. As a general rule, the active voice is better unless the passive voice improves the flow of sentences or the writer wants to de-emphasize what the actor did. For more on the effective use of the active and passive voice see 5.1 in *Just Writing*.

EXAMPLE

The phrase "prior consent" has been construed to include explicit and implied consent but not constructive consent. *See Williams v. Poulos*, 11 F.3d 271, 281 (1st Cir. 1993); *Griggs-Ryan v. Smith*, 904 F.2d 112, 119 (1st Cir. 1990). In our case, no explicit consent was given by Ms. Johnson. Although Ms. Johnson was told that calls were intercepted, she did not explicitly agree to the interception of her calls.

Sentence 1:

The phrase "prior consent" has been construed to include explicit and implied consent but not constructive consent. *See Williams v. Poulos*, 11 F.3d 271, 281 (1st Cir. 1993); *Griggs-Ryan v. Smith*, 904 F.2d 112, 119 (1st Cir. 1990).

In writing this sentence, the writer has used the passive voice. Instead of using the actor (the courts) as the subject of the sentence, the writer has used "prior consent" as the subject. The sentence would have been better if the writer had written, "The courts have construed the phrase 'prior consent' to include explicit and implied consent but not constructive consent."

Sentence 2:

In our case, no explicit consent was given by Ms. Johnson.

Sentence 2 is another sentence in which the writer has used the passive voice. Instead of saying Ms. Johnson did not give explicit consent, the writer has said that explicit consent was not given by Ms. Johnson. This sentence would have been easier to read and understand if the writer had written "In our case, Ms. Johnson did not give explicit consent."

Sentence 3:

Although Ms. Johnson was told that calls were intercepted, she did not explicitly agree to the interception of her calls.

In this sentence, the writer has used the passive voice in the dependent clause ("Although Ms. Johnson was told that calls were intercepted") and the active voice in the main clause ("she did not explicitly agree to the interception of her calls.") It would have been better to write both the dependent and the main clause using the active voice.

"Although Elite told Ms. Johnson that it would monitor some of her calls, Ms. Johnson did not explicitly agree to these interceptions."

2. Nominalizations

You have created a nominalization when you turn a verb into a noun. Although there are times when you will want to use a nominalization, if you overuse them they can make your writing harder to read and understand. In the following sentence, the words "application" and "conclusion" are nominalizations.

EXAMPLE

Application of the same principles dictates the **conclusion** that there was no implied consent.

To make this sentence better, identify the actor and then, in the verb, specifically state what action that actor has taken or will take.

EXAMPLE

If the court **applies** the same principles, it will **conclude** that there was no implied consent.

---

3. Expletive Constructions

In an expletive construction, the phrase "it is" or "there are" is used as the subject and verb of the sentence. Although it is sometimes necessary to use such a construction (note the use of expletive constructions in this paragraph), such a construction gives the reader almost no information. It is, therefore, much better to use a concrete subject and verb—that is, a subject and verb that describe something the reader can "see" in his or her mind. See also sections 5.2 and 6.2.4 in *Just Writing*.

EXAMPLE

Expletive
It is Elite's argument that . . .

Corrected

Elite will argue that . . .

---

4. Dangling Modifiers

A dangling modifier is a modifier that does not reasonably modify anything in the sentence. For example, in the following sentence, the phrase "Applying this test" does not reasonably modify anything in the sentence. It is not "it was held" that is doing the applying.

EXAMPLE 1

Applying this test, it was held that there was no implied consent.

The dangling modifier can be eliminated if the actor is used as the subject of the sentence.

EXAMPLE 2

Applying this test, the court held that there was no implied consent.

Now the phrase "Applying this test" modifies something in the sentence: the court. For more on dangling modifiers, see section 8.6.2 in *Just Writing*.

Rule 2   Keep the Subject and Verb Close Together

Researchers have established that readers cannot understand a sentence until they have located both the subject and the verb. In addition, readers have difficulty remembering the subject if it is separated from the verb by a number of words. If a number of words separate the subject and the verb, the reader must go back and relocate the subject after finding the verb.

The lesson to be learned from this research is that, as a writer, you should try to keep your subject and verb close together. In the following examples, the subject and verb are in boldface type.

EXAMPLE 1   SUBJECT AND VERB TOO FAR APART

Similarly, the **First Circuit** in *Williams v. Poulos*, a case in which there was evidence in the record indicating that the plaintiff, a CEO, did not know that his phone calls were being intercepted, **affirmed** the trial court's granting of an injunction.

Even without the full citation, the preceding sentence is difficult to read.

EXAMPLE 2   SUBJECT AND VERB CLOSE TOGETHER

Similarly, in *Williams v. Poulos*, the **First Circuit affirmed** the granting of an injunction because there was evidence in the record indicating that the plaintiff, a CEO, did not know that his phone calls were being intercepted.

The sentence reads more smoothly if the subject (First Circuit) is placed next to the verb (affirmed). For more information on the distance between subjects and verbs, see section 5.4 in *Just Writing*.

| **Rule 3** | **Put Old Information at the Beginning of the Sentence and New Information at the End** |

Sentences, and the paragraphs they create, make more sense when the old information is placed at the beginning and the new information is placed at the end. When this pattern is used, the development progresses naturally from left to right without unnecessary backtracking.

EXAMPLE

The Spears taped and listened to about twenty-two hours of calls over a **six-week period.** Although **during this period** they did not hear anything indicating that Deal had been involved in the burglary, they did find out that she had sold a keg of beer at cost in violation of store policy and that she was having an affair with another individual.

In the first sentence the new information is that the Spears taped and listened to calls over a six-week period. Thus, this information is placed at the end of the sentence. The second sentence then starts with a reference back to this information, which is now old information, and ends with new information: what the Spears heard while listening to Deal's conversations. In particular, note the dovetailing. The first sentence ends with a reference to a six-week period, and the second sentence begins with a reference back to that time period. See the prior discussion of dovetailing and 4.3.1 in *Just Writing*.

Rule 4   Vary Both the Length of Your Sentences and the Sentence Patterns

Even if writing is technically correct, it is not considered good if it is not pleasing to the ear.

EXAMPLE 1

Ms. Johnson began working for Elite Insurance in January 2000. Ms. Johnson was told that the phones and computers should be used for business purposes only. She was also told that it was Elite's policy to monitor all of an employee's phone calls during his or her one-month training period. Calls were monitored periodically after that time to ensure that the employee was providing good service. Clients calling the office heard a message saying that their phone calls might be monitored to ensure good service.

In the above example, the writing is not pleasing because the sentences are similar in length and all follow the same pattern (subject-verb-object). Although short, uncomplicated sentences are usually better than long, complicated ones, the use of too many short sentences results in writing that sounds choppy and sophomoric. As the following example illustrates, the passage is much better when the writer varies sentence length and pattern.

EXAMPLE 2

Ms. Johnson began working for Elite Insurance in January 2000. At the time she was hired, Ms. Johnson was told that the phones and computers should be used for business purposes only. In addition, she was told that it was Elite's policy to monitor all of an employee's phone calls during his or her one-month training period and to monitor them periodically after that time to ensure that the employee was providing good service. In accordance with this company policy, clients calling the office heard a message saying that their phone calls might be monitored to ensure good service.

For more on sentence construction see Chapter 5 in *Just Writing*.

b.   Writing Correctly

For a moment, imagine that you have received the following letter from a local law firm.

Dear Student:

Thank you for submitting an application for a position as a law clerk with are firm. Your grades in law school are very good, however, at this time we do not have any positions available. Its possible, however, that we may have a opening next summer and we therefore urge you to reapply with us then.

Sincerely,

Senior Partner

No matter how bad the market is, most students would not want to be associated with a firm that sends out a five-line letter containing three major errors and several minor ones. Unfortunately, the reverse is also true. No matter how short-handed they are, most law firms do not want a law clerk who has not mastered the basic rules of grammar and punctuation. Most firms cannot afford a clerk who makes careless errors or one who lacks basic writing skills.

Consequently, at the editing stage you need to go back through your draft, correcting errors. Look first for the errors that potentially affect meaning (misplaced modifiers, incorrect use of "which" and "that") and for errors that well-educated readers are likely to notice (incomplete sentences, comma splices, incorrect use of the possessive, lack of parallelism). Then look for the errors that you know from past experience that you are likely to make.

§5.18.2   Proofreading

Most writers learn the importance of proofreading the hard way. A letter, brief, or contract goes out with the client's name misspelled, with an "or" where there should have been an "and," or without an essential "not." At a minimum, these errors cause embarrassment; at worst, they result in a lawsuit.

To avoid such errors, treat proofreading as a separate step in the revising process. After you have finished revising and editing, go back through your draft, looking not at content, organization, or sentence style, but for errors. Have you written what you intended to write?

Proofreading is most effective when it is done on hard copy several days (or, when that is not feasible, several hours) after you have finished editing. Force yourself to read slowly, focusing not on the sentence but on the individual words in the sentence. Is a word missing? Is a word repeated? Are letters transposed? You may force yourself to read slowly by covering up all but the line you are reading, by reading from right to left, or by reading from the bottom of the page to the top.

Also, force yourself to begin with the sections that caused you the most difficulty or that you wrote last. Because you were concentrating on content or were tired, these sections probably contain the most errors.

Finally, when you get into practice, don't rely on just your spelling and grammar checkers. Instead, make it a habit to have a second person proofread your work. Not only will such a person see errors that you did not, he or she is also less likely than you to "read in" missing words. Although you are responsible for every word that goes out under your name, a trusted proofreader is worth his or her weight in gold.

§5.19   A Note About Citations

As a legal writer, you have an extra burden. In addition to editing and proofreading the text, you must also edit and proofread your citations to legal authorities.

At the editing stage, focus on selection and placement of citations. Is the authority you cited the best authority? Did you avoid string cites (the citing of multiple cases for the same point)? Have you included a citation to authority for every rule stated? Did you include the appropriate signal? Have you over- or underemphasized the citation? (You emphasize a citation by placing it in the text of a sentence; you de-emphasize it by placing it in a separate citation sentence.)

In contrast, at the proofreading stage, focus on the citation itself. Are the volume and page numbers correct? Are the pinpoint cites accurate? Have you included the year of the decision and any subsequent history? Is the spacing correct?

§5.20   Final Draft of Memo

At long last, we are at the end of the process. Having been researched, drafted, revised, edited, and proofread, the final draft of the memo looks like this:

EXAMPLE   **FINAL DRAFT**

To: Charles Maier

From: Legal Intern

Date: September 8, 2002

Re: Eliza Johnson v. Elite Insurance, File No. 02-478
         18 U.S.C. § 2511: Consent to intercept or monitor phone
         calls.

Statement of Facts

Elite Insurance has contacted our office, asking whether it violated the Electronic Communications Privacy Act when it intercepted one of its employee's phone calls without her explicit consent.

Eliza Johnson began working for Elite Insurance in January 2000. When she was hired, Ms. Johnson was told that the phones and computers should be used for business purposes only. In addition, she was told that it was Elite's policy to monitor all of an employee's phone calls during his or her one-month training period and to monitor them periodically after that time to ensure that employees were providing good service to Elite's clients. In accordance with this policy, clients calling the office heard a message saying that their phone calls might be monitored to ensure good service.

In fact, Elite seldom intercepted its employees' calls. According to Eric Wilson, the office supervisor, after the training period has ended, employee calls are intercepted only two or three times a year, usually immediately before the employee's annual performance review. Although Mr. Wilson does not tell employees in advance that he will be intercepting their calls, he usually discusses the calls with them immediately after the calls have been intercepted.

Because he had information indicating that Ms. Johnson might be involved in an insurance fraud scheme, Mr. Wilson began intercepting her calls in mid-July and stopped intercepting them in mid-August. At no point during this time did Mr. Wilson tell Ms. Johnson that he was intercepting her calls or discuss the calls with her. Although his intercepting did not produce any evidence that Ms. Johnson was involved in any type of illegal activity, Mr. Wilson did overhear conversations indicating that Ms. Johnson was having an affair. On August 19, 2002, Mr. Wilson fired Ms. Johnson because she had used the phones for personal business.

Mr. Wilson intercepted the phone calls by attaching a tape recorder to an extension phone. At this point, we do not know whether when she answered the phone, Ms. Johnson heard the message warning incoming callers that their calls might be monitored. Ms. Johnson did not explicitly agree, either orally or in writing, to the interception of her calls, and she states that she did not know that her calls were being intercepted.

Issue

Under the Electronic Communications Privacy Act, 18 U.S.C. § 2511, did Ms. Johnson consent to the interception of her phone calls when (1) she was told that her phone calls would be intercepted periodically to ensure good customer service but Elite seldom monitored calls, and (2) Ms. Johnson did not know that her calls were being intercepted?

Brief Answer

Probably not. Ms. Johnson did not explicitly consent to the interception of her phone calls, and, under the circumstances, a court probably will not find implied consent. Even though Elite told Ms. Johnson that her calls might be intercepted and incoming callers heard a message warning them that their calls might be monitored, Elite did not make a practice of monitoring employees' calls. In addition, Elite's motive for intercepting the calls indicates that it did not believe that Ms. Johnson knew that her calls were being intercepted.

Discussion

18 U.S.C. § 2511 sets out two consent exceptions. Subsection 2511(2)(c) applies when the party intercepting the communication was acting under color of law, and subsection 2511(2)(d) applies when the party intercepting the communication was not acting under color of law. Because there is no evidence that Elite Insurance was acting under color of law when it intercepted Ms. Johnson's phone calls, the applicable subsection is 2511(2)(d), which reads as follows:

> (d) It shall not be unlawful under this chapter for a person not acting under color of law to intercept a wire or oral communication where such a person is a party to the communication or where one of the parties to the communication has given prior consent to such interception. . . .

The applicable language of this subsection is "where one of the parties to the communication has given prior consent to such interception."

In our case, both sides will agree that the first element, that the person giving consent be a party to the communication, is not in dispute. In each of the phone calls at issue, Ms. Johnson was one of the parties involved in the call. Thus, the only element in dispute is whether Ms. Johnson gave prior consent.

The courts have construed the phrase "prior consent" to include explicit and implied consent but not constructive consent. *See Williams v. Poulos*, 11 F.3d 271, 281 (1st Cir. 1993); *Griggs-Ryan v. Smith*, 904 F.2d 112, 119 (1st Cir. 1990). In our case, there was no explicit consent. Although Ms. Johnson was told that calls were intercepted, she did not explicitly agree to the interception of her calls. There may, however, have been implied consent.

In deciding whether there is implied consent, the courts have stated that such consent should not be cavalierly implied. *Deal v. Spears*, 980 F.2d 1153, 1157 (8th Cir. 1992); *Watkins v. L.M. Berry & Co.*, 704 F.2d 577, 581 (11th Cir. 1983). Instead, implied consent should be found only when the circumstances indicate that an individual knowingly agreed to the interception of his or her communications. *Williams v. Poulos*, 11 F.3d at 281; *Griggs-Ryan v. Smith*, 904 F.2d at 117.

In the cases in which the courts have held that the plaintiff consented to the interception, the defendant had told the plaintiff that all of his or her phone calls would be intercepted. For example, in *Griggs-Ryan v. Smith*, the defendant, the plaintiff's landlady, had repeatedly told the plaintiff that she monitored all incoming phone calls. 904 F.2d at 117. Similarly, in *Gilday v. Dubois*, 124 F.3d 277, 297 (1st Cir. 1997), each time that inmates made a phone call they heard a recorded message that told them their phone call was being intercepted and monitored. In each case, the First Circuit held that these facts were sufficient to support the trial court's order granting the defendants' motion for summary judgment.

In contrast, the courts have repeatedly held that the consent requirement is not met if the individual only knew that his or her phone calls might be monitored. For example, in *Campiti v. Walonis*, 611 F.2d 387 (1st Cir. 1979), the First Circuit affirmed the trial court's decision that there was no consent despite the defendant's argument that the plaintiff, a prisoner, should have known that his phone calls might be monitored. Similarly, in *Williams v. Poulos*, the First Circuit affirmed the granting of an injunction because there was no evidence in the record indicating that the plaintiff, a CEO, knew that his phone calls were being monitored. 11 F.3d at 281.

In addition, the courts have held that the plaintiff did not consent to the interception of his or her phone calls when the defendant's statements or actions indicated that the defendant did not believe that the plaintiff knew that his or her phone calls were being intercepted. For instance, in *Deal v. Spears*, the Spears, Deal's employers, installed a recording device on an extension phone in the hopes of catching Deal in an unguarded admission. When turned on, the recorder automatically recorded all conversations with no indication to the parties using the phone that their conversations were being recorded. *Id.* at 1155-1156. The Eighth Circuit

Court of Appeals affirmed the district court's determination that there was no consent because (1) the Spears told Deal that they might intercept her phone calls, not that they were intercepting the calls; and (2) the facts indicated that the Spears believed that Deal did not know her phone calls were being intercepted. *Id.* at 1157.

Ms. Johnson will argue that the consent element is not met because she did not know that her phone calls were being intercepted. Like the plaintiffs in *Campiti, Williams,* and *Deal,* who did not know that their calls were being intercepted, Ms. Johnson did not know that Elite was intercepting her calls. In the past, her phone calls had been monitored only in January, immediately before her annual performance review, and her supervisor had intercepted only two or three of her calls and had talked to her about those calls immediately afterwards. In addition, the facts indicate that Elite did not believe that Ms. Johnson knew that her calls were being intercepted. Just as the Spears in *Deal v. Spears* hoped to catch Deal in an admission tying her to a burglary, Elite hoped to catch Ms. Johnson in an admission tying her to an insurance fraud scheme.

In the alternative, Ms. Johnson can argue that even if she did consent to the monitoring of her phone calls to determine whether she was providing good customer service, she did not consent to the monitoring of her personal calls.

In contrast, Elite will argue that the consent element is met because Ms. Johnson had been told that her phone would be monitored periodically. Elite will begin by distinguishing *Campiti* and *Williams.* Unlike *Campiti,* in which the prisoners were never told that their calls would be intercepted, and *Williams,* in which the CEO was never told that his calls might be intercepted, Ms. Johnson was told about the company's monitoring policy. In addition, Elite can distinguish *Deal.* Unlike Deal, who never knew that any of her calls were being intercepted, Ms. Johnson knew that her calls had been intercepted in the past and that they were subject to being intercepted in the future. In fact, this case is more like *Griggs-Ryan,* the case in which the landlady repeatedly told her tenants that all incoming calls would be intercepted, than it is like any of the other cases. Just as the tenants in *Griggs-Ryan* received regular reminders about their landlady's policy, so did Ms. Johnson: The message that incoming callers received telling them that their calls were subject to monitoring should have provided Ms. Johnson with a daily reminder about Elite's monitoring policy.

In addition, Elite can argue that as a matter of public policy employers with monitoring policies like Elite's should be able to intercept employees' phone calls without explicitly telling the employees that a particular call or set of calls will be intercepted. Because employees are likely to act differently when they know a particular call is being intercepted, employers will not be able to effectively monitor the type of service their employees are providing if they must tell their employees that each call is being monitored. In addition, employers will not be able to determine whether an employee is violating a company policy or is engaged in fraud if they must tell an employee that a particular call or set of calls is being intercepted.

Ms. Johnson is likely to respond to these arguments in two ways. First, it is not clear whether she heard the message that incoming callers heard. As a result, although the message may have put incoming callers on notice, it did not put her on notice, particularly given what she knew about Elite's actual practices. Second, the statute specifically requires that an individual give prior consent. Thus, even though an employer may have an interest in intercepting an employee's phone call, that interest is not recognized under the statute.

A court will probably find that there was no implied consent because Ms. Johnson did not knowingly agree to the interception of her calls. Although Elite told Ms. Johnson that her calls were subject to periodic monitoring, the interceptions that took place were not consistent with prior company practices. In addition, Elite's own reasons for monitoring Ms. Johnson's calls indicate that it did not believe that Ms. Johnson knew her calls were being intercepted.

Conclusion

A court will probably find that Elite Insurance intentionally intercepted Ms. Johnson's telephone calls without her prior consent. Although Elite told Ms. Johnson that her calls were subject to periodic monitoring, the monitoring that took place was not consistent with prior company practices. The monitoring occurred not in January at the time of Ms. Johnson's annual performance review but in July and August. In addition, instead of monitoring only two or three calls, Elite monitored calls for four or five weeks, and instead of talking to her about a call immediately after the call, Elite only talked to her about the calls when the company fired her.

In addition, even if Ms. Johnson did consent to the monitoring of her calls to determine whether she was providing good customer service, she did not consent to the monitoring of personal calls, which, although they violated company policy, were tolerated.

Chapter 6

The Second Memorandum

This chapter builds on Chapter 5. While in Chapter 5 we showed you how to research and write a relatively simple memo, in this chapter we show you how to research and write a more difficult one. In doing so, we will review some of the material contained in Chapter 5 and introduce some new techniques: how to organize a memo that does not involve an analysis of elements, how to organize the discussion section using an integrated approach, how to use parentheticals, and how to write more concisely and precisely.

§6.1 GETTING THE ASSIGNMENT

It is now the summer after your first year of law school, and you are working for a personal injury firm in Roswell, New Mexico. One of the cases the firm is handling is an electromagnetic field (EMF) case. The facts are set out in the following memo from the senior partner.

EXAMPLE

To: Legal Intern

From: Raymond Sanchez

Date: June 11, 2002

Re: File No. 123
         Nancy and Alan Flynn

The Flynns want to know whether they have a cause of action against Pecos Power. Because there are high voltage lines behind their house, they have been unable to sell it.

151

The Flynns' house is a four-bedroom, three-bathroom, 3,500 square-foot home with a pool and garden in the backyard. From the back of the house, the Flynns have a view of El Capitan Mountain and New Mexico's spectacular sunsets. The Flynns bought the house for $35,000 in 1975.

When the Flynns bought the house, they knew that the land behind it was owned by Pecos Power. Nothing was on the land, however, and when the Flynns contacted Pecos Power, they were told that the power company had no immediate plans for the land.

In 1999, high voltage lines were erected on the land that runs behind the Flynns' home. In 2000, the lines were completed, and power began running through them. The lines are within 50 feet of the Flynns' home.

In the last two years, a number of articles discussing EMFs have appeared in the *Roswell Daily Record*, the local newspaper. Several of the articles indicated that there was at least some evidence that exposure to EMFs increased the risk of cancer or other health problems, and one article in the real estate section indicated that buyers should be wary of buying a home next to high voltage lines.

A year ago, when their youngest child left for college, the Flynns put their house on the market. They did so for three reasons: (1) they wanted a smaller home; (2) the high voltage lines obstruct their view of the mountain and sunsets, something they value; and (3) they no longer feel comfortable using their backyard pool or maintaining their large vegetable gardens because of the danger posed by the EMFs. In fact, since learning about the alleged dangers posed by EMFs, they almost never use their backyard, and they keep their grandchildren inside when they come to visit.

Almost a year later, the Flynns have still been unable to sell their house, even though they have lowered the price from $279,000 to $249,000. The Flynns' real estate agent has told them that because of all of the publicity about EMFs, many people will not buy a house near power lines because they fear that either they or their children will get cancer. Even the recent studies that indicate that power lines do not cause leukemia do not seem to have quelled people's fears.

The Flynns have had their house tested for EMFs. Although the house itself tested within safe limits, unusually high levels (21 milligauss) were found in the pool and garden areas.

Neither Mr. nor Mrs. Flynn nor their children have, or have had, cancer.

The Flynns' home is only one of two in the area that back up onto the high voltage power lines.

Because we need to get back to the clients quickly, I have asked several interns to work on this project. For your part, please determine whether the Flynns have a cause of action in nuisance.

§6.2   Preparing a Research Plan

Once again, the first step is to prepare a research plan. Before going into the library, draft a preliminary issue statement, determine what law is likely to apply, and decide what sources you are going to consult and in what order.

§6.2.1   Draft the Preliminary Issue Statement

Sometimes drafting the preliminary issue statement is difficult. In assigning the project, the attorney has not been clear about what he or she wants you to research. In these situations, you need to do two things. First, ask to see the case file. By reading through the file, you may be able to get a better feel for what you do and do not need to research. Second, ask questions, either at the time that you are given the assignment or after you have read the file or have done some initial research. Most attorneys would rather have you ask questions than spend time researching something that they did not want researched.

Fortunately, in this case, drafting the preliminary issue statement is relatively easy. In his memo, the assigning attorney, Raymond Sanchez, set out the question that he wants you to research. All you need to add are the facts. Thus, you prepare the following statement.

Preliminary Issue Statement

Do the Flynns have a cause of action in nuisance against Pecos Power when they have been unable to sell their home, which is located within 50 feet of high voltage power lines?

You quickly realize that to answer this question, you will first need to answer a number of other questions. Thinking back to your first year of law school, you remember that there are different types of nuisance. Something can be a public nuisance, a private nuisance, a nuisance per se, or a nuisance in fact. You also remember reading a case that said that actions authorized by law cannot be a nuisance, or at least a nuisance per se. Finally, you know nothing about EMFs. If you are going to be able to analyze the problem, you are going to have to find out what they are.

Thus, in addition to writing the preliminary issue statement, you decide to write down some of the other questions that come to mind. You sketch out the flowchart below.

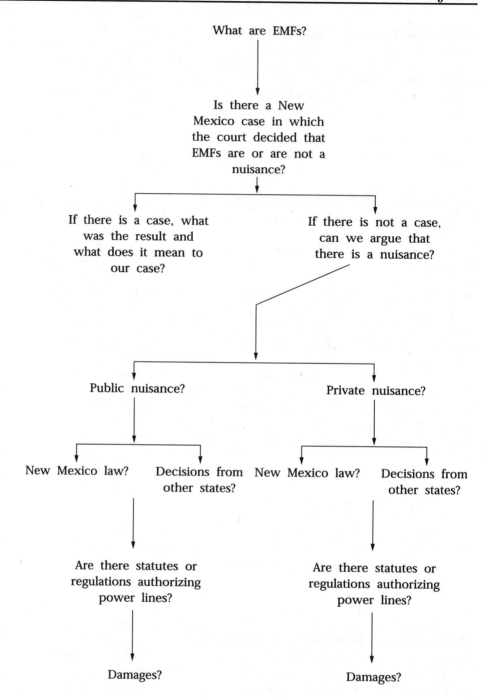

§6.2.2   Determine What Law Applies

In determining what law applies, you think, once again, back to your first-year classes. Your memory tells you that nuisance is governed by state rather than federal law. In addition, it tells you that although traditionally nuisance was a common law doctrine, many states have enacted statutes. Thus, you tentatively determine that the Flynn case will be governed by New Mexico statutes governing nuisance or, if there are no statutes, by New Mexico common law.

§6.2.3   Deciding Which Sources to Check

Like many other problems, there are a number of ways to research this problem. In fact, in thinking about which sources to check, you come up with four possible strategies.

Strategy No. 1:   Begin with *New Mexico Statutes Annotated*

- Using the *New Mexico Statutes Annotated,* locate the statutes currently in effect relating to nuisance and high voltage power lines.
- Read the statutes, looking for the sections that appear to apply.
- If no section or sections appear to apply, move to strategy 2. If a section or sections do appear to apply, continue as set out below.
- Read and analyze the applicable statutory section or sections.
- Read the Notes of Decisions following the applicable section or sections, looking for cases that appear on point, particularly for cases dealing with EMFs.
- Read the cases that appear on point.
- Cite check the cases that are on point to determine whether they are still good law and whether there are additional cases that are on point.
- Look for law review articles that are on point.

Strategy No. 2:   Begin with the *Pacific Digest*

- Look up "Nuisance" in the *Pacific Digest.*
- Read through the Notes of Decisions, looking both for statutory references and for cases that appear on point.
- Locate and read the cases and statutory sections that appear on point.
- Cite check the cases and statutes that are on point to determine whether they are still good law and whether there are additional cases that are on point.
- Look for law review articles that are on point.

Strategy No. 3:   Begin by Looking for a Law Review Article or an ALR Annotation That Is on Point

- Using either a print or online index, locate ALR annotations and law review articles that appear to be on point.
- Locate and skim either the annotations or two or three of the most recent law review articles, looking specifically for information about nuisances and EMFs.
- Look up and read the New Mexico statutes and cases cited in the articles or, if no New Mexico statutes or cases are cited, the most recent out-of-state cases discussing nuisance.
- Use either strategy 1 or strategy 2 to locate New Mexico statutes and analogous cases.

Strategy No. 4:   Begin by Running an Online Search

- Using LEXIS, Loislaw, or Westlaw, run the following search in the New Mexico cases database: "electromagnetic field" EMF/10 nuisance.
- Read and cite check any statutes and cases you locate.
- If nothing is found in the New Mexico database, revert to strategy 1, 2, or 3 above, or run the same search in a law review or an all-states database and then revert to strategy 1, 2, or 3.

In the Flynn case, all four strategies have advantages and disadvantages. If you use Strategy No. 1, you can quickly locate New Mexico's statutes relating to nuisance and high voltage power lines. In addition, by reading the nuisance statutes and Notes of Decisions following them, you can quickly eliminate public nuisance as a possible cause of action. It is unlikely that the Flynns can prove that Pecos Power maintained the lines without lawful authority; that the lines are injurious to public health, safety, morals, or welfare; or that the lines interfere with the exercise and enjoyment of public rights.

This strategy also leads you to at least some of the cases that discuss private nuisance: Some of the cases listed in the Notes of Decisions, for example, *City of Albuquerque v. State,* discuss not only the rules relating to public nuisance but also the rules relating to private nuisance. There are, however, some things that you cannot find using Strategy No. 1. Because the statutes discuss only public nuisance, the Notes of Decisions following them are not a reliable source for finding cases dealing with private nuisance. In addition, the Notes of Decisions are not a reliable way of finding EMF cases. Even if a case involved EMFs, the term "EMF" might not appear in the note.

While Strategy No. 1 provided an easy way to find the New Mexico statutes, Strategy No. 2 provides an easy way of finding New Mexico cases. When you look up "Nuisance" in the *Pacific Digest,* you find cases setting out the general rules relating both to private and public nuisance. Key numbers 1 through 58 discuss private nuisance, and key numbers 59 through 96 discuss public nuisance. Some of these cases provide citations to the New Mexico statutes. What is more difficult to find are cases that discuss EMFs. Like the Notes of Decisions following a statute, the Notes of Decisions in the digest may not set out the specific facts of a case. In addition, the Notes of Decisions do not include citations to cases outside the Pacific region or to law review articles.

Strategy No. 3 has several advantages over Strategies 1 and 2. First, several of the law review articles explain EMFs and provide citations to scientific studies. Second, several of the articles discuss EMFs as a basis for a cause of action in nuisance, providing you with a list of cases in which the courts have ruled on the issue. Finally, a number of the authors have taken a position on the issue, setting out arguments either for or against allowing EMFs as a basis for a cause of action in nuisance. What the articles do not provide, however, are citations to New Mexico statutes or to New Mexico cases that might be used to argue by analogy.

The last strategy has the advantage of providing a quick answer to what is probably the most basic question: Is there a New Mexico case in which the court has decided that EMFs are or are not a nuisance? If there is such a case, it may answer the question, and no further research would be needed. If, though, there is no such case, you will have to run the same search in a law review database or in other jurisdictions or revert to Strategy 1, 2, or 3.

As in most cases, in our example case, all four strategies lead, eventually, to the same information. Thus, in deciding where to start, you should consider the availability of the various sources, the costs associated with using those sources, and the reliability and currency of the sources. Do not, however, automatically eliminate a source because it is not readily available. An hour spent going to the nearest law library to read recent law review articles may be more cost-efficient than several hours of other types of research.

For the purposes of our problem, presume that the firm has copies of the New Mexico code and reporters, the *Pacific Digest,* and a Westlaw subscription that allows unlimited use of the New Mexico database. It does not, however, have ALR, an index to law review articles, any law reviews other than the *New Mexico Law Review,* or reporters from other states. In this situation, you decide to prepare the following research plan.

Research Plan

Preliminary Issue Statement:	Do the Flynns have a cause of action in nuisance against Pecos Power when they have been unable to sell their home, which is located 50 feet from high voltage power lines?

Jurisdiction: New Mexico

Type of Law: Statutory and common law

Step 1:   Run the following search in Westlaw's New Mexico databases: "electromagnetic field" EMF/10 of nuisance.

Step 2:   If that search produces no results, run the following search: "electromagnetic field" EMF.

Step 3:   Look up "Nuisance," "Power Companies," "Power Lines," and "Utilities" in the General Index of the *New Mexico Statutes Annotated*. Identify and read the statutes that appear on point and any cases listed in the Notes of Decisions that appear to be on point. Cite check both the statutes and cases to make sure that they are still good law.

Step 4:   If that search produces no results, look up "Nuisance" in the *Pacific Digest*. Read the Notes of Decisions, identifying the five or six cases that appear most on point. Read and cite check the cases that appear on point. Also read and cite check any cases that you locate through cite checking.

Step 5:   Go to the county law library and locate and read law review articles and out-of-state cases that appear to be on point. Cite check any of the out-of-state cases you think that you might use.

§6.3   Understanding What You Have Found

Presume that in doing the research, you have found the following:

- Several New Mexico statutes defining "public nuisances"
- Several New Mexico cases setting out the rules relating to both public and private nuisances
- Several law review articles discussing EMF litigation, including lawsuits in which the plaintiff tried to establish a cause of action in nuisance
- No New Mexico cases discussing EMFs.

Having found this material, you now must make sense of it. Although there are a number of ways of doing this, you decide to start by going back to the flowchart that you made earlier (see page 154) and answering the questions in it.

1. What Are EMFs?

As a practicing attorney, you will often need to become an instant "expert" on a particular topic. You will need to learn about a specific accounting procedure, a specific type of injury, or a specific type of technology. As a consequence, you will often need to do "non-legal legal research," locating and reading information in other fields. The trick is in knowing how much you need to know.

In the Flynn case, you do not need to know everything there is to know about EMFs; you just need to know enough about them to understand the danger they potentially pose and how they are similar or dissimilar from other "substances" that have been found to constitute a nuisance. Thus, at least at this point, it is enough to read the descriptions of EMFs set out in the law review articles. You do not need to read the reports they cite or do research in scientific or medical journals.

2. Is There a New Mexico Case in Which the Court Decided That EMFs Are or Are Not a Nuisance?

Having developed a basic understanding of EMFs, you turn to the next question: Is there a New Mexico case in which the court decided that EMFs are or are not a nuisance? Because your Westlaw searches produced no results and you did not see any references to EMFs in reviewing the Notes of Decisions in the New Mexico Code and Digest, you are confident that the New Mexico Supreme Court has not decided the issue and that there is no published decision from the New Mexico Court of Appeals. Thus, there is no mandatory authority on the issue and, when the issue reaches the New Mexico appellate courts, it will be an issue of first impression.

What you do not know, though, is whether there is any EMF litigation currently in the New Mexico trial courts. To find out whether there is such litigation, you need to consult more informal sources, for example, bar bulletins and newsletters, articles in local newspapers, other lawyers, and, possibly, various EMF websites.

After checking out some of these informal sources and not finding anything, you turn to the next level of questions.

3. Can the Flynns Argue That the EMFs Constitute a Public Nuisance?

As you discovered in doing the research, public nuisances are defined by statute. Thus, you begin your analysis by rereading the applicable statutes. The first thing you do is read through the table of contents at the beginning of the chapter and identify those sections that are potentially applicable.

In the Flynn case, only three sections are general enough to be potentially applicable: sections 30-8-1, 30-8-5, and 30-8-8. You begin by reading the most general of the sections, section 30-8-1. See Exhibit 6.1.

Although the Flynns can prove that Pecos Power knowingly created and maintained the high voltage lines, they cannot prove that it did so without lawful authority. The erection of the high voltage lines was approved by the New Mexico Public Utilities Commission. In addition, it seems unlikely that the Flynns can prove that the lines are injurious to public health or that they interfere with the exercise and enjoyment of public rights. Because it does not appear that the Flynns can establish that the lines constitute a public nuisance, you do not spend any additional time on this issue. You do not spend time trying to figure out

---

EXHIBIT 6.1

ARTICLE 8
Nuisances

Sec.		Sec.	
30-8-1.	Public nuisance.	30-8-9.	Abandonment of dangerous containers.
30-8-2.	Polluting water.	30-8-10.	Placing injurious substance on highways.
30-8-3.	Refuse defined.	30-8-11.	Illegal prescribing of medicine.
30-8-4.	Littering.	30-8-12.	Conduct offensive to public well-being.
30-8-5.	Enforcement.	30-8-13.	Unlawfully permitting livestock upon public highways.
30-8-6.	Posting; notice to public.		
30-8-7.	Public education.	30-8-14.	Highway department; agreements with owners or lessees of highway frontage; provisions.
30-8-8.	Abatement of a public nuisance.		
30-8-8.1.	Abatement of house of prostitution.		

30-8-1. Public nuisance.

A public nuisance consists of knowingly creating, performing or maintaining anything affecting any number of citizens without lawful authority which is either:

    A. injurious to public health, safety, morals or welfare; or

    B. interferes with the exercise and enjoyment of public rights, including the right to use public property.

Whoever commits a public nuisance for which the act or penalty is not otherwise prescribed by law is guilty of a petty misdemeanor.

History: 1953 Comp., § 40A-8-1, enacted by Laws 1963, ch. 303, § 8-1.

Cross references. — For polluting of water being public nuisance, see 30-8-2 NMSA 1978. For provisions on abatement of public nuisance, see 30-8-8 NMSA 1978. For conduct offensive to public well-being, see 30-8-12 NMSA 1978. For house of prostitution being public nuisance, see 30-9-8 NMSA 1978. For gambling and gambling houses being public nuisance, see 30-19-8 NMSA 1978. For provision making forest fire burning without proper precaution a public nuisance, see 30-32-1 NMSA 1978.

Nuisance must affect group of people. — A public nuisance must affect a considerable number of people or an entire community or neighborhood. Environmental Imp. Div. v. Bloomfield Irrigation Dist., 108 N.M. 691, 778 P.2d 438 (Ct. App. 1989).

Acts of municipality under governmental authority. — In the absence of a showing of fraud, collusion, or illegality, a city's constitutional and statutory authority to construct public highways and bridges constitutes a valid defense to a claim of nuisance per se. City of Albuquerque v. State ex rel. Village of Los Ranchos de Albuquerque, 111 N.M. 608, 808 P.2d 58 (Ct. App. 1991).

Acts which the law authorized to be done, if carried out and maintained in the manner authorized by law, where a public entity acts under its governmental

---

Reprinted from *New Mexico Statutes Annotated* with permission from West Group.

what the phrase "affecting any number of citizens" means, and you do not try to answer the other questions in this section of the flowchart. Although in reading the cases you will need to make sure that you interpreted the statute correctly, at this point you turn your attention to private nuisance.

4. Can the Flynns Argue That the EMFs Constitute a Private Nuisance?

Because there are no New Mexico statutes dealing with private nuisance, you turn to the cases, looking again at the cases that discussed private nuisance. In particular, you look at *Padilla v. Lawrence*, a case that appeared under a number of different subsections in the *New Mexico Digest* and that appears to be one of the key cases in New Mexico.

In reading *Padilla v. Lawrence*, you want to do a number of things. First, you want to put the case in context, determining whether the case is mandatory or persuasive authority and what the social and political context was when it was decided. Second, you want to find the rules. What test or tests did the court apply in determining whether something was a private nuisance? Third, you want to find out how the court applied the rules that it set out. What were the facts in the case, and what conclusion did the court reach when it applied the rules to those facts? Finally, you want to see what types of arguments the parties made and how the courts responded to those arguments.

Thus, you begin your reading of *Padilla v. Lawrence* by reading the caption:

101 N.M. 556

Atanacio PADILLA and Juanita Padilla and Johnny E. Padilla, Plaintiffs-Appellees, Cross-Appellants,

v.

Amy LAWRENCE and Sun Country Garden Products, a New Mexico Corporation, Defendants-Appellants, Cross-Appellees.

No. 7348

Court of Appeals of New Mexico.

June 7, 1984.

Certiorari Denied July 19, 1984.

Because *Padilla* is a Court of Appeals decision, a New Mexico trial court must apply the rules set out in the case unless one of the parties can distinguish it. The *Padilla* decision is not, however, binding on the

New Mexico Court of Appeals or the New Mexico Supreme Court. These courts can apply the rules set out in the case or modify or reject those rules.

The next step is to determine how long the case is. If it is only two or three pages long, you will probably want to read it in its entirety; if it is longer, it is better to begin by reading the syllabus and by skimming the headnotes. Because *Padilla v. Lawrence* is relatively long, you choose the second approach, reading the syllabus and headnotes to determine the causes of action, the issues on appeal, and the sections of the opinion that appear to be on point.

Text of Syllabus

Class action was brought against manure processing plant and its owner requesting an injunction, money damages based upon theories of trespass, public nuisance, private nuisance, negligence, and personal injury, and also requesting punitive damages. The District Court, Bernalillo County, Frank H. Allen, Jr., D.J., awarded plaintiffs damages for inconvenience, discomfort, and annoyance, defendants appealed, and plaintiffs cross-appealed. The Court of Appeals, Minzner, J., held that: (1) substantial evidence supported trial court's finding of private nuisance; (2) award of damages for annoyance, discomfort, and inconvenience was not abuse of discretion; (3) trial court properly refused to award damages for diminution in property value; (4) trial court properly denied injunctive relief for a continuing nuisance; (5) trial court properly dismissed public nuisance claim; (6) plaintiffs were not entitled to damages for trespass; and (7) plaintiffs were not entitled to punitive damages.

Affirmed.

What to Look For

The first thing you note in reading the syllabus is that the plaintiffs set out causes of action in both public and private nuisance. Although it does not appear that the Flynns have a cause of action for a public nuisance (see pages 159-160 in *The Legal Writing Handbook*), they may have a cause of action for a private nuisance. Thus, the case appears to be on point and you keep reading.

The second thing you note are the types of damages that were awarded. The trial court awarded the plaintiff damages for inconvenience, discomfort, and annoyance but not for diminution in property value. This may not be good news. Although the Flynns may be able to claim damages for inconvenience, discomfort, and annoyance, what they really want is to be compensated for the diminished value of their home.

After reading the syllabus, you begin reading the headnotes, looking most carefully at those that have as their heading "Nuisance." Headnotes 1 and 2, 4 through 16, and 21 set out general rules for private nuisances, and headnotes 22 and 23 set out rules for public nuisances. Because the headnotes related to nuisance are at the beginning of the opinion, you decide to begin reading the opinion at the beginning, quickly reading through the material set out below.

OPINION

MINZNER, Judge.

Atanacio Padilla, Juanita Padilla, and their son, Johnny E. Padilla ("plaintiffs"), long-term residents of Bernalillo, New Mexico, filed a class action complaint against defendant Amy Lawrence and defendant Sun Country Garden Products, a corporation ("the plant"). Lawrence is the owner of the plant, also located in Bernalillo, which processes bark and manure for the purpose of packaging soil conditioner for sale. Plaintiffs requested an injunction against the plant and sought money damages based upon theories of trespass, public nuisance, private nuisance, negligence, and personal injury. Plaintiffs also sought punitive damages.

Prior to trial, the court dismissed the class action count and plaintiffs withdrew the personal injury count. The case was tried before the trial court, which dismissed the negligence, and public nuisance claims at the close of plaintiffs' case. Following presentation of all the evidence, judgment was entered for plaintiffs on the private nuisance claim. The court refused to grant injunctive relief but awarded plaintiffs Atanacio and Juanita Padilla $10,000 each for inconvenience, discomfort, and annoyance. The court also awarded Johnny E. Padilla the sum of $2,000 for discomfort and annoyance. Although the trial court found that the value of plaintiffs' residence has been diminished by the operation of the plant, it concluded that plaintiffs failed to prove the amount of the loss. The trial court also concluded that no trespass was established and declined to award punitive damages.

What to Look For

In reading this part of the opinion, you are looking for several things: the identity of the parties, the basis for the nuisance cause of action, and what happened at trial.

When you get to this part of the opinion, the part dealing with damages, you begin reading more slowly. The news isn't as bad as you thought. The reason the plaintiffs weren't awarded damages for the diminution in the value of their property is they failed to prove the amount of their loss.

Because the heading indicates that the following section is the section of the opinion that deals with private nuisance, you slow down and read more carefully. You also begin asking yourself the following questions. How are the facts in this case similar to or different from the facts in our case? What test or tests did the court apply? What arguments did the parties make and how did the court respond to those arguments?

| **Text of Opinion** | **What to Look For** |

Text of Opinion

I. LIABILITY FOR PRIVATE NUISANCE

Plaintiffs Atanacio and Juanita Padilla own real property on which their residence is located, which is approximately 600 feet from the nearest boundary of the plant. They have resided in the house for over twenty-five years. The plant has been in operation for approximately five years. It is located in the industrial park of Bernalillo and covers over nine acres. Plaintiffs' house is among several residences near the plant. The record indicates that these residences are outside the industrial park.

The trial court heard testimony from the plaintiffs, from several of their neighbors, from plaintiffs' expert witness, and from a realtor as to the negative physical and aesthetic impact of the plant's operation on plaintiffs' enjoyment of their property. The witnesses testified that the plant's operation has resulted in plaintiffs' exposure to odors, dust, noise, and flies, which were not in evidence prior to construction and operation. The witnesses testified that an odor, variously described as that of a dead animal, of a pig pen, and of rotten fish, permeated the air, and that dust, noise, and flies were also a problem. The odor prohibited cooking in the summer, prevented use of evaporative cooling, and generally interfered with normal residential activities. Plaintiff Atanacio Padilla testified that the odor and dust caused him to have nosebleeds and fits of choking.

Mr. Padilla also testified that he and his wife finally moved from the residence in 1982 because of the problems associated with the plant's operation and that the nosebleeds and choking

What to Look For

As you read the opinion, you note that the facts in *Padilla* are similar to the facts in our case. In both instances, the plaintiffs owned their home for over 25 years and the "nuisance" was built after the plaintiffs had lived in their homes for some time. There are, however, some important differences. While the Padillas were forced to move from their home, the Flynns are still living in theirs. In addition, while everyone agrees that the noise and odors from a bark and manure processing plant are "harmful" not everyone agrees that EMFs are dangerous.

In reading this part of the opinion, you want to compare the testimony that was presented in *Padilla* with the testimony that you might be able to present. Is the evidence in *Padilla* stronger and more compelling than the evidence in the Flynn case, or is the evidence in the Flynn case stronger? You decide that the evidence can be viewed in either of two ways. On the one hand, the evidence in *Padilla* seems stronger than the evidence in the Flynn case. In Flynn, there are no odors, noise, dust, or flies, and the Flynns have not been forced to leave their home. On the other hand, the evidence in Flynn can be viewed as being stronger. While in *Padilla* the plant only caused inconvenience and discomfort, the EMFs might result in cancer and death. The problem, of course, is in establishing a causal link.

Text of Opinion	**What to Look For**

have stopped. Plaintiff Johnny E. Padilla testified that he began renting the residence at that time and that the problems continue. The realtor testified that the plant's operation caused problems that affected the property's value as a residence.

A.   *The Requirement of Unreasonableness in the Context of a Private Nuisance*

[1, 2] A private nuisance has been defined as a non-trespassory invasion of another's interest in the private use and enjoyment of land. *Scott v. Jordan,* 99 N.M. 567, 661 P.2d 59 (Ct. App. 1983). It is a civil wrong based on a disturbance of rights in land. *Jellison v. Gleason,* 77 N.M. 445, 423 P.2d 876 (1967). The elements of proof depend on whether the conduct is intentional or unintentional. Liability for intentional conduct requires that the conduct be unreasonable. *See Restatement (Second) of Torts* [hereinafter cited as *Restatement*] § 822(a) (1979).

[3, 4] We must sustain the trial court's findings and conclusions if they are supported by substantial evidence, and we must review the facts and evidence in the light most favorable to the prevailing party. *Scott v. Jordan.* Viewed in this light, the evidence would support a finding that the invasion was intentional because defendants knew or should have known that their conduct in operating the plant interfered with

It is at this point that the court begins to set out definitions and rules. Because you will need to include these rules in your memo, you begin to take notes, recording first the definition of a private nuisance. However, when you get to that portion of the opinion that sets out the elements of proof, you stop. In the Flynn case, is the conduct intentional or unintentional? At least part of the answer to this question is in the next paragraph: Conduct is intentional if the defendant knew or should have known that its conduct interfered with the plaintiffs' use and enjoyment of their land.

In applying this rule to the Flynn case, you decide that, more likely than not, a court would find that the conduct was intentional. Just as the defendants in *Padilla* should have known that their plant would interfere with the Padillas' use and enjoyment of their land, in our case Pecos Power should have known that the erection of the high voltage lines would interfere with the Flynns' use and enjoyment of their land. You do, however, decide to check the Restatement sections cited in *Padilla*.

Although this paragraph is not directly on point—the paragraph sets out the standard of review—it provides a good reminder that in *Padilla* the Court of Appeals did not review the evidence *de novo*. It only determined whether there was substantial evidence to support the trial court's findings.

Text of Opinion

plaintiffs' use and enjoyment of their land. *See Restatement* § 825(b). Evidence also supports the finding that the operation of the plant was unreasonable.

[5, 6] Defendants have argued that the trial court's finding of unreasonableness lacks substantial evidence, but they have analyzed "unreasonableness" as if the issue were negligence. Although defendants offered testimony that steps were taken to reduce the plant's negative impact on the area and that they had complied with City Council and Environmental Improvement Division requests and requirements, liability for nuisance, unlike liability for negligence, exists regardless of the degree of care exercised to avoid injury. *Wofford v. Rudick*, 63 N.M. 307, 318 P.2d 605 (1957). In the nuisance context, an intentional invasion is unreasonable if the gravity of the harm outweighs the utility of the actor's conduct, *see Scott v. Jordan; Restatement* § 826(a), or if the harm caused by the conduct is serious and the financial burden of compensating for the harm would not make continuing the conduct unfeasible, *Restatement* § 826(b). Section 826(b) of the *Restatement* recognizes that damages may be appropriate even if the utility of the activity outweighs the harm it causes. *Carpenter v. Double R Cattle Co.*, 105 Idaho 320, 669 P.2d 643 (App. 1983).

[7] The unreasonableness of intentional invasions is "a problem of relative values to be determined by the trier of fact in each case in the light of all the circumstances of that case." *Restatement* § 826 comment b. *The Restatement*, §§ 827 and 828, has suggested factors which are relevant in determining the gravity of harm[1] and the utility of conduct.[2] These factors are relevant under both Section 826(A) and Section 826(b). *See Carpenter v. Double R Cattle Co.*

What to Look For

This paragraph presents another hurdle. Presuming that the conduct was intentional, can the Flynns establish that the operation of the power lines is unreasonable? The court sets out a two-prong test: An intentional invasion is unreasonable if the gravity of harm outweighs the utility of the actor's conduct or if the harm caused by the conduct is serious and the financial burden of compensating for the harm would not make continuing the conduct unfeasible. The first prong of the test would be difficult to prove. At this point, there is no direct proof that EMFs cause cancer, and electrical power is of great social utility. The second prong of the test might be a bit easier to establish. If we can establish that the harm is serious, we may be able to prove that the cost of compensating individuals like the Flynns does not make the activity, the providing of electrical power, unfeasible. The good news is that the court did not accept the defendants' argument that there was no nuisance because the defendants had taken steps to reduce the plant's negative impact.

In this paragraph, the court discusses the two-prong test in more detail. It sets out the factors from the Restatement and then applies them to the facts of the case. As the Flynns' attorney, we need to do the same thing. We need to go through the factors, determining what each side could argue.

Text of Opinion

[8, 9] The trial court found that the operation of the plant deprived plaintiffs from enjoying the use of their property and caused plaintiffs Atanacio and Juanita Padilla to move away from their residence of twenty-five years. Further, there was evidence that the property would be difficult to sell for residential purposes and the court found that the value of the residence has been diminished. Plaintiffs Atanacio and Juanita Padilla established their home long before defendants began operating the plant, and priority of occupation is a circumstance of considerable weight in determining unreasonableness. *Schlotfelt v. Vinton Farmers' Supply Co.*, 252 Iowa 1102, 109 N.W.2d 695 (1961). Although there was evidence that the conduct was suitable to the character of the locality, and this is relevant to the question of social utility under Section 828, this evidence alone is not sufficient to require a finding of reasonableness. *Scott v. Jordan.* Further, compliance with city and agency requirements is not sufficient to require a finding of reasonableness. *Schlotfelt v. Vinton Farmers' Supply Co.*

There was substantial evidence to support the trial court's finding of unreasonableness. The finding of a private nuisance is affirmed.

1. In determining the gravity of harm, the suggested factors include the extent and character of the harm involved, the social value that the law attaches to the type of use or enjoyment invaded, the suitability of the particular use or enjoyment to the character of the locality, and the burden on the person harmed of avoiding the harm. *Restatement* § 827.

2. In determining the utility of conduct, the suggested factors include the social value that the law attaches to the primary purpose of the conduct, the suitability of the conduct to the character of the locality, and the impracticality of preventing or avoiding the invasion. *Restatement* § 828.

What to Look For

Some of the facts that the trial court relied on in *Padilla* are the same as the facts in our case. In both cases, there is evidence that the property is difficult to sell, and in both cases the plaintiffs had established their homes before the defendants began their conduct. There are, however, some differences. While the Padillas moved from their home, the Flynns have not. In addition, power plants may have more social utility than a bark and manure processing plant.

After reading *Padilla*, you read the other cases that appear to be on point. In doing so, you use similar strategies, that is, you put the cases in context, you identify the rules that the court applied, and you determine what arguments each side made and how the court responded to those arguments.

The next step is to look at the cases as a whole. Have the courts set out and applied the same rules in each case? If they have, more likely than not the court will apply the same rule in your case. If they have not, you need to look for a pattern. Can the cases be distinguished on their facts? Is the rule evolving? For example, have the courts moved from a broad to a narrow interpretation of the rule? Can the differences be explained on the basis of some underlying policy? What do the cases in which the court found for the plaintiff have in common? Similarly, what do the cases in which the court found for the defendant have in common? Preparing a chart like the ones set out in section 5.4 (Exhibits 5.4 and 5.5) can help you see patterns that you might not otherwise see.

§6.4   Constructing the Arguments

Experienced attorneys begin constructing arguments almost as soon as they receive a case. They think about what arguments they might be able to make as they talk to the client and read through supporting documents and as they read, analyze, and synthesize the statutes and cases.

Although each attorney approaches the process in a slightly different way, most attorneys do the following.

1.   They Brainstorm

At least initially, most attorneys try to identify as many arguments as possible. To do so, they try to approach the problem from several different perspectives.

(a) They analyze the law, thinking about how each side would argue each issue and sub-issue and how they would use each rule, test, and analogous case.

(b) They analyze the facts, thinking about how each side might use each fact. In addition, they think about the missing or unknown facts, the "what ifs."

(c) They think about the standard arguments that are made in this type of case. For example, they think about what type of factual, analogous case, and policy arguments they might be able to make.

(d) They think about the bigger picture. What would be the "right" or "just" way of resolving this case? What are the implications of finding for the plaintiff? for the defendant? What is the social and political context in which the case is being decided?

In *Flynn,* the list might look something like this:

Possible Arguments:

- EMFs create a risk of cancer.
- At this point, the evidence is inconclusive; some studies indicate that that there is a link between EMFs and health problems, and others don't.
- Fear of EMFs is unreasonable.
- In no other cases have the courts found that EMFs constitute a nuisance.
- The EMFs have interfered with the Flynns' use of their property.
- The lines obstruct the Flynns' view.
- Because of their fear of cancer, the Flynns no longer use their backyard.
- The Flynns should have expected that Pecos Power might erect power lines on its property.
- Unlike the Padillas, the Flynns have not been forced to move from their house.
- There are no unpleasant odors or flies. Is there noise?
- The burden of compensating the Flynns would not be substantial—all they want is to be able to sell their home.
- Any increased costs can be passed on to the ratepayers.
- The Flynns should not have to bear the cost of something that benefits everyone.
- Very few people live close to high voltage lines.
- Almost everyone lives near some sort of power line; finding for the Flynns could open the floodgates.
- It is the media that have created the fear of EMFs.

Some attorneys approach brainstorming in a very systematic way, considering each of the possibilities one by one. Others simply keep lists as they research, read, analyze, and write. Still others need to talk about the case with someone in the firm, relying on an informal oral argument to help them flesh out each side's arguments. The trick is not to stop after coming up with one possible argument, but to keep thinking about additional arguments, both that you might be able to make on behalf of your client and that the other side might make.

2. They Develop Assertions and Arguments to Support Those Assertions

As they brainstorm, most attorneys begin to develop assertions, which are usually based on the legal rules and tests. For example, in brainstorming, you might come up with the following assertions.

The Flynns' Assertion:

The harm caused by the high voltage lines is serious, and the financial burden of compensating the Flynns for the harm they have suffered would not make continuing the conduct unfeasible.

Pecos Power's Assertions:

The harm caused by the high voltage line is not serious.

In the alternative, even if the harm caused by the high voltage lines is serious, the burden of compensating everyone who lives near power lines would make continuing to provide low cost power unfeasible.

As they develop these assertions, most attorneys begin to match them with the arguments that they identified while brainstorming. What arguments support the Flynns' assertion? Pecos Power's assertions?

Arguments That Support the Flynns' Assertion

The harm is serious because

- Like the Padillas, the Flynns are no longer able to fully enjoy their home.
- The lines interfere with the Flynns' view.
- The Flynns no longer use their backyard.
- The Flynns cannot sell their home.
- EMFs create a risk of cancer.

The burden of compensating the Flynns would not make continuing the conduct unfeasible because

- All the Flynns want is to be able to sell their house.
- Very few people live close to high voltage lines.
- The company can pass costs on to customers through rate increases.
- As a matter of public policy, it is the public, not the Flynns, who should bear the cost of the harm.

Arguments That Support Pecos Power's Assertions

The harm caused by the high voltage line is not serious because

- Recent studies have not found a link between EMFs and leukemia.

- The harm is a fear of EMFs, not any actual harm from the EMFs.
- There is no reason why the Flynns cannot use their backyard.
- The Flynns knew that the land behind their home was owned by Pecos Power and that the company might erect power lines on the land.

Even if the harm caused by the high voltage lines is serious, the burden of compensating everyone who lives near power lines would make continuing to provide low-cost power unfeasible because

- Compensating the Flynns would open the floodgates to a variety of claims, not only based on high voltage lines but on all power lines and power facilities.
- Neither Pecos Power nor its customers should have to bear the burden of harms caused by unreasonable fears; if anyone is liable, it should be the media.

3.   They Evaluate the Assertions and the Arguments That Support Those Assertions

After coming up with as many assertions and arguments as they can, most attorneys take a step back and evaluate those arguments, deciding which assertions and arguments are worth making and which aren't. While in writing a brief, attorneys are selective, presenting only the strongest arguments, in writing an objective memorandum they err on the side of including rather than excluding an argument. If the memorandum is to serve its purpose, those reading it must know about all of the arguments that each side is likely to make. Thus, in the Flynn case, most attorneys would eliminate from the list only those assertions and arguments that can't pass the giggle test, for example, that it is the media that are liable for any harm the Flynns have suffered.

§6.5   DRAFTING THE STATEMENT OF FACTS

As you learned in Chapter 5 (see section 5.8), in drafting the statement of facts you want to include all of the legally significant facts and those emotionally significant and background facts that the attorney needs to understand and evaluate the case. In addition, you want to tell the attorney what facts are missing.

There are two ways to determine which facts are legally significant. Before you begin writing, you can go through the issues and subissues one at a time, identifying the facts that a court would consider in deciding those issues. Then, after you have written the first draft of your discussion section, you can go back through it, making sure that you included in your statement of facts each of the facts that you used in your discussion section. To determine which emotionally significant and background facts you need to include, think about which facts might influence the outcome of the case and which facts are needed to tell the story.

Once you have decided which facts need to be included, you can then select an organizational scheme. As a general rule, you will want to present the facts either in chronological or topical order, or you will want to use a topical scheme, presenting the facts in chronological order within each topic. Finally, in writing the statement of facts, you want to make sure that you present the facts accurately and objectively. Although in writing a brief you want to present the facts in the light most favorable to your client, you do not want to do so in an objective memorandum.

In the Flynn case, there is at least one missing fact. Although the Flynns have indicated that people will not buy their house because of its proximity to the high voltage lines, there may be another reason why the house is hard to sell. It is possible that the Flynns have not maintained the home or that there is something else in the neighborhood that makes the property hard to sell.

The only other issue in writing the statement of facts for the Flynn case is whether to include an explanation of EMFs and, if you include one, where to put it. Whether an explanation should be included depends on how much the assigning attorney and others who might work on the case know about EMFs. If they know what EMFs are, it is not necessary to include an explanation. Even though you needed to find out what EMFs were so that you could research and analyze the problem, do not automatically assume that your reader needs the same information. Where to put the explanation is a judgment call: The explanation fits equally well in the statement of facts or the discussion section.

§6.6   DRAFTING THE ISSUE STATEMENT

In Chapter 5, you saw how to draft a question presented using the "under-does-when" format. See section 5.9. After the "under," you inserted a reference to the rule of law; after the "does" or a similar word, the legal issue; and after the "when," the most significant of the legally significant facts.

Although the "under-does-when" format is the easiest format to use, many attorneys prefer the more traditional "whether" format. Under this format, the question begins with the word "whether," which is then followed by a statement of the legal question and the most significant of the legally significant facts. Although there is not a separate reference to the rule of law, a reference may be incorporated into the legal question.

EXAMPLE

Issue

Whether the Flynns have a cause of action for either public or private nuisance when Pecos Power had authorization to build the high voltage lines, the high voltage lines obstruct the Flynns' view, the Flynns no longer use their backyard because of their fear that the EMFs from the high voltage lines may cause cancer, and the Flynns have been unable to sell their home.

At first, most writers are bothered by the fact that issue statements written using the "whether" format are incomplete sentences. If you are one of those writers, remember that the format is shorthand for "The question is whether . . ." Also remember that because the complete sentence is a statement rather than a question, you need to use a period and not a question mark.

§6.7   DRAFTING THE BRIEF ANSWER

The brief answer answers the question asked in the question presented. By convention, most brief answers begin with a one- or two-word answer, which is followed by a one-, two-, or three-sentence explanation. (See section 5.10.)

In writing the brief answer, think about what you would tell the attorney if he or she stopped and asked you for the bottom line. Do the Flynns have a cause of action in nuisance? The one- or two-word answer to this question is probably not. Why not?

The Flynns do not have a cause of action for public nuisance because Pecos Power's building of the lines was authorized and because there is no evidence that the lines injure the public. In addition, while the case for private nuisance is stronger, it will be difficult to prove that the lines cause serious harm given the most recent EMF studies. Although you could say more, the more detailed explanation should be saved for the discussion section and formal conclusion.

EXAMPLE

Brief Answer

Probably not. The Flynns do not have a cause of action for public nuisance because Pecos Power was authorized to build the lines and because there is no evidence that the lines injure the public. In addition, the Flynns probably do not have a cause of action for private nuisance. The harm that the Flynns have suffered does not outweigh the social utility of the lines, and the harm that the Flynns have suffered is not serious.

---

§6.8   DRAFTING THE DISCUSSION SECTION

As you learned in Chapter 5, drafting the discussion section is a multi-stage process involving planning, drafting, revising, editing, and proof-reading. In this chapter, we walk you through the process again, showing you two other organizational plans and ways of integrating your discussion of the rules, analogous cases, and arguments.

§6.8.1   Plan the Discussion Section

In addition to the blueprint for an elements analysis (see pages 97-99 in Chapter 5), there are two other organizational plans that are commonly used: the blueprint for problems that require the balancing of competing interests and the blueprint for problems that raise issues of first impression.

When the problem requires the balancing of competing interests, one of the following blueprints usually works well. Use one of the first two blueprints when neither the statute nor the cases set out the factors that the court should consider in balancing the competing interests. Use either the third or fourth blueprints when the statute or cases set out a list of factors. Note that the third and fourth blueprints are very similar to the blueprints for a problem that involves an elements analysis.

Blueprints for a Problem That
Requires the Balancing of Competing Interests

Version 1 (Script Format)

    A. Introduce the issue and set out the general rules, including a description of the interests that are balanced.
    B. Describe the analogous cases.
    C. Set out the plaintiff's or moving party's arguments.
    D. Set out the defendant's or responding party's arguments.
    E. Evaluate each side's arguments.

Version 2 (Integrated Format)

A. Introduce the issue and set out the general rules, including a description of the interests that are balanced.
B. Describe the analogous cases.
C. Predict how the court will decide the issue.
D. Set out the reasons that support your conclusion. In doing so, set out and evaluate each side's arguments.

Version 3 (Script Format)

A. Introduce the issue and set out the general rules, including a description of the interests that are balanced and the factors that the courts consider in balancing those interests.
B. Raise and dismiss the factors that are not in dispute.
    1. Identify the factors.
    2. Explain why the factors are not in dispute.
C. Discuss the first disputed factor.
    1. Set out the rules that the court will use in evaluating this factor.
    2. Describe the analogous cases (if available).
    3. Set out the plaintiff's or moving party's arguments.
    4. Set out the defendant's or responding party's arguments.
    5. Predict how the court will "weigh" this factor.
D. Discuss the second disputed factor.
    1. Set out the rules that the court will use in evaluating this factor.
    2. Describe the analogous cases (if available).
    3. Set out the plaintiff's or moving party's arguments.
    4. Set out the defendant's or responding party's arguments.
    5. Predict how the court will "weigh" this factor.
E. Evaluate the factors and balance the competing interests.

Version 4 (Integrated Format)

A. Introduce the issue and set out the general rules, including a description of the interests that are balanced and the factors that the courts consider in balancing those interests.
B. Raise and dismiss the factors that are not in dispute.
    1. Identify the factors.
    2. Explain why the factors are not in dispute.
C. Discuss the first disputed factor.
    1. Set out the rules that the court use in deciding this factor.
    2. Describe the analogous cases (if available).

      3. Predict how the court will decide this factor.
      4. Set out the reasons that support your conclusion. In doing so, set out and evaluate each side's arguments.
  D. Discuss the second disputed factor.
      1. Set out the rules that the court will use in deciding this factor.
      2. Describe the analogous cases (if available).
      3. Predict how the court will decide this factor.
      4. Set out the reasons that support your conclusion. In doing so, set out and evaluate each side's arguments.
  E. Evaluate the factors and balance the competing interests.

In contrast, if you have a problem that involves an issue of first impression, that is, an issue that has not yet been decided in your jurisdiction, use the following blueprint.

Blueprint for a Problem
Involving an Issue of First Impression

  A. Describe the status of the law in the governing jurisdiction.
  B. Describe the rules adopted in other jurisdictions.
      1. Describe the rule adopted in the majority of jurisdictions and the reasons that the courts have given for adopting that rule.
      2. Describe the rule adopted in the minority of jurisdictions and the reasons that the courts have given for adopting that rule.
  C. Evaluate each rule and then predict which rule your jurisdiction is likely to adopt.
  D. Apply rule most likely to be adopted by the court. If the rule that court is likely to apply requires an elements analysis, use one of the blueprints for an elements analysis (see pages 97-99 in Chapter 5). If the rule that the court is likely to apply requires the balancing of competing interests, use one of the blueprints set out above.
  E. If appropriate, apply the other rules.

If the Flynn case is viewed as a nuisance problem, one of the blueprints for a problem involving the balancing of competing interests will work best. If however, the problem is viewed as an EMF problem, then the better choice would be the blueprint for a problem involving an issue of first impression. If you take the second approach, you would begin by letting the attorney know that the issue is one of first impression and then explain how the issue has been decided in other jurisdictions.

EXAMPLE 1   ORGANIZATIONAL PLAN FOR THE FLYNN MEMO IF THE PROBLEM IS VIEWED AS A NUISANCE PROBLEM

A. Introduce the two types of nuisance.
  1. Introduce the issue.
  2. Set out the test for public nuisance.
  3. Apply the test for public nuisance to the facts of our case.
  4. Set out the test for private nuisance.
B. Describe the analogous private nuisance cases.
  1. Tell the attorney that there are no New Mexico EMF cases.
  2. Describe the other New Mexico nuisance cases.
  3. Describe the EMF nuisance cases from other jurisdictions.
C. Set out the Flynns' arguments, including their factual arguments, arguments based on analogous cases, and policy arguments.
D. Set out Pecos Power's arguments, including its factual arguments, arguments based on analogous cases, and policy arguments.
E. Evaluate each side's argument and balance the competing interests.

EXAMPLE 2   ORGANIZATIONAL PLAN FOR THE FLYNN MEMO IF THE PROBLEM IS VIEWED AS AN ISSUE OF FIRST IMPRESSION

A. Introduce the two types of nuisance.
  1. Introduce the issue.
  2. Set out the test for public nuisance.
  3. Apply the test for public nuisance to the facts of our case.
B. Describe the status of law in New Mexico: New Mexico courts have never decided whether EMFs can constitute a private nuisance.
C. Describe the rules adopted in other jurisdictions.
  1. Describe the rule adopted in the majority of jurisdictions and the reasons the courts have given for adopting that rule.
  2. Describe the rule adopted in the minority of jurisdictions and the reasons the courts have given for adopting that rule or rules.
D. Evaluate each rule and predict which rule New Mexico is likely to adopt.
E. Apply the rule most likely to be adopted by the court using either the script or an integrated format.
F. If appropriate, apply the minority rule or rules.

§6.8.2   Use an Integrated Format

In each of the plans set out above, we showed you how to set out the arguments using either the script format or an integrated format. When you use the script format, you set out the rules first, the analogous cases second, the plaintiff's or moving party's arguments third, the defendant's or responding arguments fourth, and your conclusion last. Although many attorneys prefer this format because it allows them to "see" each side's arguments, other attorneys prefer a more integrated approach.

Exhibits 6.2, 6.3, and 6.4 illustrate some of the ways in which the arguments can be integrated.

In deciding whether to use the script format or a more integrated approach, consider two factors: your supervising attorney's preferences and the nature of the problem. While some problems lend themselves to a script format, others lend themselves to a more integrated approach. Whichever approach you use, however, the first step is to list each side's arguments and counterarguments. If you do not do so, your analysis is likely to be either conclusory or one-sided.

§6.8.3   Introduce and Set Out the General Rules

Whether you use the script or an integrated format, you will almost always begin the discussion section by introducing and setting out the general rules. In each instance, the goal is the same: to "set the stage" for the rest of the analysis.

EXHIBIT 6.2   **Arguments Integrated**

I.   Introductory Section

II. Discussion of First Disputed Element
    A.   Specific rules
    B.   Description of analogous cases
    C.   Mini-conclusion
    D.   Integrated discussion of both sides' arguments

III. Discussion of Second Element
    A.   Specific rules
    B.   Description of analogous cases
    C.   Mini-conclusion
    D.   Integrated discussion of both sides' arguments

EXHIBIT 6.3	Descriptions of the Analogous Cases Integrated into Each Side's Arguments

---

I. Introductory Section

II. Discussion of First Disputed Element
    A. Specific rules
    B. Mini-conclusion
    C. Plaintiff's arguments; Descriptions of analogous cases integrated into arguments
    D. Defendant's arguments; Descriptions of analogous cases integrated into arguments

III. Discussion of Second Element
    A. Specific rules
    B. Mini-conclusion
    C. Plaintiff's arguments; Descriptions of analogous cases integrated into arguments
    D. Defendant's arguments; Descriptions of analogous cases integrated into arguments

---

EXHIBIT 6.4	Descriptions of the Analogous Cases Integrated into Integrated Discussion of the Arguments

---

I. Introductory Section

II. Discussion of First Disputed Element
    A. Specific rules
    B. Mini-conclusion
    C. Integrated discussion of both sides' arguments; Descriptions of the analogous cases integrated into the arguments

III. Discussion of Second Element
    A. Specific rules
    B. Mini-conclusion
    C. Integrated discussion of both sides' arguments; Descriptions of the analogous cases integrated into the arguments

As you read in Chapter 5, sometimes the general rule is a statute. In these instances, you will introduce the statute and then set out the relevant sections.

EXAMPLE 1   **AUTHOR INTRODUCES AND SETS OUT APPLICABLE STATUTE**

18 U.S.C. § 2511 sets out two consent exceptions. Subsection 2511(2)(c) applies when the party intercepting the communication was acting under color of law, and subsection 2511(2)(d) applies when the party intercepting the communication was not acting under color of law. Because there is no evidence that Elite Insurance was acting under color of law when it intercepted Johnson's phone calls, the applicable subsection is 2511(2)(d), which reads as follows:

> (d) It shall not be unlawful under this chapter for a person not acting under color of law to intercept a wire or oral communication where such a person is a party to the communication or where one of the parties to the communication has given prior consent to such interception. . . .

The applicable language of this subsection is "where one of the parties to the communication has given prior consent to such interception."

At other times, the general rule is a common law rule. In these instances, you will introduce and then set out the common law rule.

EXAMPLE 2   **AUTHOR INTRODUCES AND SETS OUT COMMON LAW RULE**

To establish title through adverse possession, the party claiming title must establish that its possession was (1) exclusive, (2) actual and uninterrupted, (3) open and notorious, and (4) hostile and under claim of right for the statutory period. *Williams v. Howell*, 108 N.M. 225, 228, 770 P.2d 870, 873 (1989).

Whether the general rule is a statute or a common law rule, sometimes you will need to do more than just set out the rule. To set the stage, you will need to explain the policies underlying the statute or common law rule, explain the historical development of the rule, or provide the attorney with other types of background information.

EXAMPLE 3   AUTHOR EXPLAINS POLICIES UNDERLYING STATUTE AND DEVELOPMENT OF RULE

During the 1980s, private hospitals began engaging in what is commonly called "patient dumping." Faced both with the need to control costs and increasing numbers of uninsured and underinsured patients, hospitals responded by refusing to provide emergency room care to patients who could not pay. *Gatewood v. Washington Healthcare Corp.*, 933 F.2d 1037, 1039 (D.C. Cir. 1991).

Because few states imposed a duty upon private hospitals to treat patients, Congress enacted the Emergency Medical Treatment and Active Labor Act (EMTALA), 42 U.S.C. § 1395(dd). Under this Act, hospitals receiving Medicare funds must do two things. First, the hospital must screen patients to determine whether they require emergency medical treatment. Second, if a patient requires emergency medical treatment, the hospital must stabilize that patient before discharging or transferring him or her to another facility. 42 U.S.C. § 1395dd(a)-(c).

In drafting the introduction for our example case, you could take one of two approaches. If the attorneys who are likely to read the memo understand EMFs and you are treating the problem as a nuisance problem, you could start your discussion section by distinguishing trespass from nuisance. See Example 1. In contrast, if the attorneys who are likely to read the memo are not familiar with EMFs and you are treating the problem as involving a question of first impression, you could start your discussion by explaining EMFs. See Example 2.

EXAMPLE 1   APPROACH USED IF (A) ATTORNEYS KNOW WHAT EMFS ARE AND (B) PROBLEM IS TREATED AS A NUISANCE PROBLEM

Discussion	Explanation of Author's Decisions
While plaintiffs have a cause of action in trespass when their right to exclusive possession is invaded, they have a cause of action in nuisance when an invasion interferes with their right to use the land. W. Page Keeton, *Prosser and Keeton on Torts*, § 13 at 67 (5th ed. 1984).	Because the attorney asked another intern to research trespass, the author of this memo simply distinguishes trespass from nuisance.

By distinguishing trespass, the author places the discussion of nuisance in context.

In New Mexico, a nuisance can be either public or private. "Public nuisance" is defined by statute.

This sentence gives the attorney information and acts as a roadmap for the rest of the discussion. Because the attorney can raise and dismiss public nuisance as a cause of action, she discusses it first.

At this point, the author moves from a discussion of the general rules to a discussion of public nuisance, setting out the specific rules. Because most attorneys like to see the text of the applicable statutes, she quotes section 30-8-1.

§ 30-8-1 Public Nuisance
A public nuisance consists of knowingly creating, performing or maintaining anything affecting any number of citizens without lawful authority which is either
A. injurious to public health, safety, morals or welfare; or
B. interferes with the exercise and enjoyment of public rights, including the right to use public property.

N.M. Stat. Ann. § 30-8-1 (Michie 2001).

After setting out the specific rule, the author applies it. Note that she begins the paragraph with a topic sentence that sets out her conclusion.

In our case, a court is unlikely to find that the high voltage lines constitute a public nuisance. The statute is designed to protect rights held in common by the public, not the rights of private individuals to the peaceful enjoyment of their own land. *City of Albuquerque v. State*, 111 N.M. 608, 610, 808 P.2d 58, 61 (1991).

At this point, the author moves from a discussion of public nuisance to a discussion of private nuisance,

A court might, however, find that the power lines constitute a private nuisance, that is, a nontrespassory invasion of another's interest in the private use and enjoyment of land. *Padilla v. Lawrence*, 101 N.M. 556, 685 P.2d 964 (1984); *Scott v. Jordan*, 99

N.M. 567, 661 P.2d 59 (1983). Such nuisances can be either nuisances per se or nuisances in fact. A nuisance per se is conduct that is at all times a nuisance; a nuisance in fact is conduct that becomes a nuisance by reason of its circumstances, location, or surroundings. *City of Albuquerque v. State*, 111 N.M. 608, 610, 808 P.2d 58, 61-62 (1991). Because high voltage lines are not a nuisance at all times (for example, high voltage lines running through unpopulated areas are not a nuisance), the Flynns should argue that the lines are a nuisance in fact and not a nuisance per se.

setting out the specific rules for private nuisance. Once again, she begins the paragraph with a topic sentence that sets out her conclusion. She then sets out the rules, presenting more general rules related to private nuisance before more specific rules. In addition, she raises and then quickly dismisses those legal theories that are not likely to work. For example, she quickly raises and dismisses the theory that the power lines are a nuisance per se.

In determining whether conduct constitutes a nuisance in fact, the courts look at whether the conduct was intentional or unintentional. *Padilla*, 101 N.M. at 561, 685 P.2d at 968. Although the courts have not defined "unintentional conduct," they have held that conduct is intentional if the actor knew or should have known that the harm was likely to result. *Id.* For example, in *Padilla* the court held that the defendants knew or should have known that the operation of the bark and manure processing plant would interfere with plaintiffs' use of their land, and in *Scott v. Jordan* the court held that the defendant should have known that its cattle feed lot would interfere with the plaintiffs' use of their land. Although the application is not as clear in our case, a court is likely to find that the conduct was intentional. When Pecos Power

This paragraph picks up where the last paragraph left off, continuing the discussion of nuisance in fact. In discussing nuisance in fact, the author once again sets out more general rules before more specific rules. Note how the author handles the fact that the courts have never defined (or for that matter, even discussed) "unintentional conduct." Instead of hiding that information from the attorney, she tells him that the courts have never defined the phrase. Also note that, when appropriate, she applies a rule. For example, after setting out the test for intentional conduct, she applies it to the facts of our case.

erected the power lines, it knew that the lines would obstruct the Flynns' view and produce EMFs.

In this paragraph the author sets out the two-prong test that will become the focus of the analysis.

If the conduct is intentional, the courts then determine whether it is unreasonable using one of two tests: An intentional invasion is unreasonable (1) if the gravity of harm outweighs the utility of the actor's conduct; or (2) if the harm caused by conduct is serious and the financial burden of compensating for the harm would not make continuing the conduct unfeasible. *Padilla*, 101 N.M. at 561, 685 P.2d at 968 (1984).

EXAMPLE 2   APPROACH USED IF (A) ATTORNEYS DO NOT KNOW WHAT EMFS ARE AND (B) PROBLEM IS TREATED AS AN ISSUE OF FIRST IMPRESSION

Explanation of Author's Decisions

Discussion

Because the attorneys who are likely to read the memo are not familiar with EMFs, the author begins by explaining what EMFs are, where they occur, and how they are measured.

Electricity creates two types of fields. Electrical fields are produced when electrical charges are present, and magnetic fields are produced by the movement of those charges. It is the second of these types of fields, the magnetic fields, to which the term EMFs refers. *See e.g.*, Margo R. Stoffel, *Electromagnetic Fields and Cancer*, 21 Ohio N.U. L. Rev. 551 (1995).

EMFs appear everywhere that electricity is used. Thus, not only power lines but also electrical appliances such as computers, TVs, radios, hair dryers, and electric blankets emit EMFs. The strength of an EMF is measured in "gauss," or "milligauss," also known as magnetic flux density. Readings taken away from electrical appliances and wires are usually in the range of 0.1 to 4 milligauss. Although readings taken near an electrical source can be very high, they diminish rapidly as one moves away from the source. For example, a reading taken within one inch of an electric can opener might be 20,000 milligauss, while a reading taken one foot from the can opener might be 20 milligauss. Similarly, a reading taken near high voltage power lines will be much higher than a reading taken 20 feet away, and one taken 20 feet away will be much higher than one taken 100 feet away. *Id.*

At this point, the research on the effect of short-term and prolonged exposure to different levels of EMFs has been inconclusive. While some studies have linked exposure to EMFs to various types of cancer, other more recent studies have found no such link. United States Environmental Protection Agency, Questions and Answers About Electric and Magnetic Fields (EMFs) 2 (1992).

Whether EMFs from high voltage lines constitute a nuisance is an issue of first impression in New Mexico. There are no appellate level decisions and no cases currently pending in the trial or appellate courts. There have been, however, EMF cases in a number of other jurisdictions.

In the jurisdictions that have decided the issue, the courts have held that high voltage lines, and the EMFs that they produce, did not constitute either a public or private nuisance. *See e.g., Jordan v. Georgia Power Co.*, 466

After explaining EMFs, the author tells the attorneys that the issue is one of first impression in New Mexico. She then explains how other jurisdictions have decided the issue.

S.E. 601 (Ga. App. Ct. 1995); *Borenkind v. Consolidated Edison Co.*, 164 Misc. 2d 808, 626 N.Y.S.2d 414 (N.Y. Sup. Ct. 1995). In some of these cases, the court based its decision on the fact that the power lines were authorized by law. In others, it based its decision on the fact that the evidence linking EMFs to cancer was inconclusive. In still others, the court found that the plaintiffs had not proved damages.

At this point, the author picks up the discussion where it began in Example 1, setting out the general rules and then discussing public and private nuisance.

In deciding whether New Mexico will allow a cause of action in nuisance, the New Mexico courts are likely to look first at whether EMFs constitute a public nuisance and then at whether they constitute a private nuisance.

Public nuisances are defined by statute:

30-8-1 Public Nuisance
A public nuisance consists of knowingly creating, performing or maintaining anything affecting any number of citizens without lawful authority which is either . . .
C.   injurious to public health, safety, morals or welfare; or
D.   interferes with the exercise and enjoyment of public rights, including the right to use public property.

N.M. Stat. Ann. § 30-8-1 (Michie 2001).

In our case, a court is unlikely to find that the high voltage lines constitute a public nuisance. The statute is designed to protect rights held in common by the public, not the rights of private individuals to the peaceful enjoyment of their own land. *City of Albuquerque v. State*, 111 N.M. 608, 610, 808 P.2d 58, 61 (1991).

§6.8.4   Present the Analogous Cases

In Chapter 5 you saw how to set out your descriptions of analogous cases in a separate "analogous case section." Although this technique often works well, sometimes it works better to integrate your descriptions of the analogous cases into your presentation of the arguments. As a general rule, it usually works better to describe the cases in a separate section if you are relying on just one, two, or three cases, and you use the same cases in making several different arguments. In contrast, it usually works better to integrate your descriptions of the cases into the arguments if you use different cases to support different arguments. The goal is to give the attorney the information he or she needs when he or she needs it.

a.   *Integrating the Descriptions of the Analogous Cases into the Arguments*

In the following examples, the authors have integrated their descriptions of the analogous cases into the arguments. In the first example, the author sets out three paragraphs. In the first paragraph, she set out her prediction, in the second paragraph she introduces and describes analogous cases, and in the last paragraph she sets out and evaluates each side's arguments.

EXAMPLE 1

In our case, it is unlikely that a court would find that harm caused by the building of the high voltage lines outweighs the social utility of the lines.

> Author sets out her prediction.

In the cases in which the New Mexico courts have found a nuisance, the harm was more serious and the social utility of the conduct was not as great. For example, in *Padilla v. Lawrence*, 101 N.M. 556, 685 P.2d 964 (1984), the court held that a bark and manure processing plant constituted a private nuisance when, because of the noise and odors coming from the plant, the plaintiffs were forced to move out of their home. *Id.* at 569, 661 P.2d at

> Author sets out the principle that she is using the analogous cases to illustrate.

> Author describes two analogous cases.

60. Similarly, in *Scott v. Jordan*, 99 N.M. 567, 661 P.2d 59 (1963), the court held that a cattle feeding operation constituted a nuisance when, because of the dust, flies, and noxious odors, the plaintiffs could no longer enjoy their home.

The author sets out and evaluates each side's arguments.

In our case, the harm that the Flynns have suffered is less serious than the harm the plaintiffs suffered in *Padilla* and *Scott*. Although the Flynns no longer use their backyard, they have not been forced to move out of their home. In addition, although the Flynns fear that the power lines might cause cancer, neither Mr. nor Mrs. Flynn has cancer. Finally, more likely than not, a court would find that the power lines have a higher "social utility" than either a bark and manure processing plant or a cattle feeding operation.

In the next example, the author puts all of the information into a single paragraph. She begins by identifying the factor that she is discussing. She then sets out the principle that she has drawn from the cases and her descriptions of the cases that illustrate that principle. Finally, she applies the principle to the facts of her case.

EXAMPLE 2

Author identifies the factor she is about to discuss

Author sets out the principle she is using the cases to illustrate

The court will also consider the fact that the high voltage lines are authorized by law. Although this factor is not dispositive, in most of the cases in which the conduct was authorized by the law, the courts did not find that the conduct constituted a nuisance. *See e.g., Padilla v. Lawrence,* 101 N.M.

556, 685 P.2d 964 (1984). For instance, in *State v. Egolf*, 107 N.M. 315, 317, 757 P.2d 371, 372 (1988), one of the factors the court considered in finding that the building of a trout pond was not unreasonable and therefore not a nuisance was the fact that a zoning commission had found that the pond complied with zoning regulations. Similarly, in *City of Albuquerque v. State*, 111 N.M. 608, 610, 808 P.2d 58, 60-61 (1991), the court held that a river crossing project was not subject to abatement as a public nuisance because it was authorized by law and approved by concerned public agencies. *Accord, Espinosa v. Roswell Tower, Inc.*, 121 N.M. 306, 910 P.2d 940 (1995) (holding that violation of NESHAP was a public nuisance per se). Given the courts' decisions in these cases, in our case the court will probably give great weight to the fact that the lines were authorized by law and approved by the New Mexico Public Utilities Commission.

Author describes two cases in text.

Author describes a third case in a parenthetical.

Author applies rule and principle to the facts of her case.

b.   Using Parentheticals

While you will sometimes need to use several sentences or even several paragraphs to describe a case, at other times a phrase or a clause is all that is needed. In these latter instances, instead of describing the case in text, you can use a parenthetical.

As a general rule, you will want to describe a case in text when it is one of your key cases. For example, in the *Flynn* case you would want to describe both *Padilla* and *Scott* in text. If, however, a case is being offered only as additional support for a proposition or to illustrate a single point, then a parenthetical is appropriate. In the following example, the author set out the first two cases in text and a third case in a parenthetical.

The final factor the court will consider is that the high voltage lines are authorized by law. Although this factor is not dispositive, *see e.g., Padilla v. Lawrence*, the courts typically do not find that conduct constitutes a nuisance when such conduct is authorized by law. For instance, in *State v. Egolf*, 107 N.M. 315, 317, 757 P.2d 371, 372 (1988), one of the factors the court considered in finding that the building of a trout pond was not unreasonable and therefore not a nuisance was the fact that a zoning commission had found that the pond complied with zoning regulations. Similarly, in *City of Albuquerque v. State*, 111 N.M. 608, 610, 808 P.2d 58, 60-61 (1991), the court held that a river crossing project was not subject to abatement as a public nuisance because it was authorized by law and approved by concerned public agencies. *Accord, Espinosa v. Roswell Tower, Inc.*, 121 N.M. 306, 910 P.2d 940 (1995) (holding that violation of NESHAP was a public nuisance per se). Given the courts' decisions in these cases, in our case the court will probably give great weight to the fact that the lines were authorized by law and approved by the New Mexico Public Utilities Commission.

In using parentheticals, keep several "rules" in mind. First, if you are going to compare or contrast the facts in an analogous case to facts in your case, describe the analogous case in text, not in a parenthetical. Second, keep your parentheticals short. If you cannot give the attorney the information that he or she needs in a word, phrase, or clause, do not use a parenthetical. Third, make sure that in trying to present the information concisely, you do not mislead the attorney. For example, in discussing *Espinosa v. Roswell Tower, Inc.*, it is important to let the attorney know that those cases involved public and not private nuisances.

Although there is no set format for parentheticals, most take one of the following forms.

word or phrase	(cattle feed lot)
participial phrase	(holding that a cattle feed lot was a nuisance in fact)
clause	(The court held that a cattle feed lot was a nuisance in fact)

As a general rule, do not capitalize the first word of a parenthetical when using only a word, phrase, or participial phrase. Do capitalize the first word when using a complete clause or sentence. In addition, if you use one form for one parenthetical, use the same form for the other parentheticals in the same string of citations. Finally, do not overuse parentheticals. If you use too many, particularly with string citations, your memo can become difficult to read.

EXAMPLE 1   PARENTHETICALS TOO LONG AND PARALLEL CONSTRUCTION NOT USED

Accord, Espinosa v. Roswell Tower, Inc., 121 N.M. 306, 910 P.2d 940 (1995) (The court found defendant repeatedly knocked down ceilings containing asbestos from buildings it owned and dumped at least some of the debris near an abandoned city landfill and that such actions, which were in violation of NESHAP, constituted a public nuisance per se); *City of Albuquerque v. State*, 111 N.M. 608, 808 P.2d 58 (1991) (holding that a municipal highway project that involved building a bridge over the Montano River that was authorized by law and approved by governmental agencies was not subject to abatement as a public nuisance).

EXAMPLE 2   PARENTHETICAL MISLEADING BECAUSE KEY FACTS OMITTED

Accord, Espinosa v. Roswell Tower, Inc., 121 N.M. 306, 910 P.2d 940 (1995) (violation of NESHAP a nuisance); *City of Albuquerque v. State*, 111 N.M. 608, 808 P.2d 58 (1991) (bridge over river not a nuisance).

EXAMPLE 3   EFFECTIVE USE OF PARTICIPIAL PHRASES IN PARENTHETICAL

Accord, Espinosa v. Roswell Tower, Inc., 121 N.M. 306, 910 P.2d 940 (1995) (holding that violation of NESHAP was a public nuisance per se); *City of Albuquerque v. State*, 111 N.M. 608, 808 P.2d 58 (1991) (holding that bridge across river was not a public nuisance because it was authorized by law and approved by concerned public agencies).

EXAMPLE 4   EFFECTIVE USE OF CLAUSES IN PARENTHETICAL

Accord, Espinosa v. Roswell Tower, Inc., 121 N.M. 306, 910 P.2d 940 (1995) (Violation of NESHAP was a public nuisance per se); *City of Albuquerque v. State*, 111 N.M. 608, 808 P.2d 58 (1991) (Bridge across river was not a public nuisance because it was authorized by law and approved by concerned public agencies).

c. Other Reminders

In describing analogous cases, also keep the following in mind. First, make sure that your analysis is principle-based rather than case-based. Whether you set out the cases in a separate analogous case section or integrate them into your arguments, set out the principle you are using the cases to illustrate.

POOR EXAMPLE   **DESCRIPTION OF ANALOGOUS CASES IS CASE-BASED RATHER THAN PRINCIPLE-BASED**

In *Padilla*, the plaintiffs were forced to move out of their home because of the noise and odors coming from defendant's bark and manure processing plant. Similarly, in *Scott v. Jordan*, 99 N.M. 567, 661 P.2d 59 (1983), the plaintiffs could not enjoy their home because of the dust, flies, and noxious odors from the defendant's cattle feed lot. In both cases, the plaintiffs had established their homes prior to the construction of the activities alleged to be nuisances.

GOOD EXAMPLE   **SCRIPT FORMAT: DESCRIPTION OF ANALOGOUS CASES IS PRINCIPLE-BASED**

In the cases in which the New Mexico courts have found that the gravity of the harm outweighed the utility of the conduct, the harm was substantial and the social utility of the activity alleged to be a nuisance was minimal. For example, in *Padilla*, the plaintiffs were forced to move out of their home because of the noise and odors coming from defendant's bark and manure processing plant. Similarly, in *Scott v. Jordan*, 99 N.M. 567, 661 P.2d 59 (1983), the plaintiffs could not enjoy their home because of the dust, flies, and noxious odors from the defendant's cattle feed lot. In both cases, the plaintiffs had established their homes prior to the construction of the activities alleged to be nuisances.

There are several techniques you can use to come up with a topic sentence like the one set out in the previous example. In this instance, the author began with the rule: "In determining whether a use is unreasonable, the courts balance the gravity of the harm against the utility of the conduct." Because she knew she wanted to illustrate how the court applied this rule, she then wrote the following two sentence openers, the first one to introduce the cases in which the court had found that the activity constituted a nuisance and the second to introduce the cases in which the court found that the activity did not constitute a nuisance.

EXAMPLES

First Sentence Opener (To Introduce Cases in Which Court Found That Activity Was a Nuisance):

In the cases in which the New Mexico courts have found that the gravity of the harm outweighed the utility of the conduct, . . .

Second Sentence Opener (To Introduce Cases in Which the Court Found That Activity Was Not a Nuisance):

In contrast, in the cases in which the New Mexico courts have found that the gravity of the harm does not outweigh the utility of the conduct, . . .

Having written the sentence openers, the author stopped and asked herself what each group of cases had in common. Because she did not know the answer to the question, she did what attorneys often do: She went back to the cases and reread them to find out what the cases in which the court held that there was a nuisance had in common and what the cases in which the court held that there was no nuisance had in common. Then, after rereading them for this specific purpose, she returned to her writing, completing the sentences and making necessary revisions. Thus, to come up with the principle, the author read, wrote, read, and wrote.

Second, make sure that in doing principle-based analysis you do not end up writing sentences so long that they are difficult to read. Although sometimes you can say everything you need to say about a case in a single sentence, at other times you will need to use two, three, or, occasionally, even a dozen sentences. Try reading Example 1 and then, without rereading the paragraph, summarize what it says.

EXAMPLE 1

In the cases in which the New Mexico courts have found that the gravity of the harm outweighed the utility of the conduct, the harm was substantial and the social utility of the conduct alleged to be a nuisance was minimal. For example, in *Padilla*, the court held that the evidence was sufficient to support the trial court's finding that a bark and manure processing plant constituted a nuisance when, because of the noise and odors coming from the plant, the plaintiffs had been forced to move from their residence of twenty-five years, and the plaintiffs had established their home long before the defendants began operating their plant.

Because the second sentence is so long (67 words), most readers have a difficult time understanding the paragraph without rereading it. In such situations, it is better to shorten the offending sentence either by deleting unnecessary information or by dividing it into several shorter sentences.

EXAMPLE 2

Revised

In the cases in which the New Mexico courts have found that the gravity of the harm outweighed the utility of the conduct, the harm was substantial and the social utility of the activity alleged to be a nuisance was minimal. For example, in *Padilla*, the plaintiffs were forced to move out of their home because of the noise and odors coming from defendant's bark and manure processing plant.

EXAMPLE 3

Revised

In the cases in which the New Mexico courts have found that the gravity of the harm outweighed the utility of the conduct, the harm was substantial and the social utility of the activity alleged to be a nuisance was minimal. For example, in *Padilla*, the court held that the defendant's bark and manure processing plant constituted a private nuisance in fact. In reaching this conclusion, the court considered the fact that the plaintiffs had been forced to leave their home of twenty-five years because of the noise and odors coming from the plant.

§6.8.5　Present Each Side's Arguments

Whether you use the script format or the integrated format, your goal in presenting each side's arguments is the same: to tell the attorney what each side is likely to argue and how, given those arguments, a court is likely to rule. Thus, under both formats, the content should be the same. The only difference is in the way the arguments are organized.

a.　*Organizing the Arguments*

As you read in Chapter 5, when the script format is used, the arguments are presented in the order they would be presented to a judge: the moving party's arguments first, the responding party's arguments second, and the moving party's rebuttal third. In contrast, when an integrated format is used, the arguments appear as they often appear in a judicial opinion: argument by argument.

Script Format	*Integrated Format*
Moving Party's Arguments • Argument 1 • Argument 2 • Argument 3	Argument 1 • Integrated discussion of moving and responding parties' arguments
Responding Party's Arguments • Argument 1 • Argument 2 • Argument 3 • Argument 4	Argument 2 • Integrated discussion of moving and responding parties' arguments
Moving Party's Rebuttal • Counterargument 1 • Counterargument 2	Argument 3 • Integrated discussion of moving and responding parties' arguments
	Argument 4 • Integrated discussion of moving and responding parties' arguments

Thus, while under the script format the organizing principle was the "parties," under the integrated format the organizing principle is the arguments themselves.

b.   Setting Out the Arguments

When you use the script format, you begin each argument by setting out the plaintiff's or moving party's assertion. You then show how the plaintiff or moving party would use the facts, the analogous cases, or public policy to support its assertion. After you set out the plaintiff's or moving party's arguments, you then set out the other side's assertions and show how it would use the facts, the analogous cases, and public policy to support its arguments.

When you use an integrated format, you set out the same information in a different order. Instead of beginning each argument by setting out the party's assertion, you usually begin by telling the attorney how you think a court will decide the issue. You then walk the attorney through your reasoning, setting out and evaluating each side's arguments.

Compare the following examples. Example 1 shows how you might set out the arguments using the script format, and Example 2 shows how you might set out the arguments using an integrated format.

EXAMPLE 1   SCRIPT FORMAT

The author begins by setting out the Flynns' basic assertion: the high voltage power lines constitute a private nuisance. She then introduces the Flynns' first line of argument, that the harm is serious. Finally, she sets out three reasons why the harm is serious: (1) the Flynns can no longer use their backyard; (2) the lines have destroyed their view; and (3) the Flynns cannot sell their house.

The Flynns will argue that the high voltage power lines constitute a private nuisance because the harm caused by the conduct is serious and the burden of compensating for the harm would not make continuing the the conduct unfeasible.

The Flynns will argue that the harm they have suffered is serious. Like the plaintiffs in *Padilla* and *Scott*, the Flynns are no longer able to fully use their property. Because of the high level of EMFs in their backyard, they are not able to use their pool or maintain their garden without increasing their risk of cancer. In addition, the high voltage lines have destroyed their western view, one of the primary reasons that they purchased the home. Finally, the Flynns are not able to sell their home. Although they have had their home on the market for more than a year, the Flynns have not received any offers. According to their real estate agent, the recent publicity about the potential dangers of EMFs has made it difficult if not impossible to sell homes near high voltage lines.

In addition, the Flynns will argue that compensating them would not make continuing the conduct unfeasible. At this point, all that the Flynns are asking for is to be compensated for the loss of their home's value, a maximum of $272,000.

The author introduces and sets out the Flynns' second line of argument.

Finally, the Flynns will argue that, as a matter of public policy, they should not be forced to bear the loss caused by the building of high voltage lines. If the lines are of great social utility, then it is the public, not an individual landowner, who should bear the cost. By adjusting the utility company's rate structure, the cost of compensating individuals like the Flynns can be distributed among all who benefit from the high voltage lines.

The author introduces and sets out the Flynns' third line of argument.

Pecos Power will respond by arguing that the high voltage lines are not a private nuisance because, like the river crossing project in *City of Albuquerque*, in this case the lines have been authorized by law and approved by public agencies.

The author sets out Pecos Power's basic assertion: that the high voltage lines are not a nuisance. She then introduces and sets out Pecos Power's first line of argument.

In addition, Pecos Power will argue that any harm the Flynns have suffered is not serious. First, there is no evidence that high voltage lines cause cancer, and no one in the Flynn family has cancer. Second, the Flynns knew when they bought their home that the land behind their home was owned by Pecos Power and that the utility could, at any time, erect power lines on the property. Thus, the Flynns cannot complain that the lines interfere with their view.

The author introduces and sets out Pecos Power's second line of argument.

Finally, Pecos Power may argue that neither it nor its ratepayers should have to bear the cost of the public's unreasonable fears. The Flynns are having trouble selling their home not because the EMFs are dangerous but because of the public fears that they might be dangerous. If Pecos Power were forced to compensate individuals for fear of harm, it would open the floodgates to all types

The author introduces and sets out Pecos Power's third line of argument.

of claims based on unreasonable fears, such as claims that regular overhead wires or transformer boxes cause some type of harm.

The author introduces and sets out the Flynns' two rebuttal arguments.

While the Flynns will concede that the lines are authorized by law, they will argue that this fact does not prevent the court from finding that the lines are a nuisance in fact. In addition, the Flynns will argue that the studies are inconclusive. While some of the recent studies have not found a link between EMFs and childhood leukemia, other studies have found a link. In addition, EMFs may cause other health problems, such as problems with the immune system. Thus, the Flynns are acting reasonably in avoiding those areas of their property with high readings, and others are acting reasonably in deciding not to buy a home near high voltage lines.

The author predicts how the court will decide the issue.

The court will probably find that the high voltage power lines do not constitute a private nuisance. The lines are authorized by law, and the harm suffered by the Flynns is not serious. In addition, although compensating the Flynns would not impose a substantial burden on Pecos Power, it might open the door to numerous other suits.

EXAMPLE 2   AN INTEGRATED FORMAT

The author sets out her general conclusion.

It is unlikely that the court will find that the high voltage lines constitute a private nuisance.

The author sets out her conclusion for the first line of argument and then sets out and evaluates each side's arguments.

First, the court will find that the high voltage lines were authorized by law. Like the river crossing project in *City of Albuquerque,* in this case the lines have been authorized by law and approved by public agencies. Although this fact is not determinative, it does suggest that the lines are not a nuisance.

Second, more likely than not the court will find that harm caused by the high voltage lines is not serious. The Flynns allege three types of harm: (1) the high voltage lines have interfered with their use and enjoyment of the interior of their home by blocking their western view; (2) the high voltage lines have interfered with their use and enjoyment of their backyard because they fear that exposure to high EMF levels increases their risk of cancer; and (3) they have been unable to sell their home because of the high voltage lines.

The author sets out her conclusion for the second line of argument and then sets out and evaluates each side's arguments.

Although the lines do interfere with the Flynns' view, a court is unlikely to find that that harm supports an action in nuisance. When they bought the house, the Flynns knew that the property behind the house was owned by the utility company and that the company might erect lines on the property at any time.

It is also unlikely that a court will find that the Flynns' fear of EMFs is reasonable. Although the Flynns can cite studies linking EMFs to cancer and other health problems (for example, birth defects, miscarriages, and neurological dysfunctions), Pecos Power can cite studies showing no link. Finally, the fact that the Flynns cannot sell their home is related to the public's fear, not to any real evidence that EMFs cause cancer.

The court may find that the burden of compensating the Flynns would not make continuing the conduct unfeasible. The Flynns are asking to be compensated only for the cost of their home: $272,000. The court may decide, however, that compensating the Flynns would open the floodgates to a variety of other claims. The Flynns are having trouble selling their home not because the EMFs are dangerous but because of public fears that they might be dangerous. If Pecos Power were forced to compensate individuals for fear of harm, it might have to compensate indi-

The author sets out her conclusion for the third line of argument and then sets out and evaluates each side's arguments.

viduals for all types of claims based on unreasonable fears, such as claims that regular overhead wires or transformer boxes cause some type of harm. As a result, because the lines were authorized by law and the harm suffered by the Flynns is not serious, the court will probably not find that the lines are a nuisance, even though compensating the Flynns would not impose an unreasonable burden on Pecos Power.

§6.8.6   Avoid the Common Problems

When you use the script format, it is relatively easy to set out both sides' arguments. The format itself forces you to set out the moving party's arguments, the responding party's arguments, and the moving party's rebuttal. Unfortunately, it is harder to set out both sides' arguments using the integrated format. Once you have stated a conclusion, there is a tendency to set out only those arguments that support that conclusion. As a result, the supervising attorney sees only half of the analysis. Compare the following examples.

EXAMPLE 1   THE AUTHOR HAS INCLUDED ONLY ONE SIDE'S ARGUMENTS

It is not likely that a court would find that the harm the Flynns have suffered is serious. When they bought their house, the Flynns knew that the property behind the house was owned by the utility company and that the company might erect lines on the property at any time. In addition, at least at this point, there is no conclusive evidence that EMFs pose a health problem. As a consequence, the public's fear of EMFs in buying a house near high voltage lines is unreasonable.

EXAMPLE 2   THE AUTHOR HAS INCLUDED BOTH SIDES' ARGUMENTS

Second, more likely than not the court will find that harm caused by the high voltage lines is not serious. The Flynns allege three types of harm: (1) the high voltage lines have interfered with their use and enjoyment of the interior of their home by blocking their western view; (2) the high voltage lines have interfered with the Flynns' use and enjoyment of their backyard because they fear that exposure to high EMF levels increases their risk of cancer; and (3) they have been unable to sell their home because of high voltage lines.

Although the lines do interfere with the Flynns' view, a court is unlikely to find that that harm supports an action in nuisance. When they bought the house, the Flynns knew that the property behind the house was owned by the utility company and that the company might erect lines on the property at any time. It is also unlikely that a court will find that the Flynns' fear of EMFs is reasonable. Even though the Flynns can cite studies linking EMFs to cancer and other health problems (for example, birth defects, miscarriages, and neurological dysfunctions), Pecos Power can cite studies showing no link. Finally, the fact that the Flynns cannot sell their home is related to the public's fear, not to any real evidence that EMFs cause cancer.

One of the reasons that writers tend not to include both sides' arguments is that it is difficult to find ways to present those arguments without using the language "the plaintiff will argue" and "the defendant will argue." Although sometimes it can be difficult to find language that works, there are some techniques that you can use.

One of the most common techniques that writers use is to put one side's argument in a dependent clause and the other side's argument in the main clause. Thus, they might put one side's argument in a clause that begins with "although," "even though" or "despite" and the other side's argument in the main clause.

EXAMPLE

Even though the Flynns can cite studies linking EMFs to cancer and other health problems (for example, birth defects, miscarriages, and neurological dysfunctions), Pecos Power can cite studies showing no link.

The problem, of course, is that if you use this construction too often, the writing becomes repetitive. Look, for instance, at the following example.

EXAMPLE

Although the lines do interfere with the Flynns' view, a court is unlikely to find that that harm supports an action in nuisance. When they bought the house, the Flynns knew that the property behind the house was owned by the utility company and that the company might erect lines on the property at any time. It is also unlikely that a court will find that the Flynns' fear of EMFs is reasonable. **Although the Flynns can cite studies linking EMFs to cancer and other health problems** (for example, birth defects, miscarriages, and neurological dysfunctions), Pecos Power can cite studies showing no link. Finally, **although the Flynns have been unable to sell their home**, their inability to sell it is related to the public's fear and not to any real evidence that EMFs cause cancer.

The court may find that the burden of compensating the Flynns would not make continuing the conduct unfeasible. **Although the Flynns are only asking to be compensated for the cost of their home**, the court may decide that compensating the Flynns would open the floodgates to a variety of other claims.

Thus, you need to use other strategies. The following examples show some of the other techniques that you can use.

Strategy 1:   Use a Synonym

Although the Flynns can cite studies linking EMFs to cancer and other health problems (for example, birth defects, miscarriages, and neurological dysfunctions), Pecos Power can cite studies showing no link.

Even though the Flynns can cite studies linking EMFs to cancer and other health problems (for example, birth defects, miscarriages, and neurological dysfunctions), Pecos Power can cite studies showing no link.

While the Flynns can cite studies linking EMFs to cancer and other health problems (for example, birth defects, miscarriages, and neurological dysfunctions), Pecos Power can cite studies showing no link.

Strategy 2:   Use a "This, Not That" Sentence Structure

Finally, **the Flynns' inability to sell their home** is related to the public's fear, not to any real evidence that EMFs cause cancer.

**Strategy 3:   Set Out One Side's Argument in One Sentence or
Set of Sentences and the Other Side's Argument
in a Second Sentence or Set of Sentences**

The Flynns are asking to be compensated for only the cost of their home:
$272,000. The court may decide, however, that compensating the Flynns
would open the floodgates to a variety of other claims.

It is also not wrong to include an occasional "the plaintiff will
argue" or "the defendant will respond." Just make sure that you organize the arguments around the lines of argument, not each side's assertions.

EXAMPLE 1

Second, more likely than not the court will find that harm caused
by the high voltage lines is not serious. The Flynns will argue that
the harm is serious because the high voltage lines block their
western view. Pecos Power will respond by arguing that, at the
time the Flynns purchased their home they knew that land behind
it was owned by Pecos Power and that Pecos Power might use
the land at any time. Because the Flynns knew of the risk when
they purchased their home, the court is unlikely to find that the
high voltage lines have caused serious harm.

EXAMPLE 2

The more difficult question is who should bear the cost of the public's fear of buying a house near high voltage lines. The Flynns will
argue that it is the public that should bear the cost. If the lines are
of great social utility, then it is the public, not an individual
landowner, who should bear the cost. By adjusting the utility company's rate structure, the cost of compensating individuals like the
Flynns can be distributed among all those who benefit from
the high voltage lines. In contrast, Pecos Power will argue that the
public should not have to bear the cost of compensating individuals like the Flynns. The Flynns are having trouble selling their
home not because the EMFs are dangerous but because the public fears that they might be dangerous. If Pecos Power were forced

to compensate individuals who fear harm, it would open the flood-gates to all types of claims based on unreasonable fears such as claims that regular overhead wires or transformer boxes cause some type of harm.

Even when experienced attorneys use these techniques, it is easy to write arguments that are conclusory, and to make assertions but then provide only minimal support for them. Once again, compare the following examples.

EXAMPLE 1   ANALYSIS IS CONCLUSORY

In our case, it is unlikely that a court would find that the harm caused by the building of the high voltage lines outweighs the social utility of the lines. Although the Flynns have suffered some harm, that harm is not as serious as the harm the plaintiffs have suffered in other cases. *See e.g., Padilla v. Lawrence*, 685 P.2d 964 (1984); *Scott v. Jordan*, 99 N.M. 567, 661 P.2d 59 (1983).

EXAMPLE 2   ANALYSIS IS BETTER

In our case, it is unlikely that a court would find that the harm caused by the building of the high voltage lines outweighs the social utility of the lines. In the cases in which the New Mexico courts have found a nuisance, the harm was more serious and the social utility of the conduct was not as great. For example, in *Padilla*, the court held that a bark and manure processing plant constituted a private nuisance when, because of the noise and odors coming from the plant, the plaintiffs were forced to move out of their home. *Id.* at 560, 685 P.2d at 967. Similarly, in *Scott v. Jordan*, 99 N.M. 567, 661 P.2d 59 (1983), the court held that a cattle feeding operation constituted a nuisance when, because of the dust, flies, and noxious odors, the plaintiffs could no longer enjoy their home. *Id.* at 569, 661 P.2d at 60. In contrast, in our case, the Flynns are still able to live in their house and they have not become ill. Thus, the harm they have suffered is less than the harm that the plaintiffs suffered in *Padilla* and *Scott*.

EXAMPLE 3   ANALYSIS IS BETTER YET

In our case, it is unlikely that a court would find that the harm caused by the building of the high voltage lines outweighs the social utility of the lines. In the cases in which the New Mexico courts have found a nuisance, the harm was more serious and the social utility of the conduct was not as great. For example, in *Padilla*, the court held that a bark and manure processing plant constituted a private nuisance when, because of the noise and odors coming from the plant, the plaintiffs were forced to move out of their home. *Id.* at 560, 685 P.2d at 967. Similarly, in *Scott v. Jordan,* 99 N.M. 567, 661 P.2d 59 (1983), the court held that a cattle feeding operation constituted a nuisance when, because of the dust, flies, and noxious odors, the plaintiffs became ill. *Id.* at 569, 661 P.2d at 60.

    In contrast, in our case, the Flynns have suffered little harm. Unlike the Padillas, the Flynns have not been forced to leave their home and, unlike the Scotts, they have not become ill. In addition, a court is likely to find that high voltage lines have more social utility than either a bark and manure processing plant or a cattle feed lot. Thus, to win, the Flynns would have to prove that EMFs are harmful, something that plaintiffs in other jurisdictions have been unable to do. For example, in both *Jordan v. Georgia Power Co.*, 466 S.E.2d 601 (Ga. App. Ct. 1995), and *Borenkind v. Consolidated Edison Co.*, 164 Misc. 2d 808, 626 N.Y.S.2d 414 (N.Y. Sup. Ct. 1995), the courts held that the plaintiffs did not have a cause of action in nuisance because the evidence did not establish that EMFs were harmful.

In the first example, the author states his conclusion—that the court is not likely to find that the harm outweighs the social utility—but provides little support for that conclusion. It is not enough to simply assert that the harm the Flynns have suffered is less than the harm that the plaintiffs have suffered in other cases. You need to explain what harm the plaintiffs suffered in other cases and how that harm compares to the Flynns' harm.

The second example is much better. Instead of just citing the cases, the author has described them and then compared the facts in those cases to the facts in his case. He has not, however, dealt specifically with what is the Flynns' best argument: that EMFs are harmful or at least potentially harmful. While the author has done some of this in the third example, the arguments are still not as fully developed as they might be.

§6.9   Revising for Conciseness and Preciseness

In addition to revising your memo, you also need to edit it. Thus, in addition to reviewing what you have written to make sure that your content and large-scale organization are good (see section 1.4.2 in *Just Writing*) and that you have used roadmaps, signposts, and transitions effectively (see sections 2.2 and 4.1 in *Just Writing*), you also need to make sure that your sentences are well constructed (see Chapter 5 in *Just Writing*) and that your writing is both concise and precise. Every word should count, and every word should be the right word.

§6.9.1   Writing Concisely

Although writing sentences with strong subject-verb units eliminates much unnecessary language, you also need to take your red pencil to such throat-clearing expressions as "it is expected that . . ." and "it is generally recognized that . . ." and to redundancies such as "combined together" and "depreciate in value" (see sections 6.2.5 and 6.2.7 in *Just Writing*). In the following example, the language that should be deleted has been crossed out.

EXAMPLE

In contrast, ~~it is important to note that~~ the courts have usually held that an activity does not constitute a nuisance when it is ~~permitted or~~ authorized by law. For instance, in ~~the case~~ *State v. Egolf*, 107 N.M. 315, 757 P.2d 371 (1988), one ~~of the~~ factors that the court considered in finding that the building of a trout pond was not unreasonable and therefore not a nuisance was ~~the fact~~ that a zoning commission had found that the pond complied with zoning regulations.

In addition, often a sentence can be reduced to a clause, a clause to a phrase, and a phrase to a word.

EXAMPLE 1   SENTENCE IS REDUCED TO A CLAUSE

Original

The Flynns have suffered harm. Nevertheless, their harm is less than the harm suffered by the plaintiffs in *Padilla* and *Scott*.

Rewrite

The harm the Flynns suffered is less than the harm suffered by the plaintiffs in *Padilla* and *Scott*.

EXAMPLE 2   CLAUSE IS REDUCED TO A PHRASE

Original

The harm the Flynns suffered is less than the harm suffered by the plaintiffs in *Padilla* and *Scott.*

Rewrite

The Flynns' harm is less than the harm suffered by the plaintiffs in *Padilla* and *Scott.*

EXAMPLE 3   PHRASE IS REDUCED TO A WORD

Original

Without a doubt, the Flynns suffered harm.

Rewrite

Undoubtedly, the Flynns suffered harm.

---

§6.9.2   Writing Precisely

In addition to writing concisely, you also need to write precisely. You want to make sure you use the correct term, that you use terms consistently, that your subjects and verbs are paired correctly, and that in making your arguments you have compared or contrasted like things.

a.   Select the Correct Term

In the law, many words have specific meanings. For example, the words "held," "found," and "ruled" have very different meanings. In most instances, the word "holding" is used to refer to the appellate court's answer to the issue raised on appeal. In contrast, the word "found" is usually used to refer to the trial court's or jury's finding of fact.

EXAMPLE 1   "HELD" USED INCORRECTLY

For example, in *Padilla*, the court held that because of the noise and odors coming from the plant, the plaintiffs were forced to move out of their home.

EXAMPLE 2   "HELD" USED CORRECTLY

The court held that the bark and manure processing plant was a private nuisance.

EXAMPLE 3   "FOUND" USED CORRECTLY

The jury found that the plaintiffs had moved out of their home because of the noise and odors from the bark and manure processing plant.

EXAMPLE 4   "RULED" USED CORRECTLY

The court ruled that the evidence was inadmissible.

---

b.   Use Terms Consistently

In addition to making sure that you are using the correct term, also make sure that you are using terms consistently. If something is an "element," always refer to it as an element. Do not refer to it as a "factor" or a "requirement."

EXAMPLE 1   INCONSISTENT USE OF TERMS

In deciding whether the harm outweighs the social utility of the conduct, the courts consider the following **factors**:

. . .

In this case, the first **element** favors the . . .

EXAMPLE 2   CONSISTENT USE OF TERMS

In deciding whether the harm outweighs the social utility of the conduct, the courts consider the following **factors**:

. . .

In this case, the first **factor** favors the . . .

---

c.   *Make Sure Your Subjects and Verbs Go Together*

In addition to making sure that you have selected the right word and used it consistently, also make sure that the subjects of your sentences go with the verbs and objects. For instance, while courts "state," "find," "rule," and "hold," they seldom argue: It is the parties who present arguments. See section 6.1.6 in *Just Writing*. Thus, in the following sentence, the subject and verb do not go together.

EXAMPLE 1   SUBJECT AND VERB MISMATCH

While a **court** might **argue** that the lines are not a nuisance because they are authorized by law, this factor is not conclusive.

EXAMPLE 2   SUBJECT AND VERB GO TOGETHER

While **Pecos Power might argue** that the lines are not a nuisance because they are authorized by law, this factor is not conclusive.

---

d.   *Compare or Contrast Like Things*

In setting out the arguments, you will often want to show how your case is similar to or different from other cases. For instance, you will want to compare or contrast the facts in your case to those in another case. In making this comparison, make sure that you are comparing like things. For example, do not compare a case name to a party or a party to a fact.

In the following example, the author has not compared like things. She has compared a case (*Padilla*) to parties (the Flynns). Remember that when "Padilla" is italicized, it is a reference to the case. When the name is not italicized, it is a reference to the parties.

EXAMPLE   AUTHOR HAS NOT COMPARED LIKE THINGS

Unlike *Padilla,* the **Flynns** have not been forced to leave their home.

EXAMPLE   AUTHOR HAS COMPARED LIKE THINGS

Unlike the Padillas, the Flynns have not been forced to leave their home.

For checklists for critiquing a memo, see Chapter 5.

EXAMPLE   SAMPLE MEMO

To: Raymond Sanchez

From: Legal Intern

Date: June 21, 2002

Re: File No. 123
            Nancy and Alan Flynn

Statement of Facts

The Flynns want to know whether they have a cause of action against Pecos Power. Because there are high voltage lines behind their house, the Flynns have been unable to sell it.

The Flynns purchased their four bedroom, three bathroom, 3500 square foot home in 1975. From the back of the house, the

Flynns have a view of El Capitan Mountain and New Mexico's spectacular sunsets. When the Flynns bought the house, they knew that the land behind their home was owned by Pecos Power. Nothing was on the land, however, and when the Flynns contacted Pecos Power, they were told that it had no immediate plans for the land.

In 1999, Pecos Power erected high voltage lines on the land that runs behind the Flynns' home. In 2000 the lines were completed, and power began running through them. The lines are within 50 feet of the back of the Flynns' house.

In the last two years, a number of articles discussing EMFs have appeared in the *Roswell Daily Record*, the local newspaper. Several of the articles indicated that there was at least some evidence that exposure to EMFs increased the risk of cancer or other health problems, and one in the real estate section indicated that buyers should be wary of buying a home next to high voltage lines.

A year ago, the Flynns put their house on the market. They did so for three reasons: (1) they wanted a smaller home; (2) the high voltage lines have obstructed their view of the mountain and sunsets, something they value; and (3) they no longer feel comfortable using their backyard pool or maintaining their gardens because of the danger posed by the EMFs. In fact, since learning about the alleged dangers posed by EMFs, they almost never use their backyard, and they keep their grandchildren inside when they come to visit.

Almost a year later, the Flynns have still been unable to sell their house, even though they have lowered the price from $279,000 to $249,000. The Flynns' real estate agent has told them that because of all of the publicity about EMFs, many people will not buy a house near power lines because they fear that either they or their children will get cancer. Even the recent studies that indicate that power lines do not cause leukemia do not seem to have quelled people's fears.

The Flynns have had their house tested for EMFs. Although the house itself tested within safe limits, unusually high levels (21 milligauss) were found in the pool and garden areas. The Flynns' home is only one of two in the area that back up onto the high voltage power lines.

Neither Mr. nor Mrs. Flynn nor their children have, or have had, cancer.

Issue

Whether the Flynns have a cause of action for either public or private nuisance when Pecos Power had authorization to build the high voltage lines, the high voltage lines obstruct the Flynns' view, the Flynns no longer use their backyard because of their fear that the EMFs from the high voltage lines may cause cancer, and the Flynns have been unable to sell their home.

Brief Answer

Probably not. The Flynns do not have a cause of action for public nuisance because Pecos Power was authorized to build the lines and because there is no evidence that the lines injure the public. In addition, the Flynns probably do not have a cause of action for private nuisance. The harm that the Flynns have suffered does not outweigh the social utility of the lines, and the harm that the Flynns have suffered is not serious.

Discussion

Electricity creates two types of fields. Electrical fields are produced when electrical charges are present, and magnetic fields are produced by the movement of those charges. It is the second of these types of fields, the magnetic fields, to which the term EMFs refers. *See e.g.*, Margo R. Stoffel, *Electromagnetic Fields and Cancer*, 21 Ohio N.U. L. Rev. 551 (1995).

EMFs appear everywhere that electricity is used. Thus, not only power lines but also electrical appliances, such as computers, TVs, radios, hair dryers, and electric blankets emit EMFs. The strength of an EMF is measured in "gauss," or "milligauss," also known as magnetic flux density. Readings taken away from electrical appliances and wires are usually in the range of 0.1 to 4 milligauss. Although readings taken near an electrical source can be very high, they diminish rapidly as one moves away from the source. For example, a reading taken within one inch from an electric can opener might be 20,000 milligauss, while a reading taken one foot from the can opener might be 20 milligauss. Similarly, a reading taken near high voltage power lines will be much higher than a reading taken 20 feet away, and one taken 20 feet away will be much higher than one taken 100 feet away. *Id.*

At this point, the research on the effect of short-term and prolonged exposure to different levels of EMFs has been inconclusive. While some studies have linked exposure to EMFs to various types of cancer, other more recent studies have found no such link. United States Environmental Protection Agency, Questions and Answers About Electric and Magnetic Fields (EMFs) 2 (1992).

Whether EMFs from high voltage lines constitute a nuisance is an issue of first impression in New Mexico. There are no appellate decisions, and there are no cases currently pending in the trial or appellate courts. There have been, however, EMF cases in a number of other jurisdictions.

In the jurisdictions that have decided the issue, the courts have held that high voltage lines, and the EMFs that they produce, did not constitute either a public or private nuisance. *See e.g., Jordan v. Georgia Power Co.*, 466 S.E. 601 (Ga. App. Ct. 1995); *Borenkind v. Consolidated Edison Co.*, 164 Misc. 2d 808, 626 N.Y.S.2d 414 (N.Y. Sup. Ct. 1995). In some of these cases, the courts based their decisions on the fact that the power lines were authorized by law. In others, the courts based their decisions on the fact that the evidence linking EMFs to cancer was inconclusive. In still others, the courts found that the plaintiffs had not proved damages.

In deciding whether New Mexico will allow a cause of action in nuisance, the New Mexico courts are likely to look first at whether EMFs constitute a public nuisance and then at whether they constitute a private nuisance.

A. Do EMFs Constitute a Public Nuisance?

"Public nuisance" is defined by statute:

30-8-1 PUBLIC NUISANCE

A public nuisance consists of knowingly creating, performing or maintaining anything affecting any number of citizens without lawful authority which is either . . .

E.   injurious to public health, safety, morals or welfare; or
F.   interferes with the exercise and enjoyment of public rights, including the right to use public property.

N.M. Stat. Ann. § 30-8-1 (Michie 2001).

In our case, a court is unlikely to find that the high voltage lines constitute a public nuisance. The statute is designed to protect rights held in common by the public, not the rights of private individuals to the peaceful enjoyment of their own land. *City of Albuquerque v. State*, 111 N.M. 608, 610, 808 P.2d 58, 61 (1991). A court might, however, find that the power lines constitute a private nuisance.

B. Do EMFs Constitute a Private Nuisance?

A private nuisance is a nontrespassory invasion of another's interest in the private use and enjoyment of land. *Padilla v. Lawrence*, 101 N.M. 556, 685 P.2d 964 (1984); *Scott v. Jordan*, 99 N.M. 567, 661 P.2d 59 (1983). Such nuisances can be either nuisances per se or nuisances in fact. A nuisance per se is conduct that is at all times a nuisance; a nuisance in fact is conduct that becomes a nuisance by reason of its circumstances, location, or surroundings. *City of Albuquerque v. State,* 111 N.M. 608, 610, 808 P.2d 58, 61-62 (1991). Because high voltage lines are not a nuisance at all times (for example, high voltage lines running through unpopulated areas are not a nuisance), the Flynns should argue that the lines are a nuisance in fact, not a nuisance per se.

In determining whether conduct constitutes a nuisance in fact, the courts look at whether the conduct was intentional or unintentional. *Padilla,* 101 N.M. at 561, 685 P.2d at 968. Although the courts have not defined "unintentional conduct," they have held that conduct is intentional if the actor knew or should have known that the harm was likely to result. *Id.* For example, in *Padilla* the court held that the defendants knew or should have known that the operation of the bark and manure processing plant would interfere with plaintiffs' use of their land, and in *Scott v. Jordan,* the court held that the defendant should have known that its cattle feed lot would interfere with the plaintiffs' use of their land. Although the application is not as clear in this case, a court is likely to find that the conduct was intentional. When Pecos Power erected the power lines, it knew that the lines would obstruct the Flynns' view and produce EMFs.

When the conduct is intentional, the courts then determine whether it is unreasonable using one of two tests: An intentional invasion is unreasonable (1) if the gravity of harm outweighs the utility of the actor's conduct or (2) if the harm caused by the conduct is serious and the financial burden of compensating for the harm would not make continuing the conduct unfeasible. *Padilla,* 101 N.M. at 561, 685 P.2d at 968 (1984).

1. Does the Gravity of the Harm Outweigh the Utility of the Conduct?

In our case, it is unlikely that a court would find that harm caused by the building of the high voltage lines outweighs the utility of the high voltage lines. In the cases in which the New Mexico courts have found a nuisance, the harm was more serious and the social utility of the conduct was not as great. For example, in *Padilla,* the court held that a bark and manure processing plant constituted a private nuisance when, because of the noise and odors coming from the plant, the plaintiffs were forced to move out of their home. *Id.* at 560, 685 P.2d at 967. Similarly, in *Scott v. Jordan,* 99 N.M. 567, 661 P.2d 59 (1983), the court held that a cattle feeding operation constituted a nuisance when, because of the dust, flies, and noxious odors, the plaintiffs became ill. *Id.* at 569, 661 P.2d at 60. In contrast, in our case the Flynns have suffered little harm. Unlike the Padillas, the Flynns have not been forced to leave their home and, unlike the Scotts, they have not become ill. In addition, a court is likely to find that high voltage lines have more social utility than either a bark and manure processing plant or a cattle feed lot.

2. Is the Harm Caused by the Conduct Serious, and Does the Financial Burden of Compensating for the Harm Make Continuing the Conduct Unfeasible?

More likely than not the court will find that harm caused by the high voltage lines is not serious.

The Flynns allege three types of harm: (1) the high voltage lines have interfered with their use and enjoyment of the interior of their house by blocking their western view; (2) the high voltage lines have interfered with their use and enjoyment of their backyard because they fear that exposure to high EMF levels increases their risk of cancer; and (3) they have been unable to sell their home because of the high voltage lines.

Although the lines do interfere with the Flynns' view, a court is unlikely to find that that harm supports an action in nuisance. When they bought the house, the Flynns knew that the property behind the house was owned by the utility company and that the company might erect lines on the property at any time.

It is also unlikely that a court will find that the Flynns' fear of EMFs is reasonable. Although the Flynns can cite studies linking EMFs to cancer and other health problems (for example, birth defects, miscarriages, and neurological dysfunctions), Pecos Power can cite studies showing no link. Finally, the fact that the Flynns cannot sell their home is related to the public's fear, not to any real evidence that EMFs cause cancer.

In contrast, the court may find that the burden of compensating the Flynns would not make continuing the conduct unfeasible. The Flynns are asking to be compensated only for the cost of their home. The court may, however, decide that compensating the Flynns would open the floodgates to a variety of other claims. The Flynns are having trouble selling their home not because the EMFs are dangerous but because of the public fears that they might be dangerous. If Pecos Power were forced to compensate individuals for fear of harm, it might have to compensate individuals for all types of claims based on unreasonable fears, such as claims that regular overhead wires or transformer boxes cause some type of harm. As a result, because the harm suffered by the Flynns is not serious, the court will probably not find that the lines are a nuisance even though compensating the Flynns would not impose an unreasonable burden on Pecos Power.

More likely than not, the court will find two other arguments persuasive. Although the fact that the lines were authorized by law is not determinative, the fact that the lines were authorized supports Pecos Power's assertion that the lines are not a nuisance. In addition, the court will probably find persuasive the fact that the other jurisdictions that have considered the issue have decided that EMFs do not constitute a nuisance.

Conclusion

It is unlikely that the court will find that the EMFs constitute either a public or a private nuisance. The EMFs do not constitute a public nuisance. Public nuisances are governed by statute, and the statute is designed to protect rights held in common by the public, not the rights of private individuals to the peaceful enjoyment of their own land.

In addition, the Flynns probably do not have a cause of action for private nuisance. First, the harm that the Flynns have suffered does not outweigh the social utility of the lines. The Flynns have not been forced to move out of their home, and the social utility of the lines is very high. Second, the harm that the Flynns have suffered is not serious. The Flynns knew that the property behind their home was owned by Pecos Power and that the company might build power lines on it. In addition, at this point there is no conclusive evidence that EMFs cause cancer. As a result, the court may find that the Flynns' decision not to use their backyard is unreasonable. Thus, even though compensating the Flynns for the value of their home would not make it impracticable to operate the high voltage lines, the court may decide that compensating the Flynns would open the door to other claims based on individuals' unreasonable fears.

Chapter 7

The Opinion Letter

What happens to an objective memorandum once it is completed? In some instances, the attorney uses it to prepare for a meeting with the client. The attorney reads the memo and then conveys the information to the client orally. More frequently, however, the attorney uses the memorandum to write an opinion letter to the client.

§7.1   AUDIENCE

Although the primary audience for an opinion letter is the client, there may be a secondary audience. The letter may be read not only by the client but also by an interested third party or, in some cases, by the other side. Consequently, in writing the letter, you must write for both the client and for anyone else who may read the letter.

§7.2   PURPOSE

For a moment, assume that the audience is the client and no one else. In writing to that client, what is your purpose? Is it to inform? To persuade? To justify the bill? To keep the client? Should you be giving the client only your conclusions, or should you be giving the client the information that he or she needs to reach his or her own conclusions?

Your role is determined, at least in part, by your state's Rules of Professional Conduct. The following rules are representative.

Rule 1.4   Communication . . .

(b) A lawyer shall explain a matter to the extent reasonably necessary to make informed decisions regarding the representation.

Rule 1.13   Client Under a Disability

(a) When a client's ability to make adequately considered decisions in connection with the representation is impaired, whether because of minority, mental disability, or for some other reason, the lawyer shall, as far as reasonably possible, maintain a normal client-lawyer relationship with the client.

Rule 2.1   Advisor

In representing a client, a lawyer shall exercise independent professional judgment and render candid advice. In rendering advice, a lawyer may refer not only to law but to other considerations such as moral, economic, social, and political factors that may be relevant to the client's situation.

§7.3   CONVENTIONS

Just as convention dictated the content and form of the objective memorandum, convention also dictates the content and form of the opinion letter. Most opinion letters have (1) an introductory paragraph identifying the issue and, most often, the attorney's opinion; (2) a summary of the facts on which the opinion is based; (3) an explanation of the law; (4) the attorney's advice; and (5) a closing sentence or paragraph. Note the similarities between the objective memorandum and the opinion letter.

Objective Memorandum	*Opinion Letter*
heading	name
	address
	file reference
	salutation
question presented	introductory paragraph
brief answer	opinion
statement of facts	summary of facts on which opinion is based
discussion section	explanation
conclusion	advice
	closing

§7.3.1   The Introductory Paragraph

In writing the introductory paragraph, you have two goals: to establish the appropriate relationship with the reader and to define the issue or goal. In addition, you will often include substantive information. When the news is favorable, you will almost always want to set out your opinion in the introductory paragraph.

Because the introductory paragraph is so important, avoid "canned" openings. Do not begin all of your letters with "This letter is in response to your inquiry of . . . " or "As you requested . . . ." Instead of beginning with platitudes, begin by identifying the topic or issue. Compare the following examples.

EXAMPLE 1   POOR INTRODUCTORY PARAGRAPH

This letter is in response to your inquiry of September 10, 2002. I have now completed my research and have formed an opinion. The issue in your case is whether you can enforce your "contract" with the McKibbins. It is my opinion that you can.

EXAMPLE 2   BETTER INTRODUCTORY PARAGRAPH

Since our meeting two days ago, I have researched the Uniform Commercial Code's Statute of Frauds. Based on this research, I believe that your oral contract with the McKibbins is enforceable under the exception for specially manufactured goods.

EXAMPLE 3   BETTER INTRODUCTORY PARAGRAPH

I have researched your potential claim against the McKibbins, and I think that you will be pleased with the results.

The first two sentences of Example 1 could be used to open almost any letter. The sentences could have been typed into the computer, with the attorney filling in the blanks with the appropriate information each time that he or she writes a letter. Because these types of sentences subtly suggest to the reader that he or she is just one more client to whom the attorney is cranking out a response, most successful attorneys avoid them. Instead, like the authors of Examples 2 and 3, they personalize their openings.

§7.3.2   Statement of the Issue

Although you need to identify the issue, you do not want to include a formal issue statement. The under-does-when format used in office memos is inappropriate in an opinion letter.

In deciding how to present the issue, keep in mind your purpose, both in including a statement of the issue and in writing the letter itself. You are including an issue statement because you want the client to know that you were listening and because you want to protect yourself. Thus, you include a statement of the issue for both rhetorical and practical reasons. You use it to establish a relationship with the client and to limit your liability.

Look again at the examples above. In each, how did the writer present the issue?

In Example 1, the attorney was explicit in setting out the issue. He states: "The issue in your case is whether you can enforce your 'contract' with the McKibbins." The issue statement is not as readily identified in Examples 2 and 3. Instead of setting out the issue, the writers simply identify the topic that they researched.

§7.3.3   Opinion

The client is paying you for your opinion. It is, therefore, essential that you include your opinion, or conclusion, in the letter.

When the news is good, you will usually put your opinion in the introductory paragraph; having had his or her question answered, the client can then concentrate on the explanation. You may, however, want to use a different strategy when the news is bad. Instead of putting your opinion "up front," you may choose to put it at the end, hoping that having read the explanation, the client will better understand the conclusion.

Whatever your opinion, present it as your opinion. Because you are in the business of making predictions and not guarantees, never tell the client that he will or will not win. Instead, present your opinion in terms of probabilities: "The court will probably find that the goods were specially manufactured." "It is not likely that you would win on appeal."

§7.3.4   Summary of the Facts

There are two reasons for including a summary of the facts. As with the statement of the issue, the first is rhetorical: You want the client to know that you heard his or her story. The second is practical. You want to protect yourself. Your client needs to know that your opinion is based on a particular set of facts and that if the facts turn out to be different, your opinion might also be different.

Just as you do not include all of the facts in the statement of facts written for an objective memorandum, you do not include all of the facts in an opinion letter. Include only those that are legally significant or that are important to the client. Because the letter itself should be short, keep your summary of facts as short as possible.

§7.3.5   Explanation

Under the rules of professional responsibility, you must give the client the information that he or she needs to make an informed decision. It is essential, therefore, that you give not only your opinion but also the basis for your opinion. The explanation section is not, however, just a repeat of the discussion section from your memorandum. It is usually much shorter and much more client-specific.

When the explanation requires a discussion of more than one or two issues, you will usually want to include a roadmap. See section 2.2.1 in *Just Writing*. Before beginning your explanation, outline the steps in the analysis.

EXAMPLE 1   ROADMAP

> As a general rule, only written contracts are enforceable. Because your contract was not in writing, it will be enforceable only if the court finds that the exception for specially manufactured goods applies. For this exception to apply, we must prove that the rugs were "specially manufactured," that they were not suitable for sale in the ordinary course of your business, and that you had . . .

EXAMPLE 2   ROADMAP

> If you decide to go to trial, the court must decide two questions. The first is whether your actions constitute an assault. If the court finds that they do, it must then determine whether Mr.

Hoage was damaged. For you to be held liable, both questions must be answered affirmatively.

Having outlined the steps, you can then discuss each step in more detail.

The amount of detail will depend on the question, the subject matter, and the client. Although there are exceptions, as a general rule, do not set out the text of the statute or include specific references to cases. Instead, just tell the client what the statutes and cases say, without citations to authority.

After explaining the law, do some basic application of law to fact. If a particular point is not in dispute, explain why it isn't; if it is in dispute, summarize each side's arguments. The difference between the analysis in an objective memorandum and in an opinion letter is a difference in degree, not kind. In each instance, give the reader what he or she needs—nothing more and nothing less.

§7.3.6   Advice

When there is more than one possible course of action, include an advice section in which you describe and evaluate each option. For example, if there are several ways in which your client could change its business operations to avoid liability, describe and evaluate each of those options. Similarly, if your client could choose negotiation over arbitration or arbitration over litigation, describe and evaluate each option. Having described the options, you can then advise the client as to which option you think would be in his or her best interest.

§7.3.7   Concluding Paragraph

Just as you should avoid canned openings, also avoid canned closings. Instead of using stock sentences, use the concluding paragraph to affirm the relationship that you have established with the client and to confirm what, if anything, is to happen next. What is the next step and who is to take it?

§7.3.8   Warnings

Some firms will want you to include explicit warnings. They will want you to tell the client that your opinion is based on current law and on the facts currently available and that your opinion might be different if the facts turn out to be different. Other firms believe that these warnings, when set out explicitly, set the wrong tone. Because practice varies, determine which approach your firm takes before writing the letter.

In writing your letter you can use the modified semi-block format, the full block (the date, the paragraphs, and the signature block are not indented), or the modified block (paragraphs are not indented but the date and signature block are). For examples of each format, see *Webster's Legal Secretaries Handbook* (2d ed., 1996).

§7.4   WRITING STYLE

It is not enough that the law be stated correctly and that your advice be sound. The client must be able to understand what you have written.

Like other types of writing, a well-written letter is well organized. As a general rule, you will want to present the information in the order listed above: an introductory paragraph in which you identify the issue and give your opinion followed by a summary of the facts, the explanation of the law, your advice, and a concluding sentence or paragraph. You will also want to structure each paragraph carefully, identifying the topic in the first sentence and making sure that each sentence builds on the prior one. Transitions are also important. Use them to keep your reader on track and to make the connections between ideas explicit.

Also take care in constructing your sentences. You can make the law more understandable by using concrete subjects and active verbs and relatively short sentences. When longer sentences are needed, manage those sentences by using punctuation to divide the sentence into shorter units of meaning.

Finally, remember that you will be judged by the letter you write. Although clients may not know whether you have the law right, they will know whether you have spelled their name correctly. In addition, most will note other mistakes in grammar, punctuation, or spelling. If you want to be known as a competent lawyer, make sure that your letters provide the proof.

§7.5   TONE

In addition to selling competence, you are selling an image. As you read each of the following letters, picture the attorney who wrote it.

EXAMPLE   LETTER A

Dear Mr. and Mrs. McDonald:

This letter is to acknowledge receipt of your letter of February 17, 2002, concerning your prospects as potential adoptive parents.

The information that you provided about yourself will need to be verified through appropriate documentation. Furthermore, I am sure that you are cognizant of the fact that there are considerably more prospective adoptive placements than there are available adoptees to fill those placement slots.

Nonetheless, I will be authorizing my legal assistant to keep your correspondence on file. One can never know when an opportunity may present itself and, in fact, a child becomes unexpectedly available for placement. If such an opportunity should arise, please know that I would be in immediate contact with you.

Very sincerely yours,

Kenneth Q. Washburn, III
Attorney at Law

EXAMPLE   LETTER B

Dear Bill and Mary,

Just wanted you to know that I got your letter asking about adopting a baby. I can already tell that you two would make great parents. But, as you probably know, there are far more "would be" parents out there than there are babies.

But I don't want you to lose hope. You might be surprised. Your future little one may be available sooner than you think. It has happened before! And you can be sure that I'll call you the minute I hear of something. Until then, I'll have Marge set up a file for you.

All the best,

Ken Washburn

EXAMPLE   LETTER C

Dear Mr. and Mrs. McDonald:

Your letter about the possibility of adopting a baby arrived in my office yesterday. The information in your letter indicates that you would be ideal adoptive parents. However, I am sure that you realize that there are more couples who wish to adopt than there are adoptable babies. For this reason, you may have to wait for some time for your future son or daughter.

Even so, occasionally an infant becomes available for adoption on short notice. For this reason, I will ask my legal assistant to open a file for you so that we can react quickly if necessary. Because we do not know exactly when an infant will become available, I recommend that we begin putting together the appropriate documentation as soon as possible. In the meantime, please know that I will call you immediately if I learn of an available infant who would be a good match for you.

Sincerely,

Kenneth Washburn

§7.5.1   Checklist for Critiquing the Opinion Letter

I. Organization

- The information has been presented in a logical order: The letter begins with an introductory sentence or paragraph that is followed, in most instances, by the attorney's opinion, a summary of the facts, an explanation, the attorney's advice, and a concluding paragraph.

II. Content

- The introductory sentence identifies the topic and establishes the appropriate relationship with the client.
- The attorney's opinion is sound and is stated in terms of probabilities.
- The summary of the facts is accurate and includes both the legally significant facts and the facts that are important to the client.
- The explanation gives the client the information that he or she needs to make an informed decision.
- The options are described and evaluated.
- The concluding paragraph states who will do what next and sets an appropriate tone.

III. Writing

- The client can understand the letter after reading it once.
- When appropriate, the attorney has included roadmaps.
- The paragraph divisions are logical, and the paragraphs are neither too short nor too long.

- Signposts and topic sentences have been used to tell the client where he or she is in the explanation and what to expect next.
- Transitions and dovetailing have been used to make clear the connections between sentences.
- In most sentences, the writer has used the actor as the subject of the sentence.
- In most sentences, the subject and verb are close together.
- The writer has used the passive voice when he or she wants to emphasize what was done rather than who did it or when the passive voice facilitates dovetailing.
- In most sentences, the old information is at the beginning of the sentence and the new information is at the end.
- The writer has varied both sentence length and sentence structure so that each sentence flows smoothly from the prior sentence.
- The writing is concise: When appropriate, sentences have been reduced to clauses, clauses to phrases, and phrases to words.
- The writer has used language precisely: The writer has selected the correct term and used that term consistently.

§7.6.   SAMPLE CLIENT LETTERS

EXAMPLE 1

Confidential
Attorney-Client Communication

July 30, 2002

Ms. Marian Walter
1234 Main Street
Wichita, KS 67218

File No. 0192002

Dear Ms. Walter:

 Since our meeting on July 22, 2002, I have researched the law regarding your legal right to vacate your current location before the expiration of your lease. If you decide to move out before the end of your lease and your landlord, Prairie Antiques, files a lawsuit to collect the unpaid rent, you can probably win the lawsuit. You should, however, consider some of your other options.

Because my opinion is based on the following facts, please contact me if I have left out a fact or misstated a fact.

In June 2001, you received a brochure advertising an "elegant antiques mall" that was certain to attract "the most discriminating clients." When you met with the leasing agent, Joann Carter, she told you that the mall would house antique stores and that the mall was designed to attract adults, not children. In August 2001, you signed a five-year lease. The lease stated that the remaining spaces would be rented to antique stores or other retail businesses.

Between August 2001 and November 2001, five other upscale antique stores moved into the mall. The landlord was, however, unable to rent the remaining eight spaces to other antique dealers. As a result, between February and April 2002, the landlord leased four of the other spaces to other types of businesses. It leased one of the spaces to a video arcade and three others to second-hand stores. Since these stores moved into the mall, there have been children with skateboards in the mall area, and you have experienced a 20 percent decrease in profits. In addition to making oral complaints, on May 1, 2002, you sent a letter to the landlord notifying it that you believe that it violated the terms of your lease when it leased spaces in the mall to the video arcade and second-hand stores.

If you vacate the premises and default on the lease, Prairie Antiques may file a lawsuit against you to recover the rent due for the remaining months of the lease. If this happens, you can argue that Prairie Antiques "constructively evicted" you when it leased to the arcade and second-hand stores. A constructive eviction is different from an actual eviction. An actual eviction occurs when the landlord literally takes the premises away from the tenant; a constructive eviction occurs when the landlord interferes with a tenant's right to use the premises for their intended purpose. It will be up to the jury to decide whether the circumstances surrounding your case constitute constructive eviction.

To establish that you have been constructively evicted, you will need to prove four things. First, you must prove that Prairie Antiques violated the lease agreement. Prairie Antiques will argue that, under the lease, it had the right to lease to retail stores and an arcade and thrift shops are retail stores. Although the lease does allow Prairie Antiques to lease to retail stores, you may argue that both parties understood the language in the lease to mean that Prairie Antiques could lease to antique stores and other "upscale" retail establishments, for example, an upscale jewelry store or restaurant. Based on the language in the brochure and the statements made by the leasing agent, a jury should conclude that the landlord violated the lease by leasing the other spaces to the video arcade and second-hand stores.

Second, you must prove that when Prairie Antiques leased the vacant spaces to a video arcade and second-hand stores, it substantially interfered with your ability to use your leased space. Although there have been cases in which the courts have found that a landlord substantially interfered with a tenant's use of its leased space when the landlord rented to an incompatible business, there are other cases in which the court found that the landlord did not substantially interfere. The key seems to be whether the landlord's act caused a loss of profits. Thus, to prove substantial interference, we will have to show that Prairie Antiques caused your loss of profits when it leased the vacant spaces to the arcade and the second-hand stores. Although we should be able to do this, Prairie Antiques will try to prove that your losses are the result of other factors, such as the seasonal nature of your business, a general decline in business in the area, or your own business practices.

Third, you must prove that you gave Prairie Antiques notice of the problem and an opportunity to correct it. You should be able to meet this requirement: In addition to making oral complaints, you also sent a letter, and you have given Prairie Antiques several months to correct the problem.

Finally, you must prove that you vacated the premises within a reasonable amount of time after complaining to the landlord. If you vacate the premises by September 1, 2002, the jury will most likely find that you have met this requirement.

Although you should be able to prove that you have been constructively evicted, litigation is expensive and stressful, and there are no guarantees. As a result, you should consider some of your other options.

One option is to stay and pay rent. Although this option avoids the expense and stress of litigation, you may lose your right to claim that you have been constructively evicted. As I indicated earlier in this letter, one of the requirements for constructive eviction is that you move out within a reasonable time. In addition, if your loss in profits continues, it may be impractical to stay in business.

A second option would be to try to sublease your space to another business. Although your lease requires that you obtain Prairie Antiques' approval before you sublet your space, the courts have said that a landlord cannot withhold approval except for good cause. The risk associated with this option is that you may be liable for unpaid rents if the new tenant fails to make payments.

A third option is to try to negotiate an early termination of the lease on the grounds that Prairie Antiques has violated the lease by leasing to the arcade and second-hand stores. I can try to do this for you or, if you want to minimize your costs, you can do it on your own.

A fourth option would be to file a lawsuit against Prairie Antiques for breach of contract. Although you should be able to win this lawsuit and recover your lost profits, such a lawsuit would be expensive and, once again, there are no guarantees.

Unfortunately, none of these options are very good. As a result, you need to balance your desire to move out of the mall against the potential costs. Although there is a good chance that your landlord will not sue you, under our state's statute of limitations, it has six years to file a lawsuit. Thus, you would have to live under the cloud of potential litigation for a number of years.

Please contact my office to schedule an appointment to talk in more detail about your options. I look forward to meeting with you.

Sincerely,

Attorney at Law

EXAMPLE 2

**Confidential
Attorney-Client Communication**

November 18, 2001

Onlinebooks.com
6524 Industrial Parkway South
Tampa Bay, Florida 33607

Dear Ms. Brooks:

You have asked if Onlinebooks may ask job applicants whether they have back problems or have used more than five days of sick leave during the past year. My research indicates that the Americans with Disabilities Act (ADA) prohibits the asking of such questions. You can, however, ask questions that will help you determine whether an applicant can perform the essential job requirements.

Onlinebooks employs "pickers," that is, individuals who pick books off shelves, place them in a box, and then place the box on a conveyor belt. Pickers must be able to climb, reach, and lift boxes weighing up to thirty pounds. In the past, some of the individuals you have hired as pickers have not been able to do all parts of the job or have used substantial amounts of sick leave for back or other health problems. Thus, you want to ask job applicants about whether they have back problems and about how they use sick leave.

The ADA prohibits employers from discriminating against qualified job applicants who are disabled. More specifically, the ADA prohibits employers from asking applicants questions that are designed to "weed out" individuals who have a disability or who suffer from a chronic illness. As a result, Onlinebooks cannot ask job applicants about whether they have back problems or about their use of sick leave.

The ADA does not, however, prohibit an employer from asking qualified job applicants whether they can, with or without reasonable accommodations, perform the essential functions of the job for which they are applying. Therefore, Onlinebooks may describe the essential functions of the job and then ask applicants whether they can perform those functions. For example, you may tell applicants that pickers must be able to climb, reach, and lift thirty-pound boxes and then ask them whether they can perform each of these tasks. In addition, Onlinebooks may ask applicants to demonstrate that they can do each of these tasks.

If an applicant asks for a reasonable accommodation, Onlinebooks must grant that accommodation unless doing so would impose an unreasonable burden on Onlinebooks. For example, if an applicant asks to be allowed to wear a back support or to use a handcart to move heavy boxes longer distances, you should grant the request unless doing so would create an unreasonable burden on the company. You would not, however, need to grant an employee's request to be exempted from carrying boxes weighing over, for example, ten pounds.

In addition, the ADA does not prohibit employers from asking applicants about their work histories. Thus, although you may not ask applicants how much sick leave they used in the last year, you may ask them about their attendance records. In doing so, you just need to make sure that the questions are designed to collect information about the applicants' work records, not to determine whether the individual is disabled or suffers from a chronic illness.

In conclusion, although you may not ask applicants whether they have back problems, you may ask them whether they can, with or without reasonable accommodations, perform the essential functions of the job. In addition, although you may not ask applicants about their use of sick leave, you may ask them about their attendance records as long as your questions are not designed to collect information about whether the person is disabled or suffers from a chronic illness.

If you have any additional questions, please feel free to contact me.

Sincerely,

Attorney at Law

Glossary of Terms

Active voice. Active voice is the quality of a transitive verb in which the action of the verb is performed by the subject: "Judges decide cases." (See passive voice.)

Analogous case. An analogous case is a case that is factually similar to the client's case. An argument based on an analogous case is an argument in which the attorney compares or contrasts the facts in a factually similar case with the facts in the client's case.

Analysis. When you analyze something, you examine it closely, identifying each part and determining how the parts are related. In law, there are two types of analysis: statutory analysis, which involves the close examination of a statute, and case analysis, which involves the close examination of a case.

Case law. Although the term "case law" is often used to refer to common law, in fact its meaning is broader. It refers to all court decisions, including those interpreting or applying enacted law.

Case briefing. Case briefing is a technique used to analyze a court's written opinion. A case brief usually contains a summary of the facts, a statement of the issue(s), the court's holding, and the court's rationale.

Citation (also Cite). The convention for identifying legal (and non-legal) resources. Typically, a citation has some numerical components (*e.g.,* volume numbers and pages for cases and secondary sources; titles and sections for statutes and regulations), as well as an alphabetic abbreviation (usually identifying the case reporter, book title or code name). A complete citation should identify for the user what governing body made the law, when it made the law, and where the law can be located.

Dicta. Comments made by a court that are not directly related to the issue before it or that are not necessary to its holding are dicta. Such comments are often preceded by the word "if": "If the evidence had established . . . ." Although in some cases dicta are easily identifiable, in other cases they may not be. If the issue is broadly defined, the statement may be part of the court's holding; if the issue is narrowly defined, the statement is dicta. Compare with **Holding.**

Dovetailing. Dovetailing is the overlap of language between two sentences that creates a bridge between those two sentences. Dovetails are often created by moving the connecting idea to the end of the first sentence and the beginning of the second sentence, repeating key words, using pronouns to refer back to nouns in an earlier sentence, and using "hook words" (this, that, these, such) and a summarizing noun.

Elements analysis. When you do an elements analysis, you systematically analyze a set of requirements set out either in a statute or as part of a common law doctrine by determining whether, given a particular set of facts, each requirement is met.

Emotionally significant fact. An emotionally significant fact is one that, while not legally significant, may affect the way the judge or jury decides the case.

Enacted law. Enacted law is law created by the legislative or executive branches. Statutes and regulations are enacted law.

Finding. A finding is a decision on a question of fact. For example, a trial court judge may find a defendant incompetent to stand trial, or a jury may find that the defendant officer was armed. (Compare with **Holding.**)

Headnote. A headnote is a one-sentence summary of a rule of law found at the beginning of a court's opinion. Because headnotes are written by an attorney employed by the company publishing the reporter in which the opinion appears and not the court, they cannot be cited as authority.

Holding. A holding is the court's decision in a particular case. "When the court applied the rule to the facts of the case, it held that . . . ." Thus, a holding has two components: a reference to the applicable rule of law and a reference to the specific facts to which that rule was applied. Because the holding is the answer to the legal question, it can be formulated by turning the issue (a question) into a statement. Compare with **Dicta.**

Integrated format. The phrase "integrated format" refers to a method of organizing the discussion section of an objective memorandum. Instead of using the script format, in which the discussion section is organized around the arguments that each side makes, the writer organizes the discussion around legal principles or points.

Key number. An indexing tag assigned by West to the headnotes of cases published in its reporters. A key number consists of two components: a topic (the broader subject area components) and the key number (a narrow issue within the topic). Topics are identified by word; key numbers, by number. A West digest is an alphabetical arrangement of topics and key numbers containing the headnotes indexed under those key numbers.

Legalese. Legalese is a broad term used to describe several common features of legal writing such as the use of archaic language, Latin terms, boilerplate language, and long and convoluted sentences. "Legalese" is usually a pejorative term.

Legally significant fact. A legally significant fact is a fact that a court would consider significant either in deciding that a statute or rule is applicable or in applying that statute or rule.

Mandatory authority. Mandatory authority is law that a court must apply in deciding the case before it.

Nominalization. Nominalization is the process of converting verbs into nouns (determine → determination).

Paragraph block. A paragraph block is a group of two or more paragraphs that together develop a point within a larger document.

Paragraph coherence. A paragraph has coherence when the various points raised in the paragraph are connected to each other. Common connecting devices include repetition of key words, transitional phrases, parallelism, and pronouns.

Paragraph unity. A paragraph has unity when all the points raised in the paragraph are related to one larger point, the paragraph's topic.

Parallel citation. An alternative cite for a case citation. Many state decisions are published in a state reporter as well as a regional reporter. The two citations for the same case are considered "parallel." Some decisions (such as those of the United States Supreme Court) have more than one parallel cite. Other decisions have no parallel cite.

Passive voice. Passive voice is the quality of a transitive verb in which the subject receives rather than performs the action of the verb: "Cases are decided by judges." (See active voice.)

Persuasive authority. Persuasive authority is law or commentary that a court may consider in deciding the case before it.

Plain English. Plain English is the term used to describe a movement to encourage the use of simple, straightforward language (in professions such as law) that is readily understandable by lay people. In other countries, the same movement is referred to as the "Plain Language Movement."

Policy argument. A policy argument is one in which the attorney argues that a particular interpretation of a statute, regulation, or common law rule is (or is not) consistent with current public policy, that is, the objective underlying a particular law. For example, child custody laws usually seek to provide stability for children; environmental laws usually try to balance the interests of developers and preservationists.

Primary authority. The law itself. Primary authority includes constitutions, statutes, cases, regulations, and other government-created law. Primary authority can be contrasted with secondary authority, which is description of or comment on the law.

Raise and dismiss. You can raise and dismiss issues, elements, and arguments. In each case, both sides will agree on the point; therefore, extensive analysis is not necessary. However, a writer goes through the raise-and-dismiss process to assure the reader that the point was considered.

Reporter. A set of volumes containing judicial decisions. The reporter is the final form of publication for judicial decisions (the first being the slip opinion; the second, the advance sheet). The decisions in a reporter are published chronologically.

Roadmap. Roadmaps are introductory paragraphs that give readers an overview of an entire document or a section of a document.

Rule. The rule is the legal standard that the court applies in deciding the issue before it. In some cases, the rule will be enacted law (a constitutional provision, statute, or regulation); in other cases, it will be a court rule (one of the Federal Rules of Civil Procedure); and in still other cases, it will be a common law rule or doctrine. Although in the latter case the rule may be announced in the context of a particular case, rules are not case-specific. They are the general standards that are applied in all cases. (Compare with **Test.**)

Secondary authority. Description of or comment on the law (primary authority). Sources of secondary authority include treatises, law review articles, legal encyclopedias, and restatements. Secondary authority never has binding effect, but it can be used as persuasive authority based on its reasoning or the eminence of its author.

Signposts. Signposts are words and phrases that keep readers oriented as they move through a document. Transitional phrases, particularly ones like "first," "second," and "third," are the most common signposts. Topic sentences can also be considered a type of signpost.

Standard of review. "Standard of review" refers to the level of scrutiny an appellate court will use to review a trial court's decision. For example, in *de novo* review the appellate court does not give any deference to the decision of the trial court; it decides the issue independently. In contrast, when the standard of review is abuse of discretion, the appellate court defers to the trial court, reversing its decision only when there is no evidence to support it.

Statute. A law enacted by the legislative branch of federal and state governments (municipal and county enactments are called ordinances). Statutes can be contrasted with common law (or case law), which is made by decisions of the judicial branch.

Synthesis. When you synthesize, you bring the pieces together into a coherent whole. For example, when you synthesize a series of cases, you identify the unifying principle or principles.

Term of art. Although sometimes used to describe any word or phrase that has a "legal ring" to it, "term of art" means a technical word or phrase with a specific meaning. "Certiorari" is a true term of art; "reasonable person" is not.

Test. Although the words "rule" and "test" are sometimes used interchangeably, they are not the same. A test is used to determine whether a rule is met. (Compare with **Rule.**)

Topic sentence. A topic sentence is the sentence in a paragraph that introduces the key point in the paragraph or that states the topic of the paragraph. Topic sentences are often the first sentence in a paragraph.

Index